Wrestling with Doubt

*Theological Reflections on
the Journey of Faith*

Frank D. Rees

A Liturgical Press Book

THE LITURGICAL PRESS
Collegeville, Minnesota

www.litpress.org

Cover design by Greg Becker

Library of Congress Cataloging-in-Publication Data

Rees, Frank D., 1950–
    Wrestling with doubt : theological reflections on the journey of faith / Frank D. Rees.
        p.   cm.
    Includes bibliographical references and index.
    ISBN 0-8146-2590-8 (alk. paper)
    1. Faith.   2. Belief and doubt.   I. Title.

BT771.3.R44   2001
231'.042—dc21   00-049560

Contents

Foreword

This book seeks to address a confusion which has troubled many people for a long time. Too many people have been led to think that doubt is incompatible with faith. Since, almost naturally, they have found themselves doubting, they have imagined they were not people of faith. In fact, wrestling with doubt can be the expression of active and creative faith.

Two of my own experiences illustrate the point. I was conversing with a friend one day while holding in my hand a book with the title *Christian Doubt*. She asked simply, "Can there be such a thing?" She had been taught that to be a Christian involves not doubting; consequently, there can be no such thing as Christian doubt.

I began wrestling with the nature of doubt early in my teens. I was a philosophically inclined young person and my Bible class teacher was a person to whom I felt I could voice my questions. One day I asked him, "What is God?" His well-intentioned reply was: "You can't ask that question. You can ask 'Who is God?' but not 'What is God?'" I didn't accept his answer at the time, and I still don't.

Christian faith can live with questions and doubts. It is simply misleading and often damaging to tell people that there are some questions they may not ask, or to suggest that if they do wrestle with questions and doubts they do not have faith. The thesis of this book is that questioning and doubt are ambiguous experiences, which may indicate an absence of faith or an attempt to evade commitment, but they may also indicate genuine engagement with God, in what I will call the divine conversation. These insights arise from many years of study, from numerous pastoral conversations, both in my years in congregational ministry and with students in many places, and finally from my experience as a teacher of theology. In all these dimensions of my life, I have found that wrestling with doubt can be a very positive and creative dimension of faith. Furthermore, the kind of faith that tries to avoid doubt is frequently shown to be a faith that does not last, especially in the face of suffering and difficulties.

Many people who know intuitively that doubt is a vital part of their faith struggle to articulate this insight, because their ideas of God and of faith itself are drawn from a different kind of theological perspective. They may not have the intellectual "tools" to integrate their ideas and their experience. This book offers a new way of thinking about God and about our life journey, which allows that there can be times of confusion, questioning, and doubt, as well as times of clear belief and joyful celebration. The key to understanding doubt is to recognize the context of our doubt and our faith in divine conversation.

This study is dedicated to those many people who have had the honesty and courage to share with me their faithful doubts and to engage with mine. A crucial element in the journey was my doctoral study on this theme at the University of Manchester. Dr. David Pailin was my advisor for that project, and his guidance and friendship are gratefully acknowledged. My teaching colleagues at Whitley College have encouraged me through the years when I have tried to write and rewrite this book, amidst the demands of teaching and administration. Several have read and helpfully critiqued drafts of various chapters, for which I thank them. Finally, my wife, Merilyn, and our children, Lachlan, Nicholas and Felicity, have lived with and at times endured "the doubt book," always supporting me when my self-doubt overtook the project and urging me to persist. For their faithfulness and companionship in the journey I am most grateful. I am hopeful that this work will contribute something to their own participation in the divine conversation.

Frank D. Rees
November 2000

1

The Modern Problem with Doubt

The problem with doubt—at least for the modern mind—is that we don't know what to make of it. But that is just the point. Doubt is precisely the situation which obtains when we don't understand, and doubt is something we do not really understand. We don't know what to make of it; we are in doubt about doubt.

Resolving doubt seems to be a particular concern in the arena of religion or faith. Here, perhaps more than in any other aspect of our lives, we encounter the frontiers of our understanding. The existence and nature of God, the transcendent uncreated ground and source of all life, is for us the ultimate mystery. In response, a strong measure of doubt would seem appropriate, as the recognition of our unknowing. Yet throughout Christian history, doubt has been seen as inappropriate. Teachers and pastors have enjoined their people not to doubt, while theologians have sought to explain how faith is to be understood in a way that overcomes doubt. The popular Peace Prayer of Francis of Assisi asks that where there is doubt we may sow faith, while H. E. Fosdick's hymn "God of Grace and God of Glory" laments that "fears and doubts too long have bound us." In his widely read book *Doubt: Faith in Two Minds*, Os Guinness begins with a chapter arguing for the necessity of doubt to keep faith alive.[1] Authentic faith requires understanding, with good reasons, that Christianity is true and "scientific doubt" is the intellectual force which helps us to establish such understanding.

[1] Os Guinness, *Doubt: Faith in Two Minds* (Berhamsted: Lion Publishing, 1976).

Once we reach this understanding, however, Guinness sees no further constructive role for doubt. The remaining chapters of his book offer a pathology of doubts, explaining how they arise from poorly formed faith. Then for each type of doubt he offers pastoral remedies and advice on how to overcome doubt.

These paradoxical features of the relation of doubt and faith are well displayed in Graham Greene's satirical novel *Monsignor Quixote*.[2] The renegade priest Quixote admires his companion, Sancho, who maintains his Marxist dogma without doubt. Quixote thinks that some of his parishioners really do believe, while his own faith is "riddled with doubts." Sancho, on the other hand, is privately disillusioned with his dogma and considers that the priest is truly a man of faith. We are left with the question: which is the person of faith, the dogmatist or the doubter? In the theological literature about doubt, as we shall see in later chapters, similar ambiguities emerge. An approach which eschews all doubt often harbors a covert element of doubt, while many who accept or welcome doubt do so in the strength of a quite positive faith.

These initial observations suggest that a very basic ambivalence and ambiguity surround our theme. One of the difficulties here is the confusion about the term itself. Exactly what do we mean by "doubt"? Our answer here is equivocal, for the very word "doubt" carries several different meanings. Literally it means to be of two opinions or to be in two minds. The element of two-ness is central here, for to be in doubt is an experience or situation which has several possible meanings and can lead to various outcomes. If I am in doubt about something, I may investigate it further and resolve by doubt, or I may reject the idea altogether. On the other hand, I may leave the matter undecided, perhaps because I do not know how to arrive at a resolution. Doubt is an ambiguous experience or attitude.

The *Pocket Oxford Dictionary* offers a range of meanings for doubt as a noun: "1. uncertainty; undecided state of mind; 2. cynicism; 3. uncertain state; 4. lack of full proof or clear indication."

Similarly the verb has a range of meanings: "1. feel uncertain or undecided about; 2. hesitate to believe; 3. call into question."[3]

The various meanings of the word "doubt," ranging from cynicism to a hesitancy about or before believing something, suggest to us that

---

[2] Graham Greene, *Monsignor Quixote* (London: Penguin Books, 1983) esp. 205–6.
[3] Della Thompson, ed., *The Pocket Oxford Dictionary* (Oxford: Clarendon Press, 1992).

we should not enter a theological discussion of doubt with a simple idea of its meaning or significance. The term itself is equivocal; the experience is ambiguous. It is necessary to look to the context or situation, in any given instance or usage, before we decide exactly what is meant by the word in that situation. This applies to its usage in the Bible, as well as in other discourses. To be in doubt may mean a cynical attitude or a skeptical lack of trust, or it may indicate a desire for more information or clearer understanding in order to formulate a definite attitude and stronger commitment.

The situation is further complicated by the every-day language association of the terms "faith" and "belief." In the English language, a strong identification of faith and belief has developed, at least in part because these two nouns must share the one verb. In ordinary language, the verb for faith is "to believe." Many conceptual difficulties arise from this limitation. People of faith are often called "believers," and the inference is easily drawn that since doubt is the antonym of belief it is also the opposite of faith. Here we can identify one of the crucial issues to be explored in this study. Is faith to be understood essentially in terms of belief? To the extent that it is, doubt is incompatible with faith. But then the difficulty is to explain how we can come to a state of belief which excludes or overcomes doubt. On the other hand, if faith is not to be so strongly identified with belief, how can it include both belief and doubt?

All these considerations suggest the need for a careful study of the nature and significance of doubt and its relation to faith. As we begin, it will be helpful to identify several crucial features of the context in which our study is undertaken. The first of these is the dominant role of doubt in the philosophical and cultural developments of the modern era.

Faith and Doubt in the Modern Era

Although doubt and the question of its significance have clearly been present from the earliest times in Christian thought, it can reasonably be argued that doubt and its relationship to faith is a modern problem. It is a problem *of* and *for* modern thought, which developed around the ideal of certainty, with human consciousness as the measure of what can be known. In this context, trust in the mystery of God is a highly dubious matter. Either faith excludes doubt, and thus becomes a kind of certainty—how this is possible needs to be explained—or faith includes doubt, which seems to suggest that faith is in some way beyond reason, and that in itself makes it questionable to the modern perspective.

In his outstanding study of eighteenth- and nineteenth-century theology, *Modern Faith and Thought,* Helmut Thielecke begins with the contention that the modern period in Western thought can be characterized in terms of doubt. "If I were to reduce the common theme to a short formula I would say that the 18th and 19th centuries, along with the preparatory and succeeding systems, are centuries of doubt."[4]

The modern period, beginning with the eighteenth century, can be described as a time when human thought and understanding turned inward, toward an awareness of the self as knowing subject. This "turn to the subject" has often been characterized in terms of a fundamental "split" in the experience or consciousness of human subjects. In speaking of a "split" it is presumed that in some sense people previously knew or experienced reality, including their perceptions or apprehensions of God, as a unified whole. Aquinas, for example, developed his philosophy of knowledge, his metaphysics and his theology on the idea of integrated orders of truth and reason, from the natural to the divine. While some levels of truth may not be immediately apprehended by human beings (e.g., divine reason), nonetheless they were conceived of as parts of a single reality. With the Enlightenment, however, came a deep questioning of what can be known by human persons for ourselves, without any reference to received wisdom, tradition, or (worst of all) ecclesiastical tutelage.

As a consequence there arose a division between what can be known immediately, i.e., our own experiences, and any other purported objects of knowledge. This "split" or division gives rise to doubt. Much that was previously claimed to be knowledge of metaphysical and divine realities now came into question. What is real? What can be known? These are some of the basic questions of modern thought.

The philosophical tenor of the period was set by René Descartes, whose work *Discourse on the Method of Rightly Conducting the Reason, and Seeking Truth in the Sciences* introduces a method of systematic doubt.[5] From his attempt to doubt everything, Descartes discovers an

---

[4] Helmut Thielecke, *Modern Faith and Thought,* trans. Geoffrey W. Bromiley (Grand Rapids, Mich.: Eerdmans, 1990) 34.

[5] René Descartes, *Discourse on the Method of Rightly Conducting the Reason,* and *Seeking Truth in the Sciences* (1637), trans. John Veitch, Everyman's Library Edition (London: Dent, 1912).

immediate certainty, expressed as "I think, therefore I am." Here we see in immediate proximity the central features of modern thought: the turning inward to discover the nature of knowledge from within human experience, the doubt of what had previously been thought to be knowledge, and a sense of "split" between the self and those outward sources of "knowledge."

Thielecke argues that theological doubt in the modern period takes four basic forms: doubt of God's mercy, doubt of God's justice, epistemological doubt, and pragmatic doubt.[6]

Doubt of God's mercy is especially represented by Luther. This is the last "medieval" form of doubt, in that it does not arise from empirical observation of the world around us but from the human struggle to accept divine justice. Luther did not question the existence or knowledge of God. What is in question is whether God can be trusted.

Doubt of God's justice goes further than doubt of God's mercy, to question God's government of the world. Experience sometimes seems to contradict the idea of God as the creative source and foundation of all reality and ultimately gives rise to secularist thinking, in which the laws of nature become the criterion for reality. Any purported acts of God must fit within these laws.

This form of doubt in the modern era arises directly from particular events and experiences, Thielecke suggests. He discusses the Lisbon earthquake of 1755 in which between thirty thousand and sixty thousand people lost their lives. In a context where Leibniz had recently put the view that this is the best of all possible worlds, this event not only shook the earth and buildings. It was also, Thielecke says, "an earthquake in the shaky religious world." Happenings such as this not only gave rise to doubt, they also affected the way that doubt was expressed. In the psalms, for example, the questions about God's justice are addressed to God and lead to an expression of trust in God. Now that very prayer is questionable. Why pray, what is the point?[7]

This "mutation" has come about as a consequence of another quite fundamental change. Whereas previously believers implied or presumed that we are to learn from God about the nature of justice, now a concept of justice is taken to be self-evident. We learn what justice is from our knowledge of the world around us or from our own reasoning.

[6] Thielecke, *Modern Faith and Thought*, 34–48.
[7] Ibid., 36–8.

The actions of God are then evaluated against this concept of justice and how we expect the world to be.

It is, however, epistemological doubt which most characterizes the modern era. This doubt concerns the character of all religious knowledge. Various forms of questioning gave rise to this form of doubt. For example, the historical foundations of various articles of faith came into question. What reliable historical knowledge do we have of the life of Jesus? In the intellectual climate of the eighteenth and nineteenth centuries, philosophy and theology were concerned for knowledge that did not involve the sacrifice of intellectual integrity. Nothing should be believed on the basis of tradition alone. People should believe only those things which could be well grounded in some form of evidence, usually taken to be historical in form. All other matters fall under epistemological doubt.

It is important to recognize that the emergence of theological doubt in these forms is not necessarily to be identified with rationalism. One of the great thinkers of this period was Friedrich Schleiermacher, whose attempt to establish the credibility of faith to its "cultured despisers" was not an appeal to rational demonstrability but to the uniqueness of our religious sensibility. Neither does this movement of doubt signal a wholesale rebellion or willful rejection of God. Rather, Thielecke argues, it evidences a genuine searching for a faith that is well grounded and is consistent with the modern world and is worthy of the dignity of human persons.[8]

The final form of modern doubt is pragmatic doubt. This way of thinking is better characterized as political than theological. Here religious ideas are no longer evaluated in terms of truth; rather, they are assessed in terms of their adequacy or usefulness in the social situation. Thielecke sees the emergence of ideology as a governing influence in almost all modern societies as the major expression of this form of doubt. While Marxism is perhaps the most obvious example, the overriding concern with economics in present societies can be seen as further evidence of this form of doubt.

Within this overall context of doubt and new enquiry, the critical task for theology was to give some account of the truth-claims inherent in Christianity as a system of belief. On what grounds can Christianity commend itself as true and reasonable—or does faith require a commit-

---

[8] Ibid., 40.

ment against reason? Since reason was considered that which dignifies our humanity, to set religious belief against reason was to challenge human dignity and, in a sense, to set God against human beings. Whereas in earlier periods an appeal might be made to divine revelation as a basis for belief, "above" what can be known by human reasoning, this avenue was no longer available within the Enlightenment perspective. John Locke (1632–1704), in his *Essay Concerning Human Understanding*, had argued that divine revelation could operate to enlarge or inform human reason, but it would not violate our reason. Furthermore, though Locke believed that revelation may inform us about things reason alone cannot establish, reason has the final say. Locke argued that when we are presented by a claim to divine revelation, we must consult our reason "to examine whether it be a revelation from God or no," and if reason finds it to be revealed by God, "reason then declares for it as much as for any other truth, and makes it one of her dictates."[9]

Locke's approach laid the foundation for the modern understanding of religion. If there are sufficient grounds for the commitment of faith, these must be found within human experience, within the domain of what we can know, not from "beyond." For Locke this did not preclude the possibility of divine revelation, but it did set a limit to the authority to be attributed to such revelation.

As a result, in the Enlightenment period several new approaches emerged to explain how faith overcomes doubt and commends itself as a reasonable and responsible commitment. We now turn to a consideration of two of these, in the thought of Immanuel Kant and Søren Kierkegaard. In these thinkers we see illustrated the two broad options available within the modern approach to faith and doubt. On the one hand, faith is limited to the "bounds" of reason, while on the other the paradoxical or "irrational" nature of faith is embraced and doubt is overcome through a form of consciousness called "subjectivity."

Two Modern Approaches to Faith: Kant and Kierkegaard

Immanuel Kant (1724–1804) was *the* philosopher and, in a particular sense, theologian of the Enlightenment period. He lived in Prussia

---

[9] John Locke, *An Essay Concerning Human Understanding*, vol. 2, book 4, ch. 18: "Of Faith and Reason and Their Distinct Provinces," Everyman's Library Edition (London: Dent, 1947) 287.

and was in his way a devout person, though he had serious concerns about the organized religion of his day. Kant held up the ideal of the autonomous human being who was free and responsible, not accepting the imposed traditions of Church law. The autonomous person sought, through human understanding, a basis for morality and, in Kant's case, for faith in God.

Against the background of centuries of dogmatic teaching by the churches, Kant was concerned to formulate a purely rational understanding of the nature of the human person, particularly of our intellectual, moral, and religious capacities.

As regards the nature of the human mind, what we can know and how we know it and, given that framework, what we can say about the nature of the physical world, Kant wrote his most famous work, *Critique of Pure Reason*. The nature of our moral commitments and how we can make practical judgments in particular situations and yet be guided by rational or "universal" principles is the subject of Kant's *Critique of Practical Reason*.

Concerning our religious commitments, Kant wrote a quite different work, *Religion within the Limits of Reason Alone*.[10] The thrust of the argument is to proceed from our moral experience to an understanding of God as the moral law-giver. In common with other thinking of the time, Kant's is a very deistic view of God. If God is known at all in Kant's thought, it is through the moral law within human understanding.

The book begins with the question of human evil and asks whether we are inherently evil, or if there is a more fundamental capacity for good in our nature. Kant thinks there is, and by following our reason we can proceed to a form of true religion in which we strive for the coming of God's kingdom. We do this by each taking responsibility for ourselves, for our autonomous will—and not by becoming subservient to the dictates of any formal religious system. We must do what is right and good and therefore, according to Kant's moral philosophy, of universal worth. When we act in this way, the "commonwealth of moral law" becomes the foundation of God's kingdom. In short, the reign of God is a situation in which all people live according to such universalizable principles, rather than being guided by self-interest. Human beings have the potential to be such rational moral agents.

---

[10] Immanuel Kant, *Religion within the Limits of Reason Alone* (1793), trans. Theodore M. Green and Hoty H. Hudson (New York: Harper & Brothers, 1960).

What, then, has God to do with all this? According to Kant, though human beings have the potential to work out what the kingdom of God means for us, we do not always exercise our reason in this way. Many of us are simply too indolent to do this. In light of this weakness, God has sent to us the person of Jesus Christ, who is "the incarnation of the good." Christ reveals to us the nature and meaning of morality. His life is like a "demonstration model" of the kingdom of God. People will therefore find it instructive to read about Jesus' life and teachings, to help them find and do what is right. But for Kant there is nothing in historical or revealed religion that can add to reason, at least to what reason, properly developed (like Kant's!) could work out for itself. If we pursue true morality, it will lead us to the same conclusions and moral commitments and the same quality of life that serves the coming of God's reign.

There are many things that might be said in critical appraisal of Kant's version of religion "within the limits of reason alone." We will limit ourselves to two central observations. First, as a representation of human life and religious experience, and in common with Kant's moral philosophy, this work seems to take insufficient account of human weakness, especially weakness of will. As a principle of morality, the "categorical imperative" seems vulnerable to human self-delusions: we can convince ourselves that we are acting according to universalizable principles, when in reality we are not. Kant seems to have nothing to say about how people can avoid or overcome moral weakness. It is all left as a matter of ought. The difficulty is to show that we can do what we ought to do. The prospect of a moral society is entirely dependent upon the enlightened good will and moral efforts of human beings. When this is offered as a vision of what we may hope for—the kingdom of God—it seems a remote hope indeed. It should also be said that Kant's religion is scarcely recognizable as a rendition of the gospel message Jesus preached.

This leads to the second criticism, which concerns the specifically theological content of Kant's view of religion. As Theodore Greene has argued, Kant actually has very little room for God in his religion. He refuses any place for what we might call devotion to God, and for the action of God within human lives. God is not known personally.[11] Kant's whole religious theory is anthropocentric. We might add that

[11] Theodore Greene, introduction to Immanuel Kant, *Religion within the Limits of Reason Alone* (New York: Harper Torchbooks, 1934) lxxvi.

Kant's view of Christ has the same import. Though Christ is helpful to us, as the incarnation of the good, he is not essential, for we could in fact work out what the kingdom of God means for ourselves, and we must bring that situation about by our own moral efforts. Few Christians would be satisfied with this understanding of Christ as an illustration or demonstration of the good life.

The crucial failing is the absence of any distinctively *religious* experience which might allow for a knowledge of God as real and as powerful as Kant's own appreciation of the moral law. It is this dimension of religious experience, a sense of encounter with God, which leads people to be convinced about their faith and to act upon those convictions. Such faith changes people and makes them do what they know is right. In short, Kant has substituted his own moral sensibility for religion, and the moral law for God. On this basis we have to conclude that Kant's account of "religion within the limits of reason alone" is not an adequate explanation of the nature and basis of faith. It does not include the crucial personal elements which define and give life to Christian faith, and in so doing fails to give an account of how faith lives with or overcomes doubt. Kant's version of religion may claim to be certain, in a rational form of certainty, but it does so at the expense of those aspects of religion which give it its distinctive life and meaning.

There are two immediate points of similarity between the thought of Kant and that of the Danish philosopher and theologian Søren Kierkegaard (1813–55). Both were highly critical of the formal religion of their time and each sought to redefine the focus of Christian faith, within the parameters of human consciousness. Whereas Kant defines faith in terms of reason, for Kierkegaard faith is an existential state, which he termed "subjectivity."

Kierkegaard was especially critical of "schools" of thinking and systems of ideas behind which people could hide. For him this was a way of avoiding the costly personal encounter of faith. In common with other Enlightenment thinkers, he wanted people to be themselves, to be responsible for themselves and think their own ideas. This was one reason he published many of his works pseudonymously, lest people become his disciples.

In his *Philosophical Fragments,* Kierkegaard discussed the question of how faith relates to knowledge.[12] In contrast to the prevailing argu-

---

[12] Søren Kierkegaard, *Philosophical Fragments,* trans. Niels Thulstrup (Princeton, N.J.: Princeton University Press, 1962).

ments about revelation, reason, and the value of historical knowledge (about Jesus, especially), Kierkegaard argued that it was necessary to cut through all that preoccupation with the knowing mind. Truth, knowing the truth, is a completely different sort of relationship, a different state of being.

To explain the nature of faith, he introduced what he called "the absolute paradox": in order to be our teacher, God has appeared amongst us as an individual human being. The incarnation of God in Christ is paradoxical in two ways. Here God reveals the absolute unlikeness: that we should see that we are not like God—as Kierkegaard says in other places, there is "an infinite qualitative distance" between God and humankind. On the other side, this same act of incarnation not only shows the distance but also makes possible a new relationship which "does away with the absolute unlikeness, in absolute likeness."

Our reason finds this impossible to conceive. That is the nature of the paradox. It is not just an apparent contradiction: it is something that reason cannot handle. Kierkegaard describes the response of reason to the paradox in terms of *offense,* which he sees as a necessary stage preliminary to faith.

The heart of the book seeks to describe the response which the paradox positively seeks. Negatively, the paradox—the incarnation—cannot be understood, analyzed, or grasped by an objective, disengaged person. Positively, it can be met, related to, and received. Here Kierkegaard talks of "the Moment": in that moment of transformation, reason and paradox meet and a third element enters—not offense, but faith.

Such faith it is not historical knowledge. To be an eyewitness is not what makes one a disciple. Equally, faith is not an act of the will, a matter of making yourself believe. Once again this would put the matter entirely in the hands of the person, as a controlling agent. Positively, the "condition" (which is one of the unusual terms Kierkegaard uses to describe faith) is a gift: "The God gave to the disciple the condition that enables him to see him, opening for him the eyes of faith."[13]

While faith is a gift, receiving this gift involves us in not doing various things. First it means not remaining in the offense of reason. Next it involves us in not doubting, where doubt means not making any response at all. Thus it means trusting. The reality is that in face of the paradox, we do not have the kind of knowledge that might satisfy reason:

[13] Ibid., 80.

faith is always open to doubt, yet it does not doubt. We live with this paradox, this lack of logical or objective certainty, and we can only do so in terms of being a disciple.

In a later work, *Concluding Unscientific Postscript,* Kierkegaard further explains that to live in faith means maintaining *subjectivity.* Subjectivity is the opposite of the objective, uninvolved, controlling function of reason or the will: in subjectivity we are engaged, we respond, we learn, we are changed: we are the disciple, we receive, and this is what it means to have faith.

For Kierkegaard, then, faith can be genuinely centered upon Christ, rather than upon "objective propositions" or the doctrines of an institutionally organized religion, only when the believer remains constantly aware of the objective uncertainty and risk of faith. To have faith then requires that we engage *in a constant recognition of doubt.* To be aware of doubt keeps faith alive and real. In an evocative image of the risk of faith, he once wrote, "If I wish to preserve myself in faith I must constantly be intent upon holding fast to the objective uncertainty, so as to remain out upon the deep, over seventy thousand fathoms of water, still preserving my faith."[14] While doubt is something to be overcome in the "passionate inwardness" of faith, faith itself can be lively and vital only so long as it is aware of and is stimulated by doubt.

As we have seen, faith as subjectivity inherently means that it is a gift, a response to the approach of God, represented by Kierkegaard as "the paradox." The only thing a person can do to receive faith is to make themselves available to the paradox, in order to be confronted by it. One critical question which arises here is whether it necessarily follows that people will receive "the condition" of faith. It seems not, for not all who have attended to the life of Christ have become disciples. Though Kierkegaard might argue that these have not truly made themselves open to the paradox as disciples willing to be taught, or have become stuck in the "offense" of reason, this would suggest that faith is dependent upon an appropriate attitude or volition on the part of the potential disciple.

There are other difficulties with Kierkegaard's account of the origin and nature of faith. Not many Christians would recognize the object of

---

[14] Søren Kierkegaard, *Concluding Unscientific Postscript,* trans. David F. Swenson (Princeton, N.J.: Princeton University Press, 1941). See especially chapter 2, "Truth Is Subjectivity," 182–209. A valuable discussion of Kierkegaard's understanding of faith and its relation to doubt can be found in Louis Dupre, *Kierkegaard as Theologian* (London: Sheed and Ward, 1964) ch. 4.

their faith in his description of "the absolute paradox." Nor can we agree with his argument that faith is not in any way shaped or informed by historical knowledge about Jesus. The idea that Jesus of Nazareth was the incarnation of God is itself dependent upon such information. Finally, it is questionable whether faith can be or needs to be set in such strict opposition to reason. Kierkegaard's argument here seems to be unnecessarily dialectical, as a technique for avoiding explanation of how we come to faith.

These difficulties serve to illustrate the broader criticism that Kierkegaard has not in fact explained how faith "overcomes" doubt. He insists that faith is a commitment which does not doubt, in spite of a sea of uncertainty, yet he seems to allow no place in faith for rational foundations which might support and give direction to that commitment. In contrast to Kant, Kierkegaard's analysis sees faith as lively and personally engaged, with clear evidence of what Greene calls religious devotion. But Kierkegaard's account of how we come to this commitment is far from convincing, and this leaves open the question of doubt and how it relates to faith. It is notable that each of these accounts of faith involves a quite inadequate christology. In both instances Jesus' life functions at most as a revelatory illustration of a human life available to the presence or purposes of God.

We have examined briefly two seminal responses to the distinctively modern challenge of doubt. Each seeks to explain, from within the parameters of human experience, how we come to faith and how faith is fully consistent with our dignity as human beings. The difficulty we have found, however, is that a completely rational account of faith seems devoid of those essentially personal dimensions which give faith life and meaning. On the other hand, an exclusive stress on the subjectivity of faith may retain its vitality but severs it from rational foundations and thus threatens its integrity.

The dilemma for modern theology has been to explain how faith can include both a rational conviction and a lively personal commitment. A central methodological issue for theology has been whether an adequate account of faith can be given within the modern mind-set. The concern for certainty has limited the focus of theology to the human subject, whether to the critical mind or the "subjective" person. Can the knowledge of God be limited to the dimensions of human consciousness, or is there not something within the experience of God which transcends or goes beyond rational human experience? A central task of theology in the last two centuries has been to offer a coherent, critical account of what Christians claim as knowledge of God through faith. To do so, theologians have sought to develop an epistemology of faith which responds to the dilemmas posed by the modern outlook. In doing so, they have also addressed the question of how faith excludes, overcomes, or incorporates doubt.

In the next three chapters we will examine theological frameworks offered by three major contributors of the late modern era: John Henry Newman, Karl Barth, and Paul Tillich. These theologians specifically addressed the issues we have raised in this chapter and offered a distinctive account of how faith relates to doubt. For each of them, the central element in a theological response to doubt is an encounter with God—and yet they offer quite distinctive and, in some ways, contradictory accounts of the nature of faith and its relation to doubt.

2

Faith as Assent, Incompatible with Doubt

It is in the thought of John Henry Newman (1801–90), perhaps more than any other writer, that we find a sustained philosophical and theological exploration of the relationship of faith, belief, and doubt. Newman himself was well qualified for such a study. He spent a long period of his life seeking to explain the nature of his faith and his own sense of conviction. His writings on the subject are numerous, ranging from letters to people who sought his pastoral guidance through to his book *Essay in Aid of a Grammar of Assent* and the numerous papers he wrote preparatory to that work.[1] For many of his contemporaries the concept of faith itself and various "difficulties" surrounding specific Christian doctrines meant that faith could never be indubitably certain. Newman rejected this view and argued that faith must be understood as unconditional assent, a natural action of the mind in which doubt is rejected. What is highly distinctive in Newman's approach, however, is his appeal to our common experience of assent in everyday life, not only in matters of faith.

As we study Newman's thought, we shall see that he was in many ways a thoroughly modern thinker. Newman appealed to human experience as a basis for argument. "We are what we are," he declared. He grounds his theology in the encounter with God through conscience, in other words, within human experience, though unlike Kant he believes that in this way we can have knowledge of a reality beyond ourselves.

---

[1] John Henry Newman, *An Essay in Aid of a Grammar of Assent* (London: University of Notre Dame Press, 1979). Hereafter abbreviated in the text as *Grammar of Assent.*

This is crucial for Newman, for without what he called a real apprehension of God, faith lacks the essential impetus and vitality necessary for acts of devotion and morality. Thus Newman's thought can be seen as providing a way between Kierkegaard's stress on subjectivity as the essence of faith and Kant's purely "rational" religion. Newman sought to explain how faith can be rational and yet include positive vitality and commitment. Such faith, he maintained, has the distinctive feature of being incommensurate with doubt.

In his own life Newman moved from a youthful experience of evangelicalism, through his years at Oxford as an Anglican, then his conversion to Roman Catholicism in 1845. Having changed his position several times, he found it necessary to explain these moves and to ask whether he might change again. In his *Apologia Pro Vita Sua* he addressed these questions, declaring that after he became a Roman Catholic he never had one doubt.[2]

In this chapter we will examine the development of Newman's approach to faith and the various ways in which he sought to explain his certitude. Our study will focus specifically on *Grammar of Assent*. In doing so, however, we will need to consider several critical issues in the contemporary study of Newman's thought. This will lead to a critical appraisal of Newman's particular contribution to the understanding of faith and its relationship to doubt.

A number of important factors came together in Newman's understanding of religion. He was convinced that religious commitments properly involved more than a reasoned conclusion. He could never have been content with Kant's idea of a religion within the bounds of reason alone because, as he wrote in *Grammar of Assent*, "If religion is to be devotion . . . and action . . . we need something higher than a mere balance of arguments to fix and to control our minds."[3] But what exactly is this "something more"? In looking for Newman's answer, it is important to note that it is something more than, not something other than, reasoned argument. Newman did not support the view that faith is independent of the rational processes of our minds. As we shall see, his view was quite the opposite. Faith does arise from a process of reasoning, but reason alone is not sufficient to bring us to active faith.

[2] John Henry Newman, *Apologia Pro Vita Sua,* ed. with introduction by Martin J. Svaglic (Oxford: Clarendon Press, 1967) 214. Hereafter abbreviated in both text and notes as *Apologia.*

[3] Newman, *Grammar of Assent,* 193.

There are three specific factors which Newman identified as important in faith. These factors were significant aspects of his own development, and when he insists on these elements he is in part arguing on the basis of his own life story. The first of these factors is a definite dogmatic structure, a system of doctrine. Newman described his experience of evangelical conversion as a great change of thought: "I fell under the influence of a definite Creed, and received into my intellect impressions of dogma which . . . have never been effaced or obscured."[4] The importance of a dogmatic structure in faith was part of Newman's opposition to two forms of religion he saw as quite inadequate, if not dangerous. One was the "notional" religion which he saw in much Protestantism. In *Grammar of Assent* he argues that the basic requirements of notional religion are Bible reading and "living a correct life." He describes it as a religion of pious sentiment, Bible stories, and religious ideas. But for Newman it is an inferior form of religion because it lacks dogma, being "comparatively careless of creed and catechism." It induces its followers to be content with "a meagre view of revealed truth."[5] A related but distinct opponent of genuine faith, in Newman's view, is what he termed "liberalism." In *Apologia* he defined liberalism as "the anti-dogmatic principle and its developments," which were expressed in "a deep plausible scepticism."[6] Later he expounded his view of liberalism further. Liberalism involves a "false liberty of thought . . . [and] the mistake of subjecting to human judgment those revealed doctrines which are in their nature beyond and independent of it."[7]

In 1879 Newman delivered a speech in which he denounced liberalism as "the doctrine that there is no positive truth in religion, one creed is as good as another. . . . It is inconsistent with the recognition of any religion as *true*."[8] For Newman, faith involves commitment to a definite dogmatic structure, not just some ideas about sacred events in the past. For him it was essential that this dogmatic structure also had present significance, enabling a person to know the realities to which it refers and evoking a lively response.

[4] Newman, *Apologia*, 17.
[5] Newman, *Grammar of Assent*, 63.
[6] Newman, *Apologia*, 54.
[7] Ibid., 256.
[8] Meriol Trevor, *Newman,* vol. 2: *Light in Winter* (London: Macmillan and Co., 1962) 568.

Newman was also convinced, however, that religious commitments were rational. To follow a definite dogmatic creed did not require the abandonment of our critical faculties. At Oxford he had belonged to a circle known as the "Oriel Noetics," a group of logicians and philosophers who were to exercise a strong influence on his thought. The Oriel Noetics upheld a quasi-ethical standard for belief: it was considered right to assent to a proposition only to the degree justified by the supporting evidence for it. Religious beliefs were considered only probabilities, because they could not be demonstrated deductively. As a consequence these beliefs should not be held with indubitable certainty. Nonetheless there could be a "moral certainty" arising from the accumulation of evidence, a "convergence of probabilities." For this reason it was considered appropriate to develop numerous arguments or "evidences" in support of Christian belief.

Newman was initially attracted by the approach of the Oriel Noetics and indeed assisted Richard Whately, one of the leaders of the group, in the formulation of his *Elements of Logic*. But he was not wholly convinced by Whately's approach, particularly because it subjugated faith to human reason and judgment. Newman recognized the need for grounds for belief, but resisted the idea that faith is dependent upon what can be demonstrated by reason, at least by formal, syllogistic reasoning. He did not agree that we should only believe those things we could prove. For him there was a place for accepting matters on authority, if we have good reason to trust that authority. His opposition to the Noetics' account of faith and certainty was not clearly formulated, however, until *Apologia* and not expounded fully until *Grammar of Assent*. There he rejected the demand that assent must be limited to the degree or weight of supporting evidence. Faith as assent does follow a process of reasoning, but once we move to assent, Newman held, then we are certain.

This brings us to the third element in Newman's view of religion, the question of certainty. For many years this was a puzzling issue for Newman. At Easter 1848, for example, he wrote a paper entitled "Ultimate Resolution of Certainty of Faith." There he presented the problem as follows: "The *difficulty* is this: Faith is conceived to be inconsistent with *doubt*. How then can it be the result of *reasoning*? For no reasoning, in moral subjects, leads to an indubitable conclusion."[9]

---

[9] John Henry Newman, "Ultimate Resolution of Certainty of Faith." This paper, found in Packet B.9.11 of Newman's papers, is cited as Appendix III in David A. Pailin,

Against the prevailing liberalism he asserted that "there are many truths in concrete matters which no one can demonstrate, yet everyone unconditionally accepts."[10] The "rational" requirement of liberalism was unnatural and false; it was contrary to the way in which the human mind does in fact operate. *Grammar of Assent* attempts to describe a "wider logic," to show that in concrete matters we can be and are certain.

Newman's particular interest was to demonstrate the "logic" of faith, which enabled him to claim that he had no doubts. While there may be "manifold variations" of opinion in the application of specific doctrines, at the core of a living faith there must be "indefectible certitude in primary truths."[11] Faith is compatible with doubt about "secondary" aspects of religion, but at the primary level faith and doubt are incompatible. After he had finished *Grammar of Assent* Newman noted in his journal eighteen different attempts he had made to write on the certainty of faith.[12] In all these preliminary papers Newman was intending to write a work on certainty, to show how a dubitable conclusion could issue in personal certainty. It was only in 1866 that he decided to change his approach, to focus on the concept of assent rather than certainty.

Grammar of Assent

In this brief outline of *Grammar of Assent* we will need to negotiate a number of issues of interpretation which have arisen amongst scholars of Newman's thought. The book itself is divided into two main parts. The first explains how assent is related to "apprehension"; the second deals with the way assent follows upon "inference" or reasoning. As we shall see, if the exposition of Newman's thought places a stronger emphasis on either one of these parts, we receive a different view of what Newman means by faith as assent, and consequently a different understanding of how he thinks faith overcomes doubt. It will be

---

The Way to Faith: An Examination of Newman's Grammar of Assent *as a Response to the Search for Certainty in Faith* (London: Epworth Press, 1969) 206.

[10] Newman, *Grammar of Assent*, 136.

[11] Ibid., 194.

[12] John Henry Newman, *Autobiographical Writings*, ed. Henry Tristram (London: Sheed and Ward, 1956) journal entry for October 30, 1870.

important, therefore, to signal these critical elements and their implications as we proceed.

Newman wrote that in this work he was trying to explain "what the
mind does, what it contemplates, when it makes an act of faith."[13] In a
letter to Henry Beckly he explained that his main thesis is "that by the
nature of the human mind we assent absolutely on reasons which taken
separately are but probabilities."[14] For Newman *Grammar of Assent* explains how we come to believe, "absolutely" and without doubt. What,
then, are the elements of this process of assent?

Apprehension

Newman's analysis of faith begins with his identification of apprehension as the condition of assent. Newman defined apprehension as
the interpretation given to the terms of a proposition.[15] When we apprehend a proposition we grasp its sense or meaning to some degree. It
was vitally important to Newman's purpose, however, to distinguish
apprehension and comprehension. He believed that we can apprehend
and assent to propositions we do not fully understand; on the other
hand, we can understand ideas which we do not grasp as realities.

Newman distinguished two types or modes of apprehension: real
and notional. Accordingly, we may assent to a proposition as a reality
(Newman called this a real assent) or as a notion (notional assent). Unfortunately his description of the difference between these types of
apprehension is not very clear, but from the later application of the
distinction in regard to assent we can grasp it reasonably clearly. A real
apprehension, Newman says, relates to experience: "Real apprehension
is . . . in the first instance an experience or information about the concrete."[16] Such an apprehension may be of a "concrete" experience as such,
or of something remembered, or even imagined or invented, by combining elements of other real apprehensions. Newman often states that
real apprehension and real assents concern things, while notions concern the relations between things.[17] So we can say that real apprehen-

---

[13] Newman, *Grammar of Assent*, 93–4.

[14] Charles Dessain and Thomas Gornall, eds., *The Letters and Diaries of John Henry
Newman*, vol. 25 (Oxford: Clarendon Press, 1973) 266. Letter to Henry Beckly, January
1871.

[15] Newman, *Grammar of Assent*, 32.

[16] Ibid., 38.

[17] For example, pp. 44, 49, and 51.

sions concern particular things, while notional apprehensions concern conceptual relations.

The distinction between these two types of apprehension is vital for Newman's analysis of assent. H. H. Price has remarked that this distinction is Newman's "most original contribution to the epistemology of belief."[18] The way in which we apprehend a proposition gives a distinct character to our assent to it. Real apprehension, Newman argued, is stronger because things are more impressive and affective than notions. Accordingly real assents are stronger, because they concern things or the impressions things have left upon our imagination. Real assents, furthermore, are proper to the individual and have a personal character because they reflect that person's apprehension of the idea in question and their way of coming to an assent.[19] Since they depend upon personal experience, real assents create divisions between people, in the sense of inhibiting our understanding of one another, while notional assents are unlikely to have this effect.

When we ask how these elements apply to religious assents, we come to the first critical issue in the study of Newman's thought. Whereas much scholarship has been focused on his ideas of assent following informal processes of reasoning, some more recent scholarship has given greater weight to the element of apprehension. Ian Ker's recent study *Newman on Being a Christian* argues, I think rightly, that for Newman the assent of faith is vitally dependent upon the moral attitudes of a person as they apprehend religious propositions.[20] Ker draws upon earlier works, such as Newman's *Oxford University Sermons*, which argue that before a person can come to believe they must acknowledge the "antecedent probability" that Christian doctrines might be true. This acknowledgment, however, is a moral stance. It reflects what he called "first principles," which have to do with whether we expect all matters to be proven before any credence can be granted, or whether we are prepared to accept the possibility of their being true, for the sake of argument and further consideration. To be unwilling to grant this "antecedent probability" expresses an attitude of skepticism, Newman argued, for in reality "first principles" themselves cannot be proven. Thus he held there must be a moral openness to the possibility

---

[18] H. H. Price, *Belief: The Gifford Lectures Delivered at the University of Aberdeen in 1960* (London: George Allen & Unwin, 1969) 316.

[19] Newman, *Grammar of Assent*, 82–3.

[20] Ian Ker, *Newman on Being a Christian* (London: HarperCollins, 1991) ch. 1.

of religious truth before there can be any revelation. At times he actually declares that this openness to the antecedent probability of Christianity being true is what marks the difference between a good person and a bad person.[21]

In *Grammar of Assent* Newman discusses the moral foundation of faith in terms of conscience. It is the vital, enlivening factor in our religious assents. It is helpful to distinguish several specific roles of conscience in Newman's thought. The first of these concerns our apprehension of the reality of God. For Newman conscience is our religious "starting point."[22] The awareness of God through conscience is the "connecting principle" in religion, relating creature and creator, enabling us to form an elementary "image" of God as the Moral Governor and Supreme Ruler of the world. Conscience here is a medium of real apprehension, providing a necessary but not sufficient condition for real assent. In this role conscience serves to prepare the mind by creating an "anticipation" of revelation, Newman argues. He describes the way in which conscience may lead even a young child to such an apprehension of God.[23] Of itself, though, this apprehension through conscience does not create the real assent of faith. It may predispose us to believe that God is a reality, but before we actually assent in faith we must have some reason, or something which to us counts as a reason, for our assent.

Inference

Newman made a fundamental distinction between assent and inference or reasoning. He saw these as distinct acts of the mind. Inferences and conclusions are said by him to be conditional, while assent is always unconditional. Newman argues strenuously that assent is always unconditional. No example can be given of conditional assent, for even when we decide that something is only probable, our assent is categorical. It does not involve a degree of assent.[24]

---

[21] John Henry Newman, *Fifteen Sermons Preached Before the University of Oxford* (London: Rivingtons, 1884). See especially the tenth sermon, "Faith and Reason, Contrasted as Habits of Mind," pars. 33–44.

[22] Newman once wrote: "To gain religious starting points, we must interrogate our hearts, our own hearts, . . . interrogate our own consciences, interrogate, I will say, the God who dwells there." Letter to Louisa Simeon, June 25, 1869. Dessain and Gornall, eds., *Letters and Diaries*, vol. 26, 275–6.

[23] Newman, *Grammar of Assent*, 103–5.

[24] Ibid., 147.

The central issue in part two of *Grammar of Assent* is the relation between assent and inference. Newman poses what he calls a "paradox": "how it comes to pass that a conditional act leads to an unconditional." How can a process of reasoning, issuing in a conditional conclusion, lead to an unconditional assent? It is natural, instinctive, to reason and draw conclusions. We do so almost "unconsciously," that is, unselfconsciously. Furthermore, in simple matters we pass from reasoning to assent without a further thought, again almost instinctively. But the ease with which we sometimes move from inference to assent does not destroy the independence of assent, for no amount of reasoning can compel our assent. A belief (or assent) may endure after the reasoning on which it was initially founded has been refuted or abandoned. Equally we may agree that certain evidence leads to a particular conclusion and yet withhold our assent. There may be moral motives which hinder our assent, Newman suggests, quoting the saying, "A man convinced against his will is of the same opinion still."[25]

Newman's answer to this "paradox" of inferences and assent is also the basis of his answer to the question of certainty, and thus of how faith excludes doubt. We must therefore follow his argument in some detail.

Newman distinguished two forms of reasoning: formal and informal.[26] By formal reasoning he meant syllogistic reasoning, the sort of argument which is or can be set out in premises and conclusions. Newman did not consider this form of reasoning to be very useful in general. The concrete matters of daily life are too complex for syllogisms. In these matters we use informal or implicit reasoning. In informal inference we do not argue from proposition to proposition, but "from things to things, from concrete to concrete, from whole to whole."[27] In this sense the "inference" involved is implicit. This mode of reasoning is at once complex—so complex that it may not be able to be expressed—and yet simple, for we reason in this way without effort or instruction.

Not only do we reason in this informal manner, but we arrive unselfconsciously at conclusions and assents as well. We judge that a matter is "as good as proven." Our ability to derive conclusions in this way is what Newman called "the illative sense." We can sense that something is proven. In contrast to formal inference, illation does not conform to fixed and explicit procedures. Nonetheless our illative faculty

---

[25] Ibid., 143.
[26] Ibid., ch. 8.
[27] Ibid., 260.

can be improved by experience and instruction. It is also "departmen-
tal," in the sense that we may be more proficient in making correct
judgments in some areas and less expert in others.[28] The illative sense is
our ability to make judgments, to come not only to conclusions but to
convictions, in situations or matters where a formal process of reasoning is not immediately available to us.

Having identified the various types of reasoning, Newman's "paradox" or puzzle remains: How do we pass from reasoning and conclusions to the unconditional act of assent?

Assent

In his seminal study of Newman's thought, *The Way to Faith*, David
Pailin observes that it is surprising that in a "grammar" of assent Newman actually says very little about how we assent.[29] This observation
reflects Pailin's particular perspective in interpreting Newman. Though
he offers a careful exposition of *Grammar of Assent*, Pailin stresses the
element of inference and assent as personal commitment, with less
recognition of the significance Newman attributed to real apprehension of the objects of such assent. Thus when he asks how we come to
an unconditional assent from inconclusive reasoning, Pailin describes
Newman's answer as follows:

> In the end it is our will which determines whether or not our assent
> is granted. The move from antecedent reasoning to assent is a logical
> type-jump which no degree of conclusiveness can ever entail. Rea-
> soning may exert a tremendous influence upon us but ultimately it
> can never compel us to assent against our will.[30]

According to this analysis, the crucial factor in our coming to faith is
our willingness to assent, our "acceptance" of a proof as adequate. Assent
is that act of mind in which we confer this acceptance upon a conclusion. In support of Pailin's view that it is an act of will which brings us to
assent, we might cite a passage from Newman's semi-autobiographical
novel *Loss and Gain: The Story of a Convert*. Toward the end of the story
Reding, a young man in search of faith, has been logically moved to accept the Catholic faith, but is still unsure of the nature of faith. Just how

---

[28] Ibid., 267.
[29] Pailin, *The Way to Faith*, 161.
[30] Ibid., 131.

does a person come to believe? Reding asks, "What is to make him believe?" to which the reply is given:

> What is to make him believe! The will, his will. . . . If there is evidence enough to believe Scripture, and we shall see that there is, I repeat, there is more than enough to believe the Church. The evidence is not in fault; all it requires is to be brought home or applied to the mind; if belief does not then follow, the fault lies with the will.[31]

Pailin's analysis has been resisted by a number of scholars, however. Nicholas Lash retorts that "Newman never 'leapt' anywhere in his life." Lash follows the argument of John Coulson that, according to Newman, we grow into conviction rather than "leap."[32] The crucial issues here center upon the role of conscience in bringing about an unconditional assent. Just as our illative faculty "sanctions" our conclusions and judgments in concrete matters, so our conscience sanctions or prohibits our assent. There are other similarities between conscience and the illative sense: there is often no stated connection between the evidence and the judgment. The "method" or "procedure" of both is peculiar to the individual and is characteristic of the individual as a person. Both conscience and the illative sense have "authority" for us, as our own way of reaching a decision in practical matters. Finally, both improve in accuracy with experience and use.[33]

The act of assent is made under the sanction of conscience.[34] Since conscience provides us with a real apprehension of God as well as of our moral duties, it has a magisterial function. If a conclusion presented by our reason is consistent with our understanding of God, truth, right, and wrong, our assent will be commended, and vice versa. Conscience may thus exert a moral pressure to bring us to assent or to withhold our assent. It is this factor which demonstrates the personal character of assent. According to Pailin, it is by means of this personal

---

[31] John Henry Newman, *Loss and Gain: The Story of a Convert,* 6th ed. (London: Burns, Oates and Co., 1874) 384. Emphasis is Newman's.

[32] Nicholas Lash, introduction to John Henry Newman, *An Essay in Aid of a Grammar of Assent* (London: University of Notre Dame Press, 1979) 17. John Coulson, "Belief and Imagination," *Downside Review* 90 (1972) 1–14. The most substantial critique of Pailin's exposition is to be found in M. Jamie Ferreira, *Doubt and Religious Commitment: The Role of the Will in Newman's Thought* (Oxford: Clarendon Press, 1980).

[33] These similarities are in fact pointed out by Pailin, *The Way to Faith,* 163.

[34] Newman, *Grammar of Assent,* 98–9.

involvement that we make the "logical type-jump" from the logic of reasons and conclusions to the logic of personal commitments. In assenting, we are involved as persons.

This conclusion, however, far from being an exposition of Newman's thought, could be said to represent an opposite approach. Newman's entire purpose in *Grammar of Assent* was to show that the assent of faith does not involve a "jump" of logical types. On the contrary his purpose was to show that faith involves a form of reasoning which, together with a real apprehension of God, affirms and assents to what is so apprehended. The crucial issue here, in interpreting Newman, is whether we give equal weight to the role of apprehension and reasoning, in our coming to faith. Is real apprehension, as Pailin suggests, an antecedent of assent, or is it a crucial part of that assent? Real apprehension, alone, does not lead to faith; neither does a process of reasoning. Together, however, under the guidance of conscience, these elements lead a person—Newman would say "naturally"—to faith.

Thus we can see several distinct roles of a person's will or moral disposition in relation to faith. First, as we have seen, Newman held that a person can resist any assent or faith, if by disposition they are skeptical and will not allow the "antecedent probability" of Christian teaching. Second, it appears that conscience, rightly exercised, guides a person to the unconditional assent of faith, upon the basis of informal reasoning. Third, as I shall argue later, Newman seems to have implied that the will has a role to play in the maintenance or continuation of our faith as certitude. Before we can deal with this role of the will, however, we must take note of one further element in Newman's exposition of the nature of faith: the idea of complex assent.

Complex Assent

Newman distinguished between simple and complex assents.[35] In a simple assent we adhere to a belief without reservation or doubt, and without conscious deliberation. Complex assent is a more deliberate act. It is the reflexive affirmation of a simple assent: in it we assent deliberately to an existing assent, confirming that this is what we believe. Complex assent usually follows some deliberate and recognizable process of reasoning, or may be our response when one of our beliefs or assents is challenged or called into question. It is crucial for Newman's

---

[35] Ibid., 157.

entire thesis that faith is a state of complex assent, which can be described in terms of certitude.

Certitude is the psychological state of being certain, and is logically distinct from certainty, which is the quality of propositions which are proved beyond doubt. When a person is certain of a truth, Newman claims, they cannot endure the thought that the contrary opinion may be true.[36] This "magisterial intolerance" is part of the subjective condition of being certain; doubts are "put down with a high hand" as being "preposterous."[37]

Being certain is no absolute guarantee that our belief is true, however. Newman describes five deficient forms of certitude. These often take the form of bold protestations against a contrary view. The vehemence of a person's attitude or statements is no guarantee of truth. But while we can be deluded, Newman maintains that generally we can trust our certitudes. When properly founded, our complex assents can be taken to be certainties.

The question now arises: What is involved in the idea of our complex assents being "properly founded," so that we can know that our confidence is well placed? In particular, how can faith be certain? The key to Newman's account of how faith excludes doubt is his argument for the "indefectibility of certitudes."[38] Having recognized that false certitudes can occur, he now provides three "tests" for genuine certitudes. Positively, a genuine certitude follows upon investigation and proof. It is not an irrational, unreasoned judgment, but an assent based upon what is judged to be adequate proof. Second, certitudes admit of an "interior" test: along with the "magisterial intolerance" mentioned earlier certitude is "accompanied by a specific sense of intellectual satisfaction and repose." This feeling is the proper token of complex assent, and does not accompany simple assent, doubt, or inference alone. There is a peaceful sense of the issue being positively concluded. The third "test" of genuine certitudes is that they are irreversible. Newman argues, using specific examples, that someone who reverses their complex assent, that is, someone who rejects a belief of which they claimed to be certain, was in fact never certain.[39]

---

[36] Ibid., 164–5.
[37] Ibid., 178.
[38] Ibid., 181–208.
[39] Ibid., 197–200. There has been some critical discussion of this third "test" of certitudes. David Pailin argues that Newman has forgotten or failed to grasp fully his own

With these "tests" Newman places a limitation upon our certitudes. In general, probability, not certitude, must be the guide to life. Our certitudes may be few in number, but those we do have (or can have) are of the utmost importance. The probabilities of everyday life are fixed and founded upon certainties, and at the core of religion, too, there are certainties. While there may be a range of opinion in the application of various doctrines, at the core of a living faith there must be "indefectible certitude in primary truths."[40]

At this point, we can conclude this outline of Newman's view of faith as a categorical assent to those primary truths of religion, in a state of certitude. We now turn to a detailed consideration of his claim that such faith excludes doubt.

The Incompatibility of Faith and Doubt

In *Grammar of Assent* Newman says very little directly about doubt. At the beginning of the work he explains that there are three ways of "holding" propositions: we may *infer* or conclude, say, that it will rain today; we may *assent* to this conclusion; or we may suspend judgment, that is, *doubt*. Each is a distinct mental act and all three are natural to the mind.[41] It is proper to doubt in circumstances where we do not have an adequate basis for assent. In religion, however, Newman held, we do have such a basis and we can have certainty.

From some of his writings the impression may be gained that Newman was opposed to all doubt. It appears that in temperament he was intolerant of doubt and was irritated by the "slanderous" accusation that he was a doubter.[42] In one of his "Discourses Addressed to Mixed Congregations" he declared that the Church *forbids* its people to doubt.[43] It is important to recognize, however, that Newman's embargo on doubt had a specific and limited purpose. There were forms of doubt

---

distinction between certainties and certitudes. The fact that a person reverses a complex assent does not prove that they were not certain (logically)—for the proposition may yet be true. Pailin, *The Way to Faith*, 180–1.

[40] Newman, *Grammar of Assent*, 194.

[41] Ibid., 26–7.

[42] Dessain and Gornall, eds., *Letters and Diaries*, vol. 25, 181–2, 184–5. Letters to Henry Wilberforce, October 1870.

[43] Discourse XI, "Faith and Doubt," in John Henry Newman, *Discourses Addressed to Mixed Congregations* (Westminster, Md.: Christian Classics, 1966) 215, emphasis mine.

he did not prohibit. Indeed, he regarded some questioning and doubt as obligatory for educated people. We will consider each of these aspects of his position in turn.

Newman's analysis of assent provides the logical basis for his claim that faith excludes doubt. The central elements of his argument—apprehension, inference, and the unconditional nature of assent—are all relevant to establishing the incompatibility of doubt and faith. But these elements do not of themselves fully explain the nature of assent and thus the way in which faith excludes doubt. Through the activity of conscience we may have a real apprehension of God, but this alone does not produce assent. Nor does Newman's excellent account of illative reasoning explain how we come to assent, for his own thesis is that assent cannot be compelled by reasoning. If we are to appreciate fully Newman's claim that faith excludes doubt we must look to the personal and religious aspects of the incompatibility of faith and doubt. This is why Newman himself turned from trying to explain faith in terms of certainty to offering a "grammar" of assent.

The crucial issue here is Newman's understanding of the role of the will in assent. It appears from various sources that Newman makes two claims about the will: positively that the will can in some sense bring about belief or assent, and negatively that the will can hinder belief and certitude. Newman once wrote to Catherine Ward, "While there is enough evidence for conviction, whether we *will* be convinced or not depends upon ourselves."[44] For Newman, to grant our assent is an act of the will, and to withhold assent is also an act of the will. By contrast, in one of his theological papers on certainty Newman described the power of the will to hinder assent and certitude in this way: "The will cannot hinder an inference . . . but it can interfere upon the perception of the conclusion. . . . The will then, though it cannot create (force) certainty, *can stifle it*."[45] In this passage Newman does not refer to a positive act of the will, in our coming to assent, but rather to the will as having the power to suppress or limit our certitude.

Further analysis suggests that what appear to be descriptions of two distinct activities are in fact two aspects of the same general thesis. The

---

[44] Dessain and Gornall, eds., *Letters and Diaries*, vol. 12, 289. Letter to Catherine Ward, October 12, 1848.

[45] Hugo Achaval and J. Derek Holmes, eds., *The Theological Papers of John Henry Newman on Faith and Certainty*, Part 1: *Papers of 1853 on Certainty of Faith* (Oxford: Clarendon Press, 1976) 15.

role of the will in assent is not to bring about or "create" assent, as if by the infusion of some additional component, "the will." In *Grammar of Assent,* Newman's argument is that assent and certitude follow naturally upon some form of reasoning, in the case of the complex assent of certitude, consciously considered reasoning. I suggest, then, that for Newman the "role" of the will in simple assent is generally at most a permissive one: we simply assent on the basis of what appears to our illative sense to be adequate grounds. When we are certain, that is, when we confirm our simple assent, it is not that we have decided to become certain but rather that our will has not "hindered" our reflexive assent. What the will has "done" here is a negative act: it has not obstructed our certitude. Our reason has convinced us that a particular conclusion is proven and, in the absence of any conscientious objection, our reflexive assent follows.

If, however, the will can "hinder" our certitude, the implication can be drawn that at least some doubt may arise from such an activity of the will. That is to say, at least some religious doubt may have the character of a willful refusal to be certain, an interference with or interruption of the natural process by which we may arrive at certitude. This was precisely the view which Newman took of doubt.

Newman held that every person has some awareness of the reality of God through conscience, although he recognized that this knowledge of God may need to be "elicited" and that it can become dimmed and distorted.[46] Equally our natural reasoning ability can provide us with sufficient grounds for belief, even in practical matters where miscellaneous considerations are too complex for any formal demonstration or proof. With due consideration of these grounds, we can and ought to be certain, Newman held.[47] To have the complex assent of certitude, in these circumstances, is a matter of obligation, and to withhold our assent is an act of rebellion. In this context, Newman seems to have regarded the activity of the will as an unnatural interference, a disturbance of the natural process by which we come to faith and to certitude.

On this basis Newman regarded religious doubt as a turning away from our awareness of God and our natural inclinations and abilities. He recognized that this doubt may take an intellectual form: we may withhold our assent because we are preoccupied with proof, or with the

---

[46] Newman, *Grammar of Assent,* 105, also 303–4.
[47] Ibid., 218.

numerous questions and "difficulties" which arise from reflection upon the doctrinal content of faith. But at least some such intellectual perplexity, in Newman's view, is in fact a "hedging" against what we know to be true. While Newman saw a proper place for theological investigation into the basis of faith, he also saw that such questioning could be used as a "cover" to avoid the moral and personal commitment of faith. In a sermon on "Faith and Doubt" he argued that to doubt (in this sense) is to "bargain for time to come not to believe . . . to doubt or disbelieve what I hold to be an eternal truth."[48] Anyone who hesitates in this way already doubts and does not believe. Interestingly, here Newman sees doubt as an indication of unbelief, not just the suspension of judgment. In this sermon Newman depicts doubt as a form of rebellion against God and God's "oracle" the Church. Such doubt begins in "self-will and disobedience" and ends in "apostasy."[49]

A similar though rather less trenchant argument can be found in *Grammar of Assent*. As Newman saw it, faith—in common with assent in general—is an expression of our human nature. Our natural abilities enable us to make this commitment. Our illative sense leads us to conclusions of which, under the guidance and sanction of conscience, we can be certain. To resist this natural process, or to insist that it is in some sense inadequate because it does not involve formal deductive reasoning, is to oppose our created nature as human beings. For Newman the very fact that we are certain in many practical matters and without deductive proof is itself a demonstration that it is not "weakness" or "absurdity" to claim to be certain. In this context the natural is normative. In practical matters we can and ought to be certain, and it is a matter of grave responsibility to resist this natural certitude.[50]

From these considerations we may see how Newman regarded doubt. For him doubt, at least the kind of doubt we have been discussing so far, involves a willful act, an exercise of the will to hinder certitude. It should not be thought, however, that Newman regarded all doubt in this way. First it must be recognized that there was one situation in which Newman would have positively encouraged doubt of a particular kind, that is, in the instance of a person who had not yet come to the assent of faith, or those who perhaps held "liberal" or "notional" religious beliefs. We may take it that Newman would encourage such people to doubt the adequacy

[48] Newman, *Discourses Addressed to Mixed Congregations*, 216.
[49] Ibid., 218.
[50] Newman, *Grammar of Assent*, 270–3.

of their religious opinions—and to consider the arguments he had developed in *Grammar of Assent*—in the hope that they might make the real assent of faith. Newman did not oppose the kind of doubt which precedes assent and which may lead to the personal commitment of faith. It was only after a person had made such a commitment that Newman regarded doubt as unnatural and inappropriate.

Investigation and Inquiry

In addition to the doubt which may precede faith, there is another form of doubt which Newman did consider to be compatible with faith. This he termed "investigation." In *Grammar of Assent* Newman distinguished two kinds of questioning: investigation and inquiry.[51] He defines inquiry as being inconsistent with assent: "He who inquires has not found; he is in doubt about where the truth lies and wishes his present profession either proved or disproved. We cannot without absurdity call ourselves at once believers and inquirers also."[52] Newman considered that such inquiry represented a position of genuine doubt—one has never assented or has suspended one's assent.

Investigation, on the other hand, is undertaken from a position of assent. To investigate is to examine the arguments in favor of (and perhaps those against) one's belief. Newman says we can "aim at inferring a proposition, while all the time assenting to it." So for example we may continue to believe that God is the creator of all that is, and yet investigate the basis and implications of this belief. We do not necessarily abandon our belief when we engage in argument about such an item of doctrine or investigate its credibility. Indeed, Newman held that investigation of the evidence and argumentative basis of our faith is an obligation for "educated minds." Intelligent people should be theologically informed. The kind of questioning which investigation involves does not imply doubt in the sense described above. It does not require suspension of belief. If called upon to do so, a person engaged in investigation would at the same time readily grant his or her assent.

Newman makes several interesting pastoral observations in this context. First he remarks that there are people whose faith is so "delicate" that they do not understand the difference between investigation and

---

[51] Ibid., 158–61.
[52] Ibid., 159.

inquiry.[53] These persons think that "to question a truth is to make it questionable" and, because they do sometimes question their faith, they are liable to think they doubt when in fact they don't, Newman says. This seems to me an important insight. A second observation is that investigation can lead to genuine doubt and the reversal of assent.[54] It is natural to investigate our beliefs. Genuine certitude is interested in the basis of its belief, and can "investigate" because it is confident of that belief. Nonetheless, Newman warns that introspection and questioning can become habitual, and one may easily pass over from investigation to inquiry, from faith to doubt. The remnants of old disputes, arguments unanswered, and involuntary questionings may tease us, "as if we were not certain, when we are." It is necessary to resist these doubts and "put them down with a high hand, as irrational and preposterous."[55]

M. Jamie Ferreira has explored the implications of Newman's distinction between investigation and inquiry in some detail.[56] The substance of her argument is that faith is compatible with recognizing the dubitability of assent. We can recognize not only that doubt is logically possible but that "there can be arguments one way and another."[57] In support of her claim that Newman allowed this degree of doubt, Ferreira refers to one of his papers on certainty. Here Newman made what Ferreira calls "concessions" to the possibility of error. Though we have certitude we can acknowledge that certitude is not a claim to infallibility; we can admit a "mathematical chance" of error; we can listen to contrary arguments.[58] To acknowledge these doubts is not inconsistent with our assent. From these considerations Ferreira concludes that Newman allowed a "real criticizability" of faith. That is to say, to believe does not require a refusal to consider the objections to one's belief. This kind of methodological doubt does not involve suspension of assent.

---

[53] Ibid.

[54] Ibid., 160–1.

[55] Ibid., 178.

[56] Ferreira, *Doubt and Religious Commitment,* chs. 4 and 5. In her wider study of skepticism, *Scepticism and Reasonable Doubt: The British Naturalist Tradition in Wilkins, Hume, Reid and Newman* (Oxford: Clarendon Press, 1986), Ferreira offers a more positive overview of Newman's position, describing his trust in the "natural" as the means by which reasonable doubt is excluded.

[57] Ferreira, *Doubt and Religious Commitment,* 93–7 and 108–13.

[58] Achaval and Holmes, eds., *The Theological Papers,* Part 7: *Papers in Preparation for a Grammar of Assent,* 1865–1869; July 20, 1865, 122–5.

What Newman required for certitude, Ferreira argues, is not the absence of all theoretically possible doubt but the absence of all reasonable doubt. There is a significant difference between admitting that it is possible that we could be wrong and admitting that it is possible that we are wrong.[59] In the first instance we merely acknowledge the "dubitability" of our certitude. In the second we "admit" that doubt, and in so doing we have suspended our judgment, allowing that there are reasonable grounds for doubt. It is this degree of doubt which Newman ruled out as being incompatible with faith.

Ferreira's argument helps to clarify Newman's distinction. She shows that it is a very fine distinction indeed, for it is hard to see exactly how this distinction might apply, and whether in practical instances there is a real difference here. A particular weakness of Ferreira's case, however, is that she fails to maintain Newman's own crucial distinction between assent and inference. For Newman, logical objections to a conclusion are quite distinct from doubts. To allow that there are arguments for or against a proposition concerns the grounds or evidence for one's belief, not one's actual believing as such. This was what Newman meant by claiming that assent is not governed by the strength of its antecedent reasoning. Assent is absolute, categorical, even though the antecedent reasoning may be at best probable. In his own experience Newman acknowledged many "difficulties" for faith but insisted that "ten thousand difficulties do not make one doubt."[60] In that sense, then, for Newman "investigation" is not a form of doubt at all. If we take into account Newman's distinction between conclusions and assents, it becomes clear that the doubt to which Ferreira is referring to is not real doubt, at least not in the terms in which Newman wrote of doubt. This point can be seen very clearly in a later passage in the same paper from which Ferreira quoted. Here Newman argued:

> As soon as I entertain the objections adduced in a particular case as telling, not upon the proof, but on the fact itself which is the object of my certitude, then, I am no longer certain at all. This delicate sensitiveness of assent is the very differentia of certitude . . . .
>
> A first and essential characteristic, then, of certitude is, that it cannot co-exist with hesitation or doubt, or with the admission into the mind of the very supposition in any shape that it is misplaced as to its object.[61]

[59] Ferreira, *Doubt and Religious Commitment*, 110.
[60] Newman, *Apologia Pro Vita Sua*, 214.
[61] Achaval and Holmes, eds., *The Theological Papers*, July 20, 1865, 123.

The "criticizability of assents" which Ferreira has identified is in fact a criticizability of conclusions, inferences, and proofs. For Newman, to allow such criticism to affect one's assent is to begin to doubt.

The conclusion which can be drawn from Ferreira's argument is that Newman allowed, at most, an indirect dubitability or criticizability of assents, insofar as he permitted investigation and reconsideration of the grounds or reasons for them. As such Newman allowed for a process of questioning, controversy, and re-appraisal which (he recognized) could possibly lead to reversal of our assent. But genuine certitude is self-confident, he held, and will engage in this activity without hesitation or fear.

From the preceding discussion we have been able to identify the sense in which Newman considered doubt incompatible with faith, and thus to clarify the specific content of his embargo on doubt. For Newman it is required of those who genuinely believe that they adhere to their assent, even when they examine their beliefs and "investigate" the rational basis of those convictions.

Newman's embargo on doubt has three specific implications. In the first instance, Newman argued against those who insisted that we cannot have certainty in any practical matter. He regarded this insistence upon doubt as a kind of moral rebellion, a refusal "on principle" to accept the facts of our created nature. To withhold assent in instances where practical or "moral" certitude is possible is to make an illegitimate demand for rational justification. It is to demand more proof than our conscience and illative sense require, and is thus to hinder and oppose the natural functions of the mind. In faith we can have effective certitude, and to hinder this feeling is unnatural. Newman also saw that to withhold our assent when we can in fact enjoy certitude in faith has personal and religious consequences, in terms of prayer, devotion, moral action, etc. Just as assent has moral and religious aspects, so too does doubt. To withhold our assent is to become hesitant or non-committal in action and in devotion.

The second implication of Newman's view of doubt is that many people who question their faith and who perhaps think that they doubt in fact do not. Newman held that one can be certain, at a fundamental personal level, even though one is perplexed by "difficulties" and questions about the rational basis of one's convictions. The vital distinction here is between considering these difficulties as problems of "proof" and allowing them to "tell against" one's assent as such. For Newman personally, faith involved adhering to his assent in spite of many difficulties. Thus Newman's embargo on doubt was not, as is sometimes supposed, a complete prohibition of all questioning. Nor did he suggest that whoever has "difficulties" of belief does not have faith. The kind of doubt which is incompatible with faith is that which in some way refuses to be certain even though a morally sufficient basis for certitude is available.

Third, we can now see that for Newman there was an additional role for the will in maintaining our faith commitment. We have noted already the various moral and personal elements in the formation of faith, in coming to assent. Now we see that for Newman believers have an obligation to maintain their faith, not allowing difficulties and questions to tell against that commitment. In his sermons and letters, as well as his formal writing, Newman enjoins people to believe and not doubt, clearly indicating that this is a matter of choice, a decision to continue in faith.

Yet there is something paradoxical about this injunction. As we have seen, Newman held that if a person reverses a certitude, this is a sign that they were not in fact certain at all. To suggest that it is a moral choice whether or not they continue in their certitude is to imply that reversal is always a possibility, and that seems to negate the idea of certitude altogether. If people genuinely were certain, with the "indefectible" certitude Newman suggests, they would not have the choice of reversal, nor would they need an act of will to maintain their certitude.

Some of Newman's contemporary critics suggested that he had secured the "certainty" of faith by severing it from rational criticism.[62] There would appear to be some basis for this argument in Newman's embargo on doubt and his prohibition of inquiry. Investigation, as he describes it, is not so much an open quest for truth as for reasons supporting what one has already decided. Newman's response to this criticism could presumably be that if you know where the truth lies, it is foolish still to search for it. If, as Newman holds, further evidence or proof cannot add to the certainty of what is believed, to "investigate" one's belief would seem to serve no useful purpose, at least in regard to the individual who already holds that belief. This sounds very much as if reason may

---

[62] In the *Edinburgh Review* 132 (April 1870) 411–2, it was argued that Newman "secures Certitude by isolating it from the processes of thought out of which it comes." Similarly, an American reviewer concluded that by the prohibition of doubt, which Newman defended, the Roman Catholic Church "stifles thought; puts a premium on ignorance; is in open conflict with science; perpetrates its dogmas by making it sinful to call them into question." *The Biblical Repertory and Princeton Review* 43 (April 1871). Both reviews quoted in Ferreira, *Doubt and Religious Commitment,* 11.

contribute to our coming to faith, but after that cannot contribute to our faith as such, only to our ability to explain it to ourselves or others.

There is a fundamental confusion in Newman's thought here. He is insisting that since assent is categorical, investigation cannot add anything to what is already taken to be certainty. But this confuses certitude with certainty, as David Pailin has argued. One may not be able to add to one's certitude, but through rational reflection one may find better reasons for that certitude. This in fact seems to be what Newman intended, and is a legitimate contribution of reason to faith. If, however, investigation and critical thinking can affect positively our apprehension of certainty, then it is also possible that they can affect it negatively—and this is what Newman seems to have wanted to rule out. Newman seems to allow the kind of thinking which can confirm our beliefs, but wants to guarantee in advance that nothing can challenge them. This is where the distinction itself comes into question.

I am not convinced that investigation can in fact be consistently distinguished from inquiry. Clearly there may be situations where "investigation" does not involve doubt or any implicit uneasiness about one's belief. For example a person who is fully confident of their belief in the providence of God may nonetheless seek for further arguments and grounds with which to convince others. In this instance investigation is clearly distinct from inquiry. Much theological inquiry—Newman would insist that we call it investigation—is of this nature.

It is more difficult, however, to distinguish investigation and inquiry in the instance of a person who is concerned about the rational justification of their own belief. Newman describes a person in such a position when describing false certitudes: "this intellectual anxiety, which is incompatible with certitude, shows itself in our running back in our minds to the arguments on which we came to believe, in not letting our conclusion alone."[63] Here, according to Newman, "investigation" is in fact inquiry: the person who claims to be certain but who must explore repeatedly the grounds of their belief is not in fact certain at all. Yet who is to judge whether a person's questioning is investigation or inquiry? If, for example, I am wondering about the meaning of the idea of God as creator, I may indeed be perplexed about the meaningfulness of creation. In so doing, have I crossed over from investigation into inquiry—or is my questioning undertaken in authentic trust,

---

[63] Newman, *Grammar of Assent,* 167.

searching for the basis of my trust in God? It may not always be possible for me to decide this for myself. Or it may not be possible to distinguish the character of my questioning at the time. Does this mean that I should only engage in critical questioning when I already know the answers to my questions? Newman's embargo on rigorous, authentic inquiry seems to involve a level of intellectual self-limitation, which some at least would call intellectual dishonesty.

This problem leads us to a general appraisal of Newman's approach to faith and its incompatibility with doubt. Newman's account of faith has a number of important strengths. The first of these is his recognition that we can only believe what we have to some extent understood or "apprehended." Our faith then must have some propositional content. It is not mere "sentiment" or feeling. On the other hand, Newman also wished to stress that we can assent to what we do not completely understand. We do not have to comprehend the content or all the logical implications of a proposition before we can assent to it. Another strength of Newman's account of faith is his recognition of informal reasoning. He has shown that we can derive significant conclusions from processes of reasoning which cannot be expressed in syllogistic form. Newman champions the rational significance of these natural abilities, our "common sense," against the artificial standards of evidence and strict rationality propounded by liberalism. A final strength is Newman's recognition that faith is a personal matter. Our apprehension of the object of faith is personal and we reason in a highly personal, implicit manner to a conclusion and an act of assent in which we are personally committed.

Against these strengths, however, there are a number of difficulties which seriously qualify the strengths just mentioned. First is the question of whether faith itself is adequately and exhaustively explained in terms of assent. Certainly faith involves belief; there is a content to faith. But the analysis of faith as assent gives a highly individualistic and quite "intellectual" or "rationalist" impression of what faith really is. Faith cannot simply be explained as assent to statements about God. It also involves a relationship with God.[64] Perhaps something of this nature is implied in Newman's idea of real apprehension of the reality

---

[64] This point, together with other criticisms, is made by Pailin, *The Way to Faith*, 193. A similar criticism is made by John Hick in *Faith and Knowledge* (Ithaca, N.Y.: Cornell University Press, 1957); Fount Paperbacks edition (London: Collins, 1978) 90–1.

of God, but this aspect of faith is overshadowed by his concern with propositional forms of assent. In a relationship, one does not so much assent as participate. The relational elements of trust and struggle, obedience and service, worship and anguish, which seem to be parts of many people's experience of God, do not seem to have a sufficient place in Newman's picture of faith as assent. Newman values these elements, but only as consequences of our assent. As a result, his concept of faith is one dimensional. It is also too static. Newman writes of faith as if we arrive at a complex assent and thereafter we have no more to do except maintain that faith. The elements of growth and further discovery seem not to be permitted. We may learn more about the content implicit in our faith, but our assent as such is already established and must not be changed. Furthermore, when he is placing his embargo on doubt, Newman's view of faith seems to have an "all-or-nothing" character. Either we believe everything that the Catholic Church teaches or we do not believe at all. This view seems to be out of step with his own recognition that in matters of faith there are many secondary elements and lesser matters of doctrine which are open to question.

One of the major areas of debate surrounding Newman's analysis of faith concerns the role of conscience. Newman implies that every person's conscience, if attended to, will lead them to God, and indeed to the God of the Catholic faith.[65] It would be wrong to suggest that Newman was not aware of the great differences between the peoples of the world and between their religions.[66] Nonetheless in today's more pluralistic society and with a less "triumphal" view of the Christian religion, we may question whether Newman's account of conscience can be sustained. Theologically we may ask whether it is appropriate and meaningful to proceed from our feelings of moral obligation (and guilt) to a parent-figure, a "Moral Governor" and "Supreme Ruler and Judge." It is not at all clear that the feelings of conscience provide us with such knowledge. Some people may find no knowledge of God at all through conscience; others arrive at widely diverging beliefs about God. For some God is a primitive, vengeful figure; for others, a god whose favor is restricted to a select group—perhaps whites or males or "the Elect."

R. A. Naulty has asked what difference it would make to Newman's view of faith if the content of the real apprehension, through conscience,

---

[65] Newman, *Grammar of Assent*, 304, 314, 321.
[66] Ibid., 306–8; cf. 334.

identified not a God of moral demand but a God of forgiveness and benevolence.[67] This important question indicates that in addition to philosophical questions about the nature of assent, Newman's basic view of faith is theological. He understands faith as assent because he understands God and human beings to be related to one another in a particular way, namely as Moral Judge and obedient (or disobedient) subjects. The question of how faith relates to doubt is for Newman ultimately a theological question, and not only a philosophical question. In the end, a re-appraisal of Newman's view of doubt and faith leads us to the question of God and how we relate to God.

There are other critical questions about Newman's approach to faith, which we can only mention briefly. For example, against Newman's implicit trust in the natural functions of the mind, we might argue that much that seems to be natural to people is clearly not good. Destructive aggression, racial prejudice, and greed all seem "natural" human tendencies. An appeal to authority was another central feature of Newman's thought. Newman's willingness to trust implicitly the authoritative teaching of the Church as the interpreter of Scriptures and as the "oracle of God" is perhaps one of the most controversial features of his understanding of faith and doubt. Does God in fact call for unquestioning obedience in this way? Newman was right, I think, to stress the element of "the given" in faith, that is, the sense in which we assent to what has been revealed to us and what impresses itself upon us as right and true, and worthy of our devotion. But faith is not only a state of receiving. Faith must also be seen as a responsive relationship with God. Within the broad Christian tradition this relationship has included a sense of quest, a search for understanding, both of oneself and of God, and at least sometimes includes elements of struggle, even conflict. These dimensions of religious experience and tradition suggest that not all hesitation, struggle, questioning, or doubt should be seen as morally culpable rebellion against God and our created nature.

In conclusion, then, it seems that Newman has not entirely succeeded in demonstrating that faith as assent excludes doubt. We have followed his arguments and found that at crucial points his case is not convincing. In particular, we found that his distinction between investigation and inquiry was not sufficiently clear, and did not take sufficient account of the ways in which questioning can be an appropriate

---

[67] R. A. Naulty, "Newman's Conscience and God," *Colloquium* 23 (October 1990) 37–9.

part of the ongoing life of faith. Because of his static and rather individualistic concept of faith as assent, Newman has not allowed that at times people may not be able to say whether their questioning constitutes "doubt." Nor has he allowed that some struggle and questioning may be the expression of faith, in a determined commitment to know God more deeply.

Newman's *Grammar of Assent* must be recognized as a major contribution to the theological exploration of the nature of faith and its relationship to doubt. Newman sought to explain how faith arises naturally within the unhindered, conscientious experience of human beings. Yet, when analyzed in depth, it is clear that Newman's account of faith rests upon sources and authorities which are not immediately available to all people or (in Newman's view) subject to human rational judgment. In essence, Newman's view of faith and its relation to doubt is dependent upon his particular conception of God. The real apprehension of God through conscience we have found to be the essential element which enables the assent of faith. Without that element, faith would be what David Pailin calls a "logical type-jump." It is only when the moral disposition and will of a person are shaped in the ways Newman described that the assent of faith follows "naturally." In the end, we have found that Newman's account of faith and his embargo on doubt are dependent upon theological grounds, that is, upon his view of God as known through conscience. Though we can describe the various elements in faith, it is neither our reason nor our moral disposition which enables us to exclude doubt, but God.

In the next chapter we will examine the work of a theologian who took precisely this view. According to Karl Barth, it is only God's address to us as Word which creates faith and excludes doubt.

3

The Word of God:
Creating Faith, Excluding Doubt

Karl Barth, who is undoubtedly one of the most significant theologians of the twentieth century, developed a distinctive theological method which he claimed was the only way to deal with doubt. Barth was profoundly concerned with the nature of our knowledge of God, and the whole of his theology can be seen as the elaboration of what was for him the appropriate theological response to doubt.

In contrast to Newman, Barth refused to begin with human experience or the "logic" of religious commitments as the basis for his theology and his understanding of faith. Rather, he insisted that faith must be seen as a response to the prior initiative of God, and the method of theology must be appropriate to this priority also. Because of this approach, Hans Küng has argued that Barth initiated a postmodern approach to theology, by confronting "the self-consciousness of the modern subject with its self-deceptions."[1] In Barth's theology, God is the subject and faith exists within the context of God's approach to us.

Our study of Barth will begin with a consideration of some of the formative elements in his theological work, followed by a brief outline of the method which Barth claimed would overcome doubt. We

---

[1] Hans Küng, *Theology for the Third Millennium: An Ecumenical View*, trans. Peter Heinegg (London: Doubleday, 1988) 271–5.

43

will then examine critically the concept of faith which emerges from this approach.[2]

Formation of a Theologian

Karl Barth was born in Switzerland in 1886, the son of a Reformed Church pastor. He studied theology at a number of German universities and spent eleven years as a village pastor. Then he held a series of teaching positions in Germany until his expulsion by Hitler in 1935. Until his retirement in 1962 he taught theology at Basel. He died in 1968.[3]

During the years Barth was village pastor at Safenwil he conducted a lively correspondence with Eduard Thurneysen, who was pastor in a nearby village.[4] From these letters and from other biographical sources we can derive an understanding of how Barth saw his role as a minister and a clear indication of his early view of doubt and its relation to faith. Barth's experience as a pastor led him to describe faith in terms of a dialectical relationship between the "world" of the Bible or the "vista" opened up by faith, on the one hand, and the doubting, questioning attitude of the congregation, on the other. Barth saw faith as a "crisis," a point of judgment in which the congregation is confronted by the word of God and their doubting is "condemned" by the biblical call to faith. This dialectical perspective on the relationship between faith and doubt, in the context of preaching, was to be a vital factor in the development of Barth's approach to theology as such.

During 1917 and 1918 Barth wrote the first edition of his *Romans*, which is not so much a commentary on the epistle as a long essay on

---

[2] An earlier version of some elements of the argument of this chapter can be found in Frank Rees, "The Word in Question: Barth and Divine Conversation," *Pacifica* 12 (October 1999) 313–32.

[3] Two valuable biographies are Eberhard Busch, *Karl Barth: His Life from Letters and Autobiographical Texts*, trans. John Bowden (London: SCM Press, 1976), and John Bowden, *Karl Barth* (London: SCM Press, 1971). The following works provide a general account of Barth's early theological development: F. W. Camfield, "The Theology of Karl Barth as a Spiritual Movement," *Reformation Old and New: A Tribute to Karl Barth*, ed. F. W. Camfield (London: Lutterworth Press, 1947) 13–29; T.H.L. Parker, *Karl Barth* (Grand Rapids, Mich.: Eerdmans, 1970); and T. F. Torrance, *Karl Barth: An Introduction to His Early Theology* (London: SCM Press, 1962).

[4] Barth's letters to Thurneysen during the period 1914–22 and the letters of both Thurneysen and Barth (during 1921–25) have been published in *Revolutionary Theology in the Making*, ed. and trans. James D. Smart (London: Epworth Press, 1964).

the fundamental content of the Christian faith. For Barth Jesus Christ is the revelation of God the Wholly Other, who is absolutely different from us. What is revealed in Christ, Barth asserts, is that "God is in heaven and thou art on earth."[5] In this work Barth's contention was that the theology of the nineteenth century was more concerned with the history of faith or of "religion" and the religious consciousness of human beings than with the object of faith. Barth was convinced that this kind of theology failed to recognize that faith is not a human phenomenon as such but is the activity and creation of God. This central insight was to guide Barth's entire approach to faith and to theology.

At this stage, however, there were other factors in Barth's approach to theology, which I suggest are important in understanding his view of faith and doubt, and which will also be important in evaluating the theological method he eventually developed. Most significant here is his understanding of preaching and the encounter of the word of God in terms of questions.

In 1922 Barth addressed a conference of ministers on the theme "The Need and Promise of Christian Preaching."[6] The preacher, Barth argued, must speak to the congregation of "the infinite contradiction of their life" and of "the no less infinite message of the Bible." In this lecture and in another given that year Barth spoke of the two "magnitudes" confronting one another—human life and the world of the Bible.[7] These two dimensions constitute the dialectic of preaching. Barth described this dialectic by using the idea of question and answer. The people face the preacher with a question: "Is it true, this talk of a living and good God. . . . What the people want to find out and thoroughly understand is, *is it true?*"[8]

For Barth, the Bible and preaching based on the message of the Bible evoke the crisis of doubt and faith, because the Bible addresses people at precisely the point "where doubt has seized (them)."[9] The

---

[5] Karl Barth, *Epistle to the Romans,* trans. Edwyn Hoskyns (London: Oxford University Press, 1933, 1977) 10.

[6] This lecture is published in Karl Barth, *The Word of God and the Word of Man,* trans. Douglas Horton (London: Hodder and Stoughton, 1935) 97–135. A commemorative appreciation of this lecture can be found in Frank Rees, "The Need and Promise of Christian Preaching," *Evangelical Quarterly* 66 (1994) 107–23.

[7] Karl Barth "Biblical Questions, Insights and Vistas," *The Word of God and the Word of Man,* 51–96.

[8] Karl Barth, "The Need and Promise of Christian Preaching," *The Word of God and the Word of Man,* 108.

[9] Ibid., 117.

question asked by the doubting congregation is itself confronted by the biblical "riddle." The Bible's "answer" is to awaken the questioning people, not with a palliative answer but by giving their question greater depth and meaning, showing that all their previous questions were but preparation for the issue which now arises: "Are we seeking God in earnest? Are we seeking after God?" Only in the confrontation of questioning people and questioning God does the "miracle" of preaching take place.

Here we see that for Barth the relationship between faith and doubt was initially understood in terms of the task of preaching, which itself involved engagement with questions. Barth saw doubt as the natural human response to the "possibility" presented in the Bible. The task of the preacher, Barth maintained, is to evoke this doubt and to raise the "crisis" of faith by bringing home to his hearers the difference between God and themselves. But the approach of God is here described in terms of profound questioning. In critiquing Barth's theology later in the chapter, my contention will be that it is unfortunate that he abandoned this perspective on the word of God. Barth seems to be suggesting that God's word does not only come to us in the form of pronouncements or statements. God may also engage us as one who asks questions.

In 1927, while teaching at Göttingen, he published what was to be the first volume of a Christian Dogmatics. Here he presented a prolegomena for dogmatic theology. From the beginning he defines the task of dogmatics as laying the foundations for preaching.[10] The focus of theology is to be the word of God in its threefold form—as revelation in Christ, as Scripture, and as preaching. Here we see the basis of his later contention that to expound the nature and content of the word of God was the only appropriate theological response to doubt. It is not human thought or feeling but only the word of God which can create faith and expel doubt. In this volume we see the clear stress upon revelation of God's word which was to be the hallmark of Barth's later thought. We also see the beginnings of his later critique of "religion," which represents for him the misguided emphasis of Friedrich Schleiermacher upon the believing or faithful human being.[11] While Barth insists that the foundation of faith is in the address of God to human beings, he allows himself some discussion of the "conditions of the subjective possi-

---

[10] Karl Barth, *The Göttingen Dogmatics: Instruction in the Christian Faith*, trans. Geoffrey W. Bromiley (Grand Rapids, Mich.: Eerdmans, 1991).

[11] Ibid., 171–81.

bility" of revelation, explaining the nature of faith and obedience in response to God's word.

Immediately after he had finished this first volume of Christian dogmatics, Barth abandoned the work because he felt he had failed in his essential theological purpose. Whereas he had hoped to speak only of God in "contradiction" of humanity, he now felt that he had been too concerned with the human experience of that contradiction and the resulting "crisis" of faith. He had not entirely freed himself from the "egg-shells" of existentialist philosophy and phenomenology.[12] What he needed was a methodological principle which would enable him to center his theology exclusively upon God's act of revelation in Jesus Christ. The "break-through" for Barth came several years later through his study of Anselm. Eberhard Jüngel has remarked that Barth's appropriation of Anselm brought about a "complete reorientation" of the previous direction of his thinking.[13]

When Barth moved to Bonn in 1930 and began a seminar on Anselm of Canterbury, he developed what were to be crucial insights for his theological method. In 1931 he published his *Anselm: Fides Quaerens Intellectum.*[14] Barth later complained that few scholars had recognized how important this work was in the development of his thought. Here he was working "with a vital key, if not the key, to an understanding of that whole process that has impressed me more and more in my *Church Dogmatics* as the only one proper to theology."[15] Barth also claimed that he saw in Anselm "how to handle doubt in the proper way."[16]

The insights Barth derived from Anselm particularly concern the relationship between theology and faith. For Anselm, faith involves a love for God which seeks the truth, since God is the creator and source of all truth. It is part of the nature of faith to seek understanding, since

---

[12] This was how Barth described his own "well-known false start" and his "unwitting contribution" to natural theology, in his essay, "No," *Natural Theology,* Emil Brunner and Karl Barth, trans. P. Fraenkel (London: Geoffrey Bles, 1946) 70.

[13] Eberhard Jüngel, *Karl Barth: A Theological Legacy,* trans. Garrett E. Paul (Philadelphia: Westminster Press, 1986) 41.

[14] Karl Barth, *Anselm:* Fides Quaerens Intellectum, *Anselm's Proof of the Existence of God in the Context of His Theological Scheme,* trans. Ian W. Robertson (London: SCM Press, 1968).

[15] Ibid., preface to the 2d ed., 11.

[16] Karl Barth, *Evangelical Theology: An Introduction,* trans. Grover Foley (Grand Rapids, Mich.: Eerdmans, 1979) 123.

faith is a movement or commitment of the will to hold to and love God, even though we do not wholly understand God. The origin of such faith, however, does not rest with the believer. Faith comes about through "something new encountering us and happening to us from outside," through the "seed" of the word of God preached and received as grace. As a result of this encounter, the activity of faith is to remember God's actions in the past, to recognize them in the present, and to respond in love.[17] Inherent in this basic conception of faith, then, is the motivation of theology as "faith seeking understanding." It is faith itself which spontaneously seeks understanding of God.

What then is the nature of the "understanding" which faith seeks? First Barth argues that faith does not seek "confirmation" of what is already believed in order to "strengthen" its belief. Faith is not dependent upon theological understanding, nor can that understanding deliver a person from doubt. Theological answers "have no bearing on the existence of faith." Second, Barth argues, Anselm saw that the task of theology is related to the Church's confession of faith: the search for understanding is undertaken *within* the context and the limits of the Church's confession, which has a direct and specific focus in the person of Christ.[18] The task of theology concerns the understanding of the revelation of God in Christ, as mediated to us through the Scriptures and the faith of the Church. The Scriptures thus provide the basis for theological understanding and a criterion by which theological ideas may be judged.[19]

The third and most important aspect of faith's search for understanding, however, arises from the recognition of the limits of that understanding. Theological statements can never adequately express their object, the divine word. The categories and arguments by which theologians express their understanding of God are ultimately "shattered" by God. Even the most careful description of the divine reality, as apprehended in faith, will only be partially appropriate. For this reason Anselm held that theology can never achieve more than a "scientific certainty." Under the determining norm of Scripture, theologians can formulate their understanding of God; but in the final resort they must acknowledge the limitation of their knowledge. For Anselm,

---

[17] Barth, *Anselm*, 16–20.
[18] Ibid., 26–7.
[19] Ibid., 32–3.

though, this limitation serves to indicate the true nature of theology as faith in search of understanding. God can be known only through God's self-revelation. Therefore the theologian must seek God and the understanding of faith in prayer. Prayer is the *sine qua non* of Anselm's theological method, Barth argues.[20] From this aspect of his reading of Anselm, Barth came to consider that theology itself must be "a work of faith." Here Barth found the "key," which he later called the "analogy of faith," through which theology can have knowledge of the revelation of God, and anxiety and doubt can be excluded—by God.

With the insights derived from his study of Anselm, Barth set about a new work of dogmatics. This was to be a work of *Church Dogmatics,* and was named accordingly. A work of five volumes was projected. The fourth volume, on reconciliation, is incomplete and the fifth, on redemption, was never commenced. The basic reason Barth took up such an ambitious theological task was that he believed there was a need for a work of doctrinal theology which focused exclusively upon the self-revelation of God in Jesus Christ.[21] In this way Barth was moving away from the Enlightenment paradigm, with its focus on human subjectivity as the central datum of all knowledge. It is this move which justifies Hans Küng's suggestion that Barth was initiating the shift to a postmodern theology.

It is not surprising that a work as substantial and complex as *Church Dogmatics* should be the subject of much scholarly interpretation and debate. George Hunsinger has recently surveyed a number of major interpretations, each of which seeks to identify a central or governing motif of Barth's system.[22] I find Hunsinger's criticisms and conclusions convincing and his own exposition of Barth's thought in terms of "truth as mediated" through the revelation of God in Jesus Christ a helpful corrective to a number of earlier studies. While it is not possible to engage in depth with these issues of interpretation, clearly they touch

---

[20] Ibid., 35–9.

[21] Already in 1924, Barth had written to Thurneysen of the need to make "a fresh beginning" with Protestantism. *Revolutionary Theology in the Making,* 175.

[22] George Hunsinger, *How to Read Karl Barth: The Shape of His Theology* (Oxford: Oxford University Press, 1991). Hunsinger's critique addresses the following key works: Hans Urs von Balthasar, *The Theology of Karl Barth* (Garden City, N.Y.: Doubleday, 1972); Torrance, *Karl Barth;* George Berkower, *The Triumph of Grace in the Theology of Karl Barth* (Grand Rapids, Mich.: Eerdmans, 1956); and Robert Jenson, *God after God: The God of the Past and the Future as Seen in the Work of Karl Barth* (Indianapolis: Bobbs-Merrill, 1969).

upon this study and some reference will be made to several of these issues as we proceed.

Our study of the *Church Dogmatics* will concentrate on those aspects
which specifically express Barth's theological response to doubt. For
Barth the relationship between faith and doubt is the same in theology
as it is for the individual believer. Barth's theology is, then, an attempt to
show how the word of God creates faith and excludes doubt. As we follow this limited study, we will note some of the complexities of Barth's
system, yet find ourselves returning several times to the same key issues.
Barth once made this observation about his theological method, using
the image of a mountaineer circling a summit, continually gaining fresh
perspectives on the same central objective. Recognizing this, it is time
for us now to leave the foothills and begin our approach!

The Faith that Excludes Doubt: Theology of the Word of God

In the first volume of *Church Dogmatics,* Barth established the method
and perspective of his system as a whole.[23] From the beginning Barth insists that dogmatics is a work of faith made possible by the activity of the
word of God. His theme is the "priority" of the word of God. To examine this theme in a little detail, our study will concentrate on Barth's view
of faith and his account of the certainty and uncertainty of theology.
These in turn will lead us to two related topics: the theologian's struggle
with doubt and Barth's characterization of religion as unbelief.

Barth's continuous emphasis is upon the sovereign freedom of God,
who chooses to be the partner of human beings. In freedom and for
freedom, God has created us and approaches us as the Word. Thus it is
God who creates or, as Barth puts it, "determines" faith. The faith of
human beings arises from "the power which is power before faith and
without faith."[24]

Faith is not in any sense an achievement of human effort. It is
rather "the determination of human action by the being of the Church
and therefore by Jesus Christ, by the gracious address of God to man
[*sic*]."[25] In this statement we see three crucial aspects of Barth's under-

---

[23] Karl Barth, *Church Dogmatics,* vol. 1: "The Doctrine of the Word of God: Prolegomena to Church Dogmatics," 2d ed., trans. G. W. Bromiley (Edinburgh: T & T
Clark, 1975).

[24] Ibid., 1:1, 154.

[25] Ibid., 1:1, 17.

standing of faith. First, we note the Christological center: in faith, Jesus Christ, known through the Church, is the central reality. We also see Barth's stress upon the initiative of God. Faith comes about through the gracious action of God, addressing us in Christ. Third, we note that human beings are brought into the reality of faith, in response to God's word. Necessarily there is a human element in faith, an answering response which "puts into effect what the Word of God tells us," though even this dimension of faith is created by the impact of the Word.[26]

The exact nature of the human response to God's revelation is one of the issues raised in criticism of Barth's theology. Barth was not unaware of the need to show that human beings are drawn into the revelatory encounter. While he stressed the sovereign freedom of God, he wished to emphasize even more the gracious call and election of God, choosing human beings as God's covenant partners. In a number of places within *Church Dogmatics*, Barth describes aspects of human experience which he considers as appropriate responses to the Word. One such passage is the discussion of "The Christian under the universal Lordship of God the Father," which is part of Barth's doctrine of creation.[27] Here Barth describes the invitation of God to human beings to be God's creature-partners. But the creatures as such are neither able nor willing to fulfill this calling. Only through the word of God, in Jesus Christ, are humans able to relate to God in this way. Barth proceeds to describe a "dynamic attitude" which involves perceiving, understanding, and knowing God, and a readiness and willingness to cooperate. All this arises from thankfulness and works itself out in three ways: in faith, obedience, and prayer. These elements, then, describe the human element or response in faith. But Barth is adamant that these are only possible as responses to God's self-revelation.

Theological understanding of faith is not, therefore, to be concerned with analyzing the nature of belief or assent, nor with seeking a rational basis for such belief. Belief and unbelief alike are but responses to the activity of divine grace in the Word: "only in the sphere of grace is there faith and unbelief."[28] Theology is concerned with the grounds of faith, that is to say, with the prior reality of the word of God.

---

[26] Ibid., 1:1, 200. Here Barth describes the experience of the word of God, the "self-determination" which is "subject to determination by God."

[27] Ibid., 3:3 "The Doctrine of Creation," 239–46.

[28] Ibid., 1:1, 154.

It is within the context of God's self-revelation in Christ, then, that we may have knowledge of God through faith. The most urgent question that now arises, however, is how we can know that such faith is well-founded—in the terms of Barth's own early analysis, *Is it true?* This question brings us to what Barth has to say about the certainty and uncertainty of faith and theology.

The Certainty and Uncertainty of Faith

The central epistemological implication of Barth's claim that faith is the creation of the word of God is that the certainty of faith, and of theology, depend not upon the believer but upon God. To find the basis of faith, the grounds for certainty in theology, we must not look to human beings as such, but only to God. In a difficult but important passage, Barth explains the epistemological implications of his theological stance:

> If experience of the Word of God is such that it can have its basis and certainty only outside itself, then understanding of it as true and actual experience is in fact understanding of its own radical end and of the fact that there is here a real perishing and dying of man. This is the new land which opens up when one does not just consider Christian experience as a phenomenon but lets it speak for itself.[29]

Here Barth claims that genuine faith, as experience of the word of God, involves repudiation of any human capacity for knowing God. Here we see Barth attempting to break free of the Enlightenment paradigm, which saw all epistemological issues within the framework of the knowing mind, the human consciousness. For Barth, there is an "end" to human knowledge and a "death" of the human person as the object and source of theological understanding. The knowledge of God through faith is not knowledge of the phenomenon of faith but is immediate knowledge of "the farther side."

It should be noted that Barth is not only making an epistemological claim here. He is also making an ontological claim. The object of knowledge through faith is God the Lord: "it will just be true from God that human existence is engaged in acknowledgment of the Word of God."[30] Thus Barth is insisting that the experience of God's word

[29] Ibid., 1:1, 222.
[30] Ibid.

brings us to know the being and reality of something other than ourselves. We have this knowledge "from God."

It is important at this stage to clarify exactly what Barth is seeking to affirm and to deny, in making these claims for the priority of God in the epistemology of faith. One of his explicit purposes is to deny any inherent human capacity for knowing God.[31] Barth firmly opposes the idea of a special capacity or faculty of mind which is awakened, in some persons at least, when they hear the word of God, enabling them to apprehend it and thus to know God. "The certainty that dogmatics, Church proclamation and the Church itself need in relation to the possibility of knowledge of God's Word is not obtained here."[32] It is not by examining the religious person, even the experience of hearing the word of God, that theology can achieve the certainty it seeks.

This denial was a major element in Barth's vehement rejection of Emil Brunner's approach to "natural theology." In a reference to Brunner's arguments, Barth contends that without the action of God's grace human beings have no capacity for response to God: "man has completely lost the capacity for God."[33] On this basis Barth frequently describes the state of faith as being "awakened," to indicate a situation of which we had no previous awareness.

Barth was concerned that some interpreters of his theology saw him as allowing no significant place for human beings as respondents to God's word. In particular, he objected to G. C. Berkouwer's concept of the "triumph of grace," preferring to speak of "the freedom of grace," for he insisted that the approach of God sets people free.[34]

In giving a positive account of our knowledge of God, Barth introduces the concept of analogy.[35] His use of this concept has been the subject of much discussion and is the central theme of Hans Urs von Balthasar's study. In earlier periods of theological tradition, an "analogy of being" was used to develop a natural theology. The idea was that we can derive some knowledge of the being and nature of God by an analogy drawn between human beings and God. God's nature is similar to, though not the same as, human nature. Barth rejects this use of analogy in theology but introduces instead the idea of an *analogia fidei,* an analogy

---

[31] Ibid., 1:1, 214–9.
[32] Ibid., 1:1, 217.
[33] Ibid., 1:1, 238.
[34] Busch, *Karl Barth,* 381.
[35] Barth, *Church Dogmatics,* 1:1, 244–7.

of faith. The point of "analogy" here is not that we find that God is like us and so we are able to believe in God; rather, within the "analogy of faith" we become like God, our life is "conformed" to God. When a person is addressed by the word of God and is "awakened" to faith, their life becomes conformed to God. The human decision for God is itself a consequence of God's address to us.

In this context, and on this basis, Barth speaks very positively of belief and of the "self-determination" of those who believe. Believers have neither come to faith nor created their own faith: "faith has been granted to [them] through the Word." Even so that person is "not at all a block or stone in faith but self-determining man."[36] Barth insists that the believer is neither passive nor apathetic; the priority of God in creating our faith does not diminish human responsibility or freedom. It is we who act, believe, and respond in faith, even though we do this within the "bracketing" of God's self-disclosure. This "self-determination" of believers in active recognition of God's prior determination in Jesus Christ is what Barth means by the analogy of faith.

At this point, however, Barth is again confronted by the philosophical demand for criteria for knowledge and certainty. How can we know that the word we hear is in fact God's word? Are there no general epistemological criteria by which we can identify this form of knowledge as such?

Barth's contention is that the proof of the word of God "consists in the proclamation of faith."[37] To understand what Barth means by "proof" here we must turn to his longer discussion of the question of verification in volume two.[38] There Barth argues that theology and the believer can resist doubt and have certainty in faith only through various forms of participation. It should be noted that what is verified here is our knowledge of God. Barth speaks of participation in the veracity of God's revelation, through the offering of our thanks. This thankfulness involves worship as well as works of gratitude. Barth does not explain how this response of gratitude comes about. Neither does he explain how this participation can verify our experience of the word of God. He recognizes that this participation, thankfulness, and service clearly require a decision or assent—our acceptance of and commitment to what we believe is God's revelation. Even this assent, though, is created by the Word. This is what Barth means when he says that it is

---

[36] Ibid., 1:1, 244–5.
[37] Ibid., 1:1, 241.
[38] Ibid., 2:1, 9 and 209–54, esp. 218–9.

"just true from God" that we are engaged in acknowledging God's word.[39] For Barth, then, the certainty of faith consists in its origin, its source and foundation in the word of God. The assurance of faith, expressed in thankfulness and praise, depends entirely upon the activity of God through the "analogy of faith." It is only in this active, participatory, and responsive mode that faith can be certain.

We now turn to Barth's account of the uncertainty of faith. It is part of the experience of faith, properly understood, that it should be uncertain "from the human side." Faith seems to be without grounds, insecure and uncertain. In a phrase echoing Kierkegaard, Barth speaks of the life of faith as "being suspended and hanging without ground under our feet."[40] In the "decision" of faith we abandon every attempt to justify ourselves, although we are continually tempted to seek human or experiential grounds for our faith.

On the "human side" faith is and must be uncertain, for it is utterly dependent upon the activity of God as Word. What is revealed to us, according to Barth, is not that we know God but rather that God is hidden. God is known only within the limits of God's hiddenness.[41] Here human knowledge reaches its "end," but through grace we then apprehend the mystery of God.[42] Barth stresses, however, that it is not appropriate for theology to over-emphasize our inability to know God. Theology must be content to be "on the way" in its understanding and knowledge of God. Our response to the revelation of the hiddenness of God must not be regret about "how little we know"; it should rather be a thankful celebration.[43]

Here we see most clearly Barth's view of the relationship between faith and doubt. While our knowledge of God is, in a human sense, dubitable and God remains a mystery to us, nonetheless in faith we participate in the knowledge of God. We are lifted "above ourselves" in a "sober exuberance" and a true knowledge of God. While there is an ultimate uncertainty of faith, it is the nature of faith to overcome this difficulty. Under the impact of the word of God, doubt is excluded.

There is, however, a further aspect of the uncertainty of faith which must be considered. Here we are concerned with theology, the specific

---

[39] Ibid., 1:1, 222.
[40] Ibid., 2:1, 159.
[41] Ibid., 2:1, 180–4.
[42] Ibid., 2:1, 195–9.
[43] Ibid., 2:1, 210–21.

activity of faith in which we seek to formulate our understanding of the word of God. Barth deals at some length with the question of how it is possible for the human mind to grasp the word of God in conceptual terms. How can we "participate" in faith and the knowledge of God, in proclamation and in theological reflection, if we cannot describe or express that word?[44] If God remains hidden, even in self-revelation (as Barth contends), how can we know that we have rightly understood that revelation?

Barth's answer to these questions is that the gift of grace extends so far as to include the gift of an ability to conceptualize what is revealed to us.[45] Barth observes that the traditional theological resolution to this difficulty introduced a further use of the concept of analogy. There is a "partial correspondence and agreement" between our concepts and words about God and God as their object.[46] In the human work of trying to explain the content of the word of God, we must appropriate the promise "that we shall speak the truth in the analogy of truth itself."[47] For Barth, again drawing upon Anselm, the role of prayer is vital here. If in good conscience theologians are open to God's revelation, they can trust that their words about God will possess "the entire veracity which they have in God himself. . . . God lives and speaks in them."[48]

Barth held that theologians may have confidence as they use human concepts to express the word of God, but he drew back from the claim that any particular doctrinal formulation can be identified with the word of God. For Barth there remains a radical uncertainty in theology as well as in faith. Barth himself indicates on a number of occasions his own uncertainty about various aspects of doctrine. In his discussions with students, published as "Table Talk," he answers a number of doctrinal questions with an emphatic, "I don't know."[49] Barth refused to allow his own system of dogmatics to be seen as a set of doctrinal formulations to which he was permanently committed. Indeed he resisted the idea of a "system" altogether. In a famous disavowal he once wrote,

---

[44] Ibid., 2:1, 223–4.

[45] Ibid., 2:1, 223.

[46] Ibid., 2:1, 227.

[47] Ibid., 2:1, 231.

[48] Ibid.

[49] *Karl Barth's Table Talk,* recorded and edited by John D. Godsey, *Scottish Journal of Theology Occasional Papers,* no. 10 (Edinburgh and London: Oliver and Boyd, 1963) 24, 46, 47. Note also Barth's account of his changing views, 51 and 52.

"If there are 'Barthians' then I am not one of them."[50] For Barth, all doctrinal formulations, all theology, must be seen as in principle questionable and dubitable "from the human side."[51] The popular suspicion of dogmatics is, in Barth's view, well founded. In themselves, theological formulations of our knowledge of God are uncertain. We cannot be sure that we have spoken the truth about God. For Barth, it is faith, understood as this state of radical "determination" by God, which allows the theologian to say, "I don't know." There is here a faithful form of doubt. Theology does not claim to know all about God, but bears thankful witness to what can be known of the revelation and hiddenness of God.

How then can theology deal with this uncertainty without lapsing into "anxiety and doubt"? Barth's answer to this question goes right to the heart of the relationship between theology and faith, and the relationship of each to doubt. It is the theologian who must deal with the threat of doubt.

Doubt as a Threat to the Theologian

During his final year of teaching, Barth gave a series of lectures in which he sought to provide an introduction to the thought and work which had occupied his lifetime. These were published as *Evangelical Theology: An Introduction.* The book is divided into four sections, dealing first with the place of theology within the community of faith created by God's word, then with "theological existence" in wonder, concern, commitment, and faith. Next Barth discusses the "threats" to theology constituted by solitude, doubt, and temptation, and, finally, theological work involving prayer, study, service, and love. In addition to its significance as Barth's "swan song," *Evangelical Theology* has a distinctively personal character. Here more than in any other work we see the person of Barth the theologian—passionate, humorous, and self-effacing. In other ways also Barth appears to be reflecting his own experience of solitude, temptation, and doubt, as well as making his final "offering" in prayer and praise to God.

In the section of the book about threats to theology, Barth was dealing with the question of how the theologian must deal with the "ultimate

---

[50] Karl Barth, foreword to Otto Weber, *Karl Barth's Church Dogmatics,* trans. Arthur C. Cochrane (London: Lutterworth Press, 1953) 9.

[51] Barth, *Church Dogmatics,* 1:1, 21–3.

uncertainty" of theology described above. Like Newman and many other writers about doubt, Barth begins by distinguishing two forms of questioning. "Socratic doubt" is essential to theology as that discipline which asks of the credal faith of the Church, "How far is it so?" This kind of doubt is not a threat to theology. Indeed the real danger is fear of this doubt, an unwillingness to question rigorously in search of the truth.

The second form of doubt which Barth identifies also arises "from the very center of the performance of the theological task."[52] In this case, however, doubt focuses on the activity of theology itself and becomes doubt about the purpose of theology and about its object. Does theology have an object, or is it a delusion? Barth describes the life of a theologian in this position. Doubt is not unbelief, in the sense of disbelief, an overt denial or negation of faith. The doubting theologian is ambivalent about his or her calling because their own relationship to God has this character: "swaying and staggering, life in uncertainty and embarrassment about our very relationship to God's work and word."[53] Even for those who are convinced intellectually that this doubt is unfounded, who have perhaps learned from Anselm how to "handle doubt in the proper way," it is "uncannily easy" to doubt the existence of God, Barth observes. These comments are reminiscent of Newman's claim that a person who "investigates" their beliefs can easily slip into "inquiry," in which they withhold their assent. It seems probable that Barth was indicating here that he personally found the transition from Socratic doubt to genuine religious doubt was one easily made, even though he had established what he considered to be an effective theological method for dealing with that doubt and uncertainty. Indeed later in the chapter he speaks of the virtual inevitability that every theologian will in some way fall into doubt.

It is clear from this section that Barth saw the problem of doubt as a matter of the psychological disposition of the theologian. Through frustration, perplexity, and the sheer difficulty of the quest for truth, the theologian may become "embarrassed" by the apparent weakness of theology and may doubt its value and purpose.

Barth considers a number of causes of this kind of doubt. First he observes that "the principalities and powers which still reign in this age" may cause one to doubt God and thus to turn away from faith.[54] The power of the Gospel may seem nothing compared with the impor-

---

[52] Barth, *Evangelical Theology*, 117.
[53] Ibid., 119.
[54] Ibid., 120.

tance of economics, science, technology, and the many other achievements of modern humanity. Only a blind theologian would not be impressed by these things, Barth suggests.

The second possible cause of the theologian's doubt may be the Christian community itself "in its feebleness, disunity and perhaps the perverseness of the form and proclamation of his own familiar Church."[55] Experience of the "underside" of the Church can cause one to feel that everything is uncertain and regrettable. It is highly probable that there are reflections of Barth's own experience in this passage. It may be that his struggle with the "German Christians," who supported Hitler, constituted at least a temptation to doubt in this way.

Finally, Barth suggests that doubt may arise from "a structural flaw" in the theologian's private life.[56] Barth does not explain exactly what he means by this expression, though he does say that no Christian and no theologian can altogether rid themselves of this flaw. This suggests that there is some personal weakness in every theologian which makes it inevitable that we will be tempted to doubt and will in fact doubt, to some degree. We can gain some idea of what Barth means by this "flaw" from his description of two ways in which a theologian might respond to this problem. We may think we can live "dualistically," allowing ourselves a "private practice" of doubt while publicly claiming to have the "knowledge of faith." Alternatively, we may respond to this tendency to doubt with "an incomparable exclusiveness," "an unhealthy overeating" in theology. In this instance the theologian takes no interest in the everyday things of life, in sport, art, history—in humanity in general. Such an existence, Barth argues, will actually lead to doubt. If we try to isolate faith and theological understanding from humanity in general and the world to which God's word is addressed, we will in fact not know God but will fall into radical doubt and lose faith altogether.

Before leaving Barth's consideration of doubt as a threat to theology we must note the way in which, in his view, the theologian ought to deal with doubt. The crucial aspect of Barth's argument again stems from his reading of Anselm and his view of theology as faith in search of understanding. Theology must be "a work of faith" and so it is only when theologians turns to God, chiefly in prayer, and are attentive to God's personal address that they will be able to overcome the "flaw" in their own character.

---

[55] Ibid., 121.
[56] Ibid., 122–4.

The same is true of the other threats to theology. Theologians must "endure and bear" and trust in God. The final chapters of *Evangelical Theology* involve a sustained consideration of how theologians must participate in the life of faith. It is through prayer, service, and love, as well as rigorous thought and study, that we may achieve the understanding we seek. Even so this will not be our own achievement but a gift of grace.[57]

So much for Barth's discussion of doubt as a threat to theology. With regard to the life of faith more generally, Barth sees an even more sinister threat than doubt. In face of the "uncertainty" of faith described above, Barth sees the temptation of religion. Barth describes the revelation of God as the abolition of religion.[58] Religion is unbelief, quite the opposite of the faith determined by the word of God.

Religion as Unbelief

If we are to understand Barth's argument here we must begin by explaining what he means by "religion." Again his approach to his subject is conditioned by his view of the "event" of faith in the self-revelation of God. In the light of this event religion is seen as a human concern, directed against faith; indeed, religion is "the one great concern of godless man."[59] By "religion," then, Barth means every aspect of our response to God where that response is generated by independent human intention. The vital factor here is the initiative in these religious acts. For Barth religion refers to human attempts to "reach" God. Such attempts are futile, for "in view of God all our activity is in vain even in the best life . . . of ourselves we are not in a position to apprehend the truth."[60] In contrast to religion, faith requires that we abandon all such self-initiated attempts to apprehend the truth and to know God. Genuine faith will see all such religious "activity" as an attempt to resist faith.

For Barth, then, religion is a form of resistance to God. In religion, people do not listen and believe; rather, they talk, and bolt and bar themselves against revelation "by providing a substitute."[61] These claims apply also to Christianity whenever it claims to be the true religion: "all

---

[57] Ibid., 158.
[58] Barth, *Church Dogmatics*, 1:2, ch. 17: "The Revelation of God as the Abolition of Religion," 280–361, esp. 297–340.
[59] Ibid., 1:2, 300.
[60] Ibid., 1:2, 301, 302.
[61] Ibid., 1:2, 302, 303.

this Christianity of ours . . . is in its own way . . . unbelief."[62] Christianity can, in a very different sense, also be said to be the "true religion"—but only in the sense that genuine faith is possible through God's word in Christ. Where Christianity is determined by the word of God, it is possible to speak of it as true religion. In this situation, however, Christianity will not be thinking of itself as the one, true religion over against other false religions; nor will it be a self-conscious claim to be a religion at all.

For Barth, genuine faith is not concerned with itself as religious. The strength of faith lies in its abandonment to God. By contrast the weakness of religion is precisely its resistance to God through its preoccupation with humanity, even with the "religious life." The attraction of religion is precisely that here human beings "manage" the extent to which they have to do with God. In religion, we fit God into our lives, rather than allow the priority of God's gracious claim upon us.

The particular significance of Barth's characterization of religion as unbelief is his conclusion that religion leads to doubt. The weakness of religion, Barth argues, is its "non-necessity."[63] Religion is not determined by God but is conditioned by a person's own life and nature, their moral and religious feelings. As a consequence, religions vary according to cultural settings, national and even climatic contexts, and as a contextual phenomenon religions wax and wane. They are "notorious" for their illnesses, Barth says, and are always fighting for their lives.

Without revelation religious people cannot find the way to faith and do not know that their religion is in fact unbelief. In the life of the individual, participating in a religion arouses a desire for freedom, which creates doubt about the claims of that particular religion. Individuals sense disquiet and doubt because of the "non-necessity" of their beliefs. In fact, these beliefs have no ultimate significance. They are simply chosen or accidental forms of religious activity, which can be abandoned or changed without serious personal implications.

Barth then asks what it is that we abandon, if we "give up" our religion. He argues that the non-necessity of religion makes both belief and the abandonment of belief relatively easy, because those beliefs do not express a real involvement with God.[64] What we are giving up is something we in

---

[62] Ibid., 1:2, 327.
[63] Ibid., 1:2, 316.
[64] Ibid., 1:2, 317.

fact created. At its basis, religion is not a response to the reality of God but is a human activity, similar to a hobby or spare-time interest. Consequently, a change of religion does not constitute a substantial change in people's positions in life, in their relationships with God.

The problem of religion, according to Barth, is that it is not aware of its own nature as unbelief and so will not refrain from its attempts at self-justification. As a result religious people cannot defend themselves against anxiety and doubt. It is not by some adjustment of one's religious beliefs, or by trying harder or being "more committed," that doubt is to be resolved. The unbelief of religion is overcome only by the "event" of faith, the gift of grace in which the word of God is known and religion is abolished.

Several critical observations seem appropriate at this point, before I proceed to a more general evaluation of Barth's theological response to doubt. First, Barth does not justify the claim that "religion" leads to a desire for freedom from God and thus to disquiet and doubt. His claim here is a generalization, which may have considerable veracity but is nonetheless made without any specific evidence. It may be true that Barth would apply his criticism of religion to himself as much as to anyone else. Even so the claim that religion invariably leads to anxiety and doubt is one that requires further argument and cannot simply be presupposed.

Another aspect of Barth's argument here is quite problematical. The argument seems to suggest that religious belief and human religious activity are the "enemies" of genuine faith. But what exactly can this mean? Can there be faith without belief and without "religion"?

Barth seems here to refuse any value or importance to what he calls the religious person's self-determination. Yet we have noted earlier his strong affirmation of various aspects of the human response to God's word of grace, which included believing, obedience, and prayer—all essentially religious in character. Yet in this section his argument seems to be that all belief is in fact unbelief. Any self-conscious attempt to be related to God by upholding and practicing one's religious belief is in some sense an attempt at self-justification and amounts to resisting divine grace. How then is it possible to believe the gospel of grace and to serve God without falling into "unbelief"? It appears that we are left with no clear basis on which to distinguish a faithful response from the unbelief of religion.

In one further passage in *Church Dogmatics* Barth provides an indication of how he would respond to this difficulty. In volume 4.3, where he presents his doctrine of God's election and reconciliation of all humanity in Christ, Barth recognizes that some people may beg leave to question or doubt the reality of this salvation. He presents a "dialogue" between a Doubter and the Word of Grace. The Doubter acknowledges that there may be some eschatological sense in which she or he will be a redeemed person, though at present they cannot recognize themselves as such. The Word of Grace responds by affirming this honesty, but then urges the Doubter to accept this promise as true: "All honor to your honesty, but my truth transcends it. Allow yourself, therefore, to be told in truth and on the most solid grounds what you do not know, namely that you are this person in spite of what you think."[65] The basis on which a person is to accept this truth is subsequently explained as the person of Jesus Christ, addressing the Doubter. Here we see very clearly that for Barth faith is not grounded upon what we know or believe but upon the word addressed to us. To doubt is precisely to try to base one's faith upon one's own understanding or belief, rather than upon this word.

According to Barth, Christian faith is the creation of God and the existence of faith is wholly dependent upon the sovereign word of grace. As a consequence, a person who does not have faith, or one who is in doubt, cannot "become a Christian" by his or her own decision or act of intellectual assent. Equally, one who has heard the word of God and is "awakened" to faith remains in that position only insofar as they continue to hear it and to be responsive to it as God's word.

For Barth these are the "dynamics" of faith and doubt, and they apply with equal rigor to individuals and to theology. Theology can speak truthfully about God only insofar as it is an activity of faith and is concerned to hear the word of God. Theology cannot claim that it adequately understands the divine word of truth, and in this sense theology remains uncertain. Nonetheless, theology must work in hope, in the analogy of faith, and in prayer, trusting that God will reveal all that we need to know. Only in this stance can theology be free of doubt. Only in this way can faith be free of "religion" and unbelief.

It is now time to ask what are the strengths of this approach and what insights it offers for our further understanding of the nature of doubt and its relationship to faith.

We must begin by acknowledging Barth's enormous contribution to Christian theology. His system of dogmatics is extremely comprehensive

---

[65] Ibid., 4:3, part 1, 250.

both in its scope and detail, giving incisive expositions of Christian doctrines and their relations to one another, as well as lucid explanations of numerous debates in the history of Christian theology. Yet within this comprehensiveness, and the passion and vitality with which he writes, Barth has consistently maintained his basic methodological focus on the "priority" of God.

The whole of Barth's theology can be seen as a joyous celebration of the approach of God to humanity, in the person of Jesus Christ the living Word. This Word is consistently available to us and for us. The "event" character of the Word reflects God's freedom for us. At the heart of Barth's theology is a God whose freedom is expressed through being God for us and with us, as the Word which calls us into being and sustains us in grace. To have developed a theology which maintains so consistently the priority and sovereignty of God, on the one hand, and yet includes human life and the reality of history, on the other, is a major theological achievement. As we shall see, however, there are those who question that Barth has achieved the right balance between God's sovereignty and human freedom.

One of the strengths of Barth's theology is its thoroughly Christological focus. The whole system is characterized by this emphasis on the nature of God for us, as made known in Christ. As a result, the system Barth developed has the strengths of consistency with the historic formulations of faith and with the witness of Scripture, while gathering these into a coherent dogmatic scheme.

As already noted, Hans Küng has argued that Barth succeeded in breaking the modern or Enlightenment paradigm, in which the knowledge of God was limited to the perspective of human subjectivity. Whether or not Küng is right in seeing Barth as beginning the movement toward a postmodern theology, it has to be agreed that Barth has made a highly original and seminal contribution. Barth's theology gives eloquent expression to the Christian experience of faith in which, for many people, encounter with God issues in conviction and a joyous life of praise and service. In so doing, Barth emphasizes that such faith is not a human creation. He shifts the focus from the human subject, which he rightly argues is appropriate to the "existentials" of faith. People experience faith as a gift from God, not as something they have achieved. In this way, Barth shows that it is God's word which creates faith and may thus exclude doubt. It is not by human will or by a particular form of belief that doubt is overcome. If faith is to be free from uncertainty it will not be by human effort but through encounter with God.

Barth is surely right to deal with doubt in this way. Any other approach, which suggests that doubt is to be overcome through greater effort in believing or prayer, or through a clearer understanding of the content of faith, is self-defeating. Those who "try harder" in these ways betray their anxiety and doubt, all the more so because it is unacknowledged. This is what Barth saw as the insidious failing of what he called "religion." As we found with Newman, if there is to be a form of faith which excludes doubt it arises not from the logical structure of belief, or from the will of the believer, but from intense personal encounter with God.

In Barth's theology, then, the question of how faith excludes doubt is addressed through his doctrine of the self-revealing word of God. As a result, much debate about Barth's theology has been concerned with the necessity for and adequacy of his idea of revelation. Wolfhart Pannenberg, for example, has argued that Barth is right to see that our knowledge of God is dependent upon God's self-revelation, but then contends that Barth has mistaken the context and medium of that revelation. He opposes the idea of revelation as the word of God coming to us, unmediated, in history (in Jesus), Scripture, and preaching. For Pannenberg, God's revelation is mediated to us through "ultimate history," in which our reason and imagination are drawn into a recognition of God through our knowledge of history, science, the world as a whole.[66] There continues to be considerable debate about the adequacy of Barth's particular formulations of the doctrine of revelation, but more recent scholarship has returned to an affirmation of the necessity of some idea of revelation as the basis of faith and theology.[67]

One of the continuing areas of concern about Barth's theology has to do with his greatest strength, that is, his doctrine of God. The critical issues here concern both his theological method and his approach to faith as determined by the word of God. It has been argued that Barth has so emphasized the priority and sovereignty of God that in effect he has excluded the historical life of humanity and the world at

[66] Pannenberg's most recent critique of Barth and development of his own view of revelation can be found in Wolhart Pannenberg, *Systematic Theology*, vol. 1, trans. Geoffrey W. Bromiley (Grand Rapids, Mich.: Eerdmans, 1991) ch. 4, § 4, "Revelation as History and as Word of God."

[67] A concise statement of the issues and options in contemporary debate regarding the place of revelation in theology can be found in Mark I. Wallace, "Theology without Revelation?" *Theology Today* 45 (July 1988) 208–13.

large.[68] As a result, it seems that there is no room in Barth's theology for autonomous human beings, and thus for belief *or* doubt.

Barth is right to insist that faith must be seen in relational terms. In faith, we are aware of and drawn into a relationship with one who addresses us, grasps us, and is made known to us. It also seems appropriate that theology should "order" its doctrinal thinking about this reality in such a way as to ascribe to it priority, sovereign freedom, and grace. Critics have argued, though, that Barth's "word of God" is not only prior to theology and prior to faith, it is also all-sufficient. The Christological center is actually turned in upon itself as an all-embracing, all-encompassing reality. A free, reciprocal relationship between human beings and God is ultimately impossible, or at best superfluous. A number of arguments can be adduced in support of this criticism.

Stephen Sykes, for example, has argued that Barth follows the Reformation tradition in which the "objectively clarified preaching of the word" is the only sacrament of the Church.[69] As a consequence theology itself is governed by the word as received in Scripture and as proclaimed in the Church. A fundamental problem of this methodology concerns the activity of theology as a critical discipline. In the Reformed tradition dogmatic theology is seen as the "testing-ground" for the Church's self-understanding and yet, Sykes argues, it is deprived of any basis for criticism or even clarification. On the one hand, dogmatic theology is the testing-ground of the fidelity of the Church's gospel witness. At the same time this very theology is meant to be a witness to the revelation of God. This second "function" of dogmatic theology, Sykes contends, deprives theologians of any basis for criticism of their own understanding of the Gospel. The theologian is "denied . . . the right to clarify the meaning out of fear that he thereby presumes to 'control' his subject."[70] According to Sykes's analysis, in Barth's theology the "priority" of the word of God as the controlling norm of theology makes critical reflection, but especially criticism of the proclamation of the word, effectively impossible. It is not simply that historical-critical studies of the Bible are set aside, as a number of other critics allege.

---

[68] In particular, see Heinz Zahrnt, *The Question of God: Protestant Theology in the Twentieth Century*, trans. R. A. Wilson (London: Collins, 1968) ch. 4, and David E. Jenkins, *Guide to the Debate about God* (London: Lutterworth Press, 1966) ch. 4.

[69] Stephen Sykes, "Barth on the Center of Theology," *Karl Barth: Studies of His Theological Method*, ed. Stephen Sykes (Oxford: Clarendon Press, 1979) 17–54.

[70] Ibid., 52.

Theology as such is deprived of any criterion for "testing" or clarifying its understanding of the word of God.

These criticisms point to an underlying difficulty of Barth's theology, which is that the word of God seems to stand "outside" human history and is ultimately unrelated to it. Heinz Zahrnt rightly sees that the central problem here is Barth's doctrine of God. Zahrnt describes Barth's doctrine of the word as a "monologue in heaven": God speaks of himself to himself, in his Son, and through his Son he answers himself.[71] All this happens "outside" human history.[72] The critical issue here is the alleged all-sufficiency of the word of God. In his attempt to "order" his theology upon its Christological center Barth is said to have effectively denied any significance to human history as such.

Barth himself was deeply troubled by criticism of his theology in these terms. He denied that his theology amounted to "all of God and nothing of humanity." Nonetheless in 1956 he delivered a lecture in which he called for a "change of direction" in theology, to emphasize "the humanity of God."[73] Yet even here Barth was concerned not with the humanity of human beings, but of God: "It is a matter of God's sovereign togetherness with man, a togetherness grounded in Him and determined, delimited, and ordered through Him alone. . . . He exists, speaks and acts as the partner of man, though of course as an absolutely superior partner."[74]

In defense of Barth, T. F. Torrance has argued that Barth does envisage a genuine "interaction" between God and human beings.[75] In particular Barth's stress upon the incarnation arises from his concern to

[71] Zahrnt, *The Question of God,* 107–16.

[72] Ibid., 113.

[73] Karl Barth, "The Humanity of God," *The Humanity of God,* trans. John Thomas and Thomas Weiser (London: Collins, 1961 and 1967) 33.

[74] Ibid., 42. Another powerful critique of Barth's alleged "theological isolationism" can be found in Richard H. Roberts, *A Theology On Its Way? Essays on Karl Barth* (Edinburgh: T & T Clark, 1991). In a review article, however, Bruce D. Marshall has argued that Roberts and the line of criticism he pursues involves a misreading of Barth. Marshall argues that Barth sees the priority of the word of God seeking to engage with all other discourses, not to silence them or to remain apart from them. While Barth's presentation can suggest a "totalitarianism" of the word of God, what he intends, Marshall argues, is a "totality" of all things with God. Bruce D. Marshall, review of *A Theology On Its Way? Essays on Karl Barth,* by Richard H. Roberts, *Journal of Theological Studies* 44 (April 1993) 453–8.

[75] T. F. Torrance, "The Problem of Natural Theology in the Thought of Karl Barth," *Religious Studies* 6 (1970) 121–35.

emphasize that we are addressed by God and are drawn into partnership with God. The crucial difficulty seems to be that in developing a theological epistemology which appropriately emphasizes the priority of God, Barth has not given sufficient content and credibility to his idea of human beings as genuinely autonomous beings. His theology itself has been unduly limited by his epistemological method. The celebration of the word of God as the reality of God's approach to us cannot be coherently limited to this epistemology. As Paul Tillich had argued much earlier, the problem with Barth's "dialectical" theology is that it isn't dialectical enough.[76] An adequate account of faith must allow a greater mutuality in the encounter of God and human beings. To do this, however, requires a different understanding of faith—and makes possible a different understanding of doubt. It seems that Barth was aware of this need but was prevented by his own methodology from addressing it.

In considering Barth's view of faith and its relation to doubt, the crucial question is whether belief or unbelief is actually possible within his theological scheme. Only where there is freedom not to believe can there also be belief, trust, worship, and service. My contention is that faith must involve a genuine relationship in which there are two parties, each with some degree of freedom and mutual responsibility. The "priority" of the divine word in the event of revelation need not exclude the possibility of a genuine, free response. This, as we have seen, is what Barth insisted. Though God's word is epistemologically prior, there is nonetheless a crucial role for human response in "the offering of our thanks."

If we grant Barth's argument that there is room for a free response to the word of God, there is still a question about how we should understand doubt and belief, and perhaps also "religion." If faith is created exclusively by the word of God, it seems impossible that anyone to whom the word is addressed could not believe, for such unbelief or doubt would imply a faulty or in some sense ineffective act of revelation. We must take it then that if there are some who do not believe— as there surely are—this must be because for some reason God has not, as yet, addressed them, even though perhaps they have attended Church, have read the Bible, and have tried to grasp the significance of Christian teaching. It would seem, that is, that God chooses to "elect" humanity in Christ but only to include some within the immediate community

---

[76] Paul Tillich, "What Is Wrong with Dialectical Theology?" *Journal of Religion* 15 (1935) 127–45.

of faith and redemption. Why some are left in doubt and some in unbelief we cannot tell.

These, I think, are implications Barth would wish to avoid. To do so, however, requires a different view of faith in which the hearer of the word is admitted as a genuine partner, a person whose knowledge, history, and religion, whose freedom to act as an autonomous person, are taken into account. To do this would require a different kind of theology than that which Barth has developed, such as he began to envisage in his lecture on "The Humanity of God." But that in turn would require a more positive recognition of the "human side" of faith and of religious belief, allowing some genuine freedom and initiative on the part of human beings. In short, this requires an account of faith which attends to the experience of human beings, in its own right, and thus a more adequate analysis of the relationship between faith, belief, and doubt.

This brings us to Barth's specific treatment of doubt. We have seen that Barth regarded doubt as a threat to theology and to the theologian. In discussing this claim we can immediately agree with his assertion that methodological or "Socratic" doubt is essential to theology. While Barth sees an important place for rigorous questioning within theology, he does not seem to have allowed that such questioning can also be a part of the life of faith as such. When people question God, not just ideas about God, Barth sees this as a threat to faith. He seems to presume that the only appropriate responses to the word of God are belief, praise, thanksgiving, and so on. There is no place in faith (as distinct from theology) for exploration, challenge, searching, and protest. All these must be undertaken, if at all, at a second order, as theology. Questions may be asked, but they must always be questions about God, not questions of God, addressed to God.

Why Barth makes this separation between faith and theology is an interesting question. As we have seen, Barth described two ways in which a theologian might attempt to overcome doubt, first in a kind of "dualistic" existence and second by an "incomparable exclusiveness," a life in which humanity is effectively banished from the theologian's world.

Here we find a curious paradox in Barth's own life and work. It is clear from the biographies that Barth was deeply engaged with life, people, art and music, travel and recreation. Yet in his theology human experience appears not in its own right but only as the object of God's creation, election, reconciliation, and redemption. Do we not see here precisely that the kind of dualism which Barth described in *Evangelical Theology* as one of the means by which theologians seek to deal with doubt? Is Barth's concern for the certainty of theology, and his convic-tion that theology can be free from anxiety and doubt only when it centers exclusively on the word of God, in fact an indication of his own doubt? Perhaps there is here a deep uncertainty about "God's good creation" and about the efficacy of the Word to redeem this world. By concerning itself so exclusively with what he saw as the "objective" side of faith, Barth's theology has incorporated, deep within it, a measure of his own doubt and uncertainty.

The critical question is whether this is a weakness, as Barth seems to have felt it to be. I suggest that it is not a weakness at all, but should be recognized as something essential to the very character of faith and of theology. To do so, however, it is necessary to acknowledge that our experience of the word of God is subject to that same "non-necessity" which Barth attributes to religion. While we may say that in itself God's self-revelation is certain, the human apprehension and under-standing of that revelation must remain subject to the risks and uncer-tainties of historical existence. Barth acknowledged that from the "human side" there is an ultimate uncertainty in theology, yet he did not allow this recognition to penetrate his own concept of faith and the human experience of divine revelation. If, however, we do accept that our encounter with God in Christ takes place within history and is subject to the risk of doubt, this does not preclude the possibility of our faith being true. The fact that our experience of God is part of our his-torical existence does not entail that what we believe to be God's word to us cannot be genuine. What it does entail, though, is that our faith cannot be demonstrated to be true with indubitable certainty. It also entails that our account of the word of God can include many more elements of human experience. We can emphasize the priority of God's approach to us, but we can also speak of God challenging us, even per-haps God provoking us, and of ourselves as responding in exploration, questioning, and searching, as well as in service and praise. Later in this book I will argue that the biblical witness to God's approach and human responses includes a whole range of such experiences. This suggests the need for a theology which includes both the self-revealing activity of God and the human response of faith, which may include both belief and doubt. As we noted early in this chapter, Barth's experience as a preacher suggested to him that encounter with God's word can be a process of mutual questioning. It seems unfortunate that his mature theology moved away from this perspective to one in which the crea-tive potential of human response has little place.

We have now examined two accounts of faith which seek to demonstrate that faith is incompatible with doubt. Newman sought to explain how doubt is overcome through the processes of the human mind coming to faith as assent. We found that in this approach "real apprehension" of God was a crucial element in producing the certitude Newman claims is essential to faith. Barth's account of faith works in exactly the opposite way, placing all the emphasis on God's self-revelation and not concerning itself with the human experience of faith as such. We have found that neither approach can give an adequate account of the relationship of doubt and faith. In the next chapter, we will consider the work of a theologian who seeks to include both perspectives, a stress on the "objectivity" of God and upon the human experience of faith. In doing this, however, Paul Tillich argues that we must see doubt as an essential element in the "structure" of faith.

4

The Dynamics of Doubt and Faith

Paul Tillich is perhaps *the* theologian of faith and doubt. He regarded the question of doubt and its relation to faith as one of the special problems with which contemporary theology must deal. Tillich was convinced that doubt is an essential element in faith and both the methodology and content of his theological system reflect this conviction.

As in the preceding chapters, we begin with a brief consideration of Tillich's own life and the context of his thought. With Tillich, however, this aspect of our study is of special significance, for Tillich's theology arose directly out of his own experience of what he called "the human predicament." Tillich's theology is therefore of particular value for our study, because it draws upon his own experience of doubt and his life-long reflection upon the significance of doubt as a necessary element in the "structure" of faith.[1]

---

[1] The most valuable of the biographies is Wilhelm Pauck and Marion Pauck; *Paul Tillich: His Life and Thought*, vol. 1: *Life* (London: Collins, 1977). The projected second volume has not been published. A number of studies of Tillich's work include chapters or essays which relate his thought and his life. Of particular value here are the following: Rollo May, *Paulus: Reminiscences of a Friendship* (London: SCM Press, 1974) esp. chs. 4–7; Walter Leibrecht, "The Life and Mind of Paul Tillich," *Religion and Culture: Essays in Honor of Paul Tillich*, ed. Walter Leibrecht (London: SCM Press, 1959); Arne Unhjem, *Dynamics of Doubt: A Preface to Tillich* (Philadelphia: Westminster Press, 1966); "Introduction: The Theological Development and Contribution of Paul Tillich," *Paul Tillich: Theologian of the Boundaries*, The Making of Modern Theology Series, ed. Mark Kline Taylor (London: Collins, 1987); and John P. Newport, *Paul Tillich,*

Tillich's Life: The Crisis of Faith and Doubt

Paul Tillich was born near Berlin in 1886. His home life provided a rich foundation for his own appreciation of literature and the arts.[2] He studied philosophy and theology at the Universities of Berlin, Tübingen, and Halle, returning to Berlin to train for the ministry. During these years he also undertook postgraduate work on the philosophy of Friedrich Schelling.

With the outbreak of World War I he volunteered as a military chaplain and was engaged in this work until early in 1919. When released from the army, he took up a low-paid university lectureship in Berlin. During these years in Berlin, Tillich participated in the Religious Socialist movement and a group of intellectuals known as the "kairos circle."[3] For Tillich religious socialism provided an interpretation of the current intellectual and social situation in religious terms. In this context Tillich first expounded his idea of a "theology of culture" and his call for a new form of social relationships, which he called "theonomous" culture, in which individual and social life would reflect a religious dimension.[4]

Makers of the Modern Theological Mind Series (Waco: Word Books, 1984) esp. chs. 1 and 2. Tillich himself provides many valuable insights into the personal background to his thought in three autobiographical essays. The first, "On the Boundary," was first published in Paul Tillich, *The Interpretation of History* (New York: Scribners, 1936) and later republished as *On the Boundary: An Autobiographical Sketch* (London: Collins, 1967). My references are to the latter edition. The second autobiographical essay is found in the "Author's Introduction" to Paul Tillich, *The Protestant Era* (Chicago: University of Chicago Press, 1948 and London: Nisbet, 1951). My references are to the abridged edition by the University of Chicago Press, 1957. The third autobiographical sketch is Paul Tillich, "Autobiographical Reflections," *The Theology of Paul Tillich*, ed. Charles W. Kegley and Robert Bretall (New York: Macmillan, 1952).

[2] Pauck and Pauck, *Paul Tillich*, 3–16. See also Tillich's *On the Boundary*, 13–28, and "Autobiographical Reflections," 3–10.

[3] Pauck and Pauck, *Paul Tillich*, 70–5. Tillich's notion of the "kairos" is explained at length in an article called "Kairos" first published in German in 1922, and in English as chapter 2 of *The Protestant Era*, 32–51. See also Langdon Gilkey's study of Tillich's early political thought, *Gilkey on Tillich* (New York: Crossroad, 1990).

[4] Tillich's concept of theology of culture was the subject of his first public lecture, delivered before the Kant Society in Berlin, in April 1919. His notion of a "theonomous" culture is explained at length in his article "Religion and Secular Culture," *The Protestant Era*, 55–65. Tillich's book *The Religious Situation*, trans. H. Richard Niebuhr (New York: Henry Holt & Co., 1932), explained the idea of theonomy as it related to the contemporary German culture.

Tillich's career as a university teacher of philosophy and theology came to an abrupt end. In July 1932, as dean of the faculty of philosophy at Frankfurt, he confronted Nazi students and demanded they be expelled from the university. A year later, when Hitler had assumed power, Tillich's book *The Socialist Decision* was banned and he was dismissed from his post. He emigrated to the United States where he had been invited to teach at Union Theological Seminary in New York.

Tillich lived and taught at Union Theological Seminary from 1933 until 1955. In "retirement" he held positions at Harvard and the University of Chicago Divinity School, until his death in 1965. During his years in the United States, Tillich's theological work developed many of the ideas first outlined in his articles and lectures in Germany in the 1920s. His three-volume *Systematic Theology* and all his later works expounded in one way or another his concept of faith as "ultimate concern" and his distinctive understanding of the symbolic nature of religious concepts. These central features of Tillich's theology are derived from his own experience of what he called the "dynamics" of faith and doubt. If we are to understand the various aspects of the relation of doubt to faith in Tillich's work, therefore, we must follow his own pathway from the crisis of doubt to the theology of ultimate concern.

The Crisis of Doubt

It is clear from Tillich's autobiographical essays that in his early life doubt raised for him something of a personal and familial crisis. There was a strong internal association between his father's authority and the religious authority of divine revelation.[5] It seems that before World War I his doubt centered particularly on the problems raised by the historical-critical study of the Bible. On this subject he was deeply influenced by the thought of Martin Kahler. Writing late in his life, Tillich explained that Kahler applied the principle of justification by faith to the situation of modern people, whom he characterizes as being "between faith and doubt": "Kahler taught us that he who doubts any statement of the Bible and the Creed can nevertheless be accepted

---

[5] Tillich, *On the Boundary*, 37. See also Tillich's discussion of his response to various forms and systems of authority in "Autobiographical Reflections," *The Theology of Paul Tillich*, 7–9.

by God and can combine the certainty of acceptance with the actuality of even radical doubt."[6]

Even as a student Tillich had adopted this position. In a Christian student meeting the question arose whether a person could be a member of such a group if they were "in doubt." Tillich formulated the reply:

> The individual person doubts, or he does not doubt, and his doubt might even be radical, but if he takes very seriously the problem of his doubt and his faith, and struggles with the problem of the loss of faith in him, then he is a member of our fraternity.[7]

In other words, Tillich held that intellectual problems and doubts do not mean the absence of faith: what is crucial is wrestling with questions in a thoroughly concerned—"serious"—manner.

The question of the relation of doubt to faith continued to concern him. In 1913, while he worked as a pastor in Berlin, Tillich and a friend conducted "evenings of reason" in which they discussed various subjects in Christian apologetics. At one of these gatherings Tillich read a paper on "The Courage to Find the Truth," and at another "The Protest of Doubt."[8] These intellectual-theological concerns, however, were soon to be intensified by a more fundamental experience of the crisis of doubt.

Tillich's experience during World War I revealed to him "an abyss in human existence."[9] What Tillich describes here in conceptual terms was immediately experienced during the war as the death of the known world. He entered the war confident of his nation's cause and of a speedy victory, but by the end of 1915 he was resigned to a long war. He wrote that he no longer feared his own death.[10] He felt he was experiencing "the actual death of this our time" and wrote to his family, "We are experiencing . . . the end of the world order."[11] A whole civilization and culture were dying, revealing "the abyss" in human existence.

In this context Tillich's religious doubt found its broadest expression. All of reality was questionable. Tillich was overcome by a sense of

---

[6] Paul Tillich, foreword to Martin Kahler, *The So-Called Historical Jesus and the Historic, Biblical Christ,* trans. Carl E. Braaten (Philadelphia: Fortress Press, 1964) xii.

[7] Paul Tillich, *Perspectives on Nineteenth- and Twentieth-Century Protestant Theology,* ed. with an introduction by Carl Braaten (London: SCM Press, 1967) 154.

[8] Pauck and Pauck, *Paul Tillich,* 37.

[9] Tillich, *On the Boundary,* 52.

[10] Pauck and Pauck, *Paul Tillich,* 47.

[11] Pauck and Pauck, *Paul Tillich,* 51. Letter to Johannes Tillich, 10 December 1916.

the loss of God and wrote, "I have long since come to the paradox of faith without God, by thinking through the idea of justification by faith to its logical conclusions."[12] This sense of the loss of God and of "faith without God" was to be vital for his later account of the dynamics of faith and doubt. Indeed all of Tillich's theology may be seen as an exploration of "the paradox of faith without God."

In 1924 Tillich published an article called "Rechtfertigung und Zweifel"—Justification and Doubt.[13] Here Tillich developed Kahler's idea that the concept of justification by faith also applied to the situation of those who doubt. His argument here is of particular importance as it provides a number of insights into the early development of his concept of faith as ultimate concern.

Tillich began with the Lutheran interpretation of law and gospel, arguing that there is a paradox in the whole idea of justification by faith. It is only through awareness of the "demand" of the law that we may also become aware of the grace of God. It is only as sinners that we may also be justified by faith. The paradox of justification, Tillich argues, also applies to the problem of doubt. The doubter is one who has been gripped by the law or demand of truth. When this law "takes hold" of a person, with its "ruthless demand," that person may experience radical doubt.[14] Faced with such all-embracing relativity, yet sensing the "demand" for truth, the doubter experiences a crisis, not of damnation by God but rather they experience what Tillich calls the abyss of meaninglessness. The crisis of doubt is precisely the sense that one must, and yet one cannot, find any final "truth"—and so the very "demand" for truth seems to turn in upon itself into a meaningless abyss. Here, though, where doubt and meaninglessness seem overwhelming, the paradox of justification also applies: just as the sinner is justified as a sinner, so the doubter is justified as a doubter. Those who feel that they have no God, who cannot find any truth to which they

---

[12] Ibid., 54. Letter to Maria Klein, 5 December 1917.

[13] Paul Tillich "Rechtfertigung und Zweifel," first published in *Vortrage der Theologischen Konferenz* (Giessen, 1924) and now in Paul Tillich, *Gesammelte Werke*, vol. 8 (Stuttgart: Evangelisches Verlagswerk, 1970) 85–100. This paper has not to my knowledge been published in English, though Tillich refers to it a number of times in other later essays: *On the Boundary*, 48–52, and in "Author's Introduction," *The Protestant Era*, x–xii. Arne Unhjem's *Dynamics of Doubt* includes an extensive discussion of the significance of this study in Tillich's thought.

[14] Tillich, "Rechtfertigung und Zweifel," *Gesammelte Werke*, vol. 8, 89.

can be committed, are nonetheless "related" to God through their acknowledgment and implicit acceptance of the "demand" of truth.

Tillich's crucial idea is the paradox of justification of the doubter, by
God. God is seen to be with those who have no God: "What is revealed here is the God of those who have no God, the truth of those
who are without truth, the fullness of meaning for those who are bereft
of all meaning."[15] In a later summary of this argument Tillich concluded that doubt "need not separate us from God."[16]

Tillich drew a number of implications from his argument about justification and doubt. The first of these concerns the nature of faith itself.
For Tillich the "faith" by which the doubter is justified is quite different
from the faith that has been "lost," that is, the belief they can no longer
accept. The doubter's faith is their acceptance of the "demand" of truth,
the "seriousness" about the truth they lack and the meaning sought. In
these ideas we see the basis of Tillich's later concept of faith as being
conditioned by "the unconditional," in a state of "ultimate concern."

On the basis of his argument that even in radical doubt we are "related" to God, Tillich sought to identify the sense in which all intellectual
and cultural activities, including politics, art, and morality, as well as
overtly religious practices, may have religious "depth" or significance. In
his theological works Tillich searched for an interpretative key to explain
what he called the "correlation" between traditional religious concepts and
the religious meaning or "depth" which he considered to be inherent in all
human culture and experience. In this theological-philosophical search
Tillich developed a number of "principles" or broadly-defined concepts to
sketch the outlines of his "theology of culture." One such principle was his
notion of "theonomy," another the idea of "kairos," and a third was what
he called "the protestant principle." All of these principles he held to be
theologically equivalent to the doctrine of justification by faith. Tillich's
theology of ultimate concern depends fundamentally upon his conviction
that even in doubt or despair we are not "separated" from God.

The Theology of Ultimate Concern

We begin this brief outline of Tillich's approach to theology with a
consideration of Tillich's view of the nature of religious knowledge and

---

[15] Ibid., 92.
[16] Tillich, "Author's Introduction," *The Protestant Era*, x.

theological concepts, for it is in this way that he developed his unique concept of "ultimate concern."

Tillich began his theological system by distinguishing the formal criteria and the concrete norm of his theology.[17] Tillich describes what he sees as the two formal criteria of theology in terms of the notion of ultimate concern. First, as a matter of definition, the object of theology is that which concerns us ultimately. Second, what concerns us ultimately is that which determines our being or non-being, that is, it is a reality which can give us life or can threaten our being. This second criterion shows how all theological ideas have ontological significance or import. Our ultimate concern—or God—is the source and "ground" of all that is, of all being.[18]

These formal criteria are implicit in any theological system, Tillich argues. It is essential to the nature of faith and theology, though, that these formal aspects of theology take some positive or concrete form. That is to say, necessarily we perceive our ultimate concern in terms of some particular religious concepts. In Jewish thought, for example, the object of faith is understood in terms of the God of the First Commandment, while for the Christian theologian the norm of faith and theology is the New Testament claim that Jesus is the Christ. Every theology, then, has as its object that reality which ultimately defines our lives. What distinguishes theologies, and religions, is the way in which this reality is conceptualized.

The distinction between the formal criteria and the concrete norm of theology reflects the nature of faith itself. For Tillich faith is, formally, the state of being ultimately concerned. But necessarily this state is expressed or mediated through some specific content of belief and commitment, such as the confession of the Christian community. Similarly the theologian necessarily stands within a particular religious tradition and perceives the object of faith in terms of the specific religious ideas of that tradition.

A direct consequence of this formal analysis of faith as the state of ultimate concern was Tillich's claim that religious concepts must be understood as symbols. This feature of Tillich's thought is one of his

---

[17] Paul Tillich, *Systematic Theology*, vol. 1 (London: Nisbet, 1953) 4–21, 53–9. An excellent discussion of Tillich's idea of the norm of theology can be found in Mary Ann Stenger, "Paul Tillich's Theory of Theological Norm and the Problems of Relativism and Subjectivism," *Journal of Religion* 62 (1982) 359–75.

[18] Tillich, *Systematic Theology*, vol. 1, 15–17.

most helpful contributions to theology and the understanding of faith.
In a number of places Tillich explained his concept of religious symbols, in terms of six key characteristics:

    i. in common with signs, they point beyond themselves;
    ii. in contrast to signs, symbols participate in the reality to which
       they point;
    iii. symbols open up levels of reality which are otherwise closed for us;
    iv. symbols also unlock dimensions and elements of our soul which
       correspond to the dimensions and elements of reality; and thus
       open up hidden depths of our being.
    v. symbols grow out of the individual or collective unconscious and
       cannot function without being accepted by the unconscious di-
       mension of our being;
    vi. symbols cannot be invented. Like living beings they grow and
       die. They grow when the situation is ripe for them, and they die
       when they no longer evoke response.[19]

Religious concepts and doctrines must be seen as symbols, through
which we participate in and are related to our ultimate concern.

Though there has been considerable critical discussion of Tillich's
concept of religious symbols, we will confine our consideration to one
central difficulty.[20] Every system of symbols needs some initial points
of definition. We can only know what religious symbols mean if there
is some non-symbolic religious statement which limits and defines the
field of symbolic reference, in other words, some statement which
refers directly and literally to the object of faith.[21] The difficulty for
Tillich, however, was to identify even one particular non-symbolic

---

[19] Paul Tillich, *Dynamics of Faith* (New York: Harper and Row, 1957) 41–54. Tillich
explained his concept of religious symbols in two other essays: "The Religious Symbol," *Journal of Liberal Religion* 11 (1940) 13–33, and "The Meaning and Justification
of Religious Symbols," *Religious Experience and Truth,* ed. Sidney Hook (New York:
New York University Press, 1961) 3–11. Tillich's article "The Religious Symbol" is
reprinted in this volume also (301–21).

[20] The most important sources for critical discussion of Tillich's concept of symbols
are William P. Alston, "Tillich's Conception of a Religious Symbol," *Religious Experience and Truth,* ed. Hook, 12–26, and William L. Rowe, *Religious Symbols and God: A
Philosophical Study of Tillich's Theology* (Chicago: University of Chicago Press, 1968)
esp. chs. 4 and 5.

[21] Tillich acknowledged this criticism in his "Reply to Interpretation and Criticism,"
The Theology of Paul Tillich, ed. Kegley and Bretall, 334. For a review of the discussion,
see Rowe, *Religious Symbols and God,* 24–30.

theological statement. In succeeding volumes of his *Systematic Theology*, he suggested different statements as the only non-symbolic statement that can be made about God.[22] This was a problem Tillich never resolved to the satisfaction of his critics. Clearly Tillich did not regard the linguistic-philosophical debate about the meaning of religious language as a pressing issue.

Langdon Gilkey has offered a very clear exposition of Tillich's view of symbols and their function, and how this approach differs from the purely analytical-philosophical concerns of some of his critics. Gilkey's discussion demonstrates that a belief in revelation was central to Tillich's theology. Tillich's theology was based on the conviction that in numerous ways the divine life is continually being disclosed to us.[23] Gilkey's exposition helps to explain what Tillich was seeking to do with his concept of symbols. For Tillich the task of theology is not to consider the way in which theological concepts refer to their object in a detached, analytical way. Rather, his approach was phenomenological. He was seeking to explain the nature of faith by describing how religious concepts, as living symbols, enable people to participate in their ultimate concern, through what he calls the "power" of being. The success or failure of this approach to theology depends, therefore, on what Tillich called "response," that is, whether it is effective in showing particular people, who read Tillich's works or heard his theology in the form of sermons, that in their situation in life they can indeed participate in this "power of being," through the symbols and rituals of the Christian religion. If the exposition "works," as a phenomenological description, then the theology will have demonstrated its veracity.

Tillich was acutely aware, however, that for many people living in this century religious concepts, as traditionally understood, have ceased to have any meaning at all. Tillich's method of theology was intended to address this concern. He described this theological method as the method of correlation. By this method, theology "explains the contents

---

[22] In *Systematic Theology*, vol. 1, 204–5 Tillich states: "The statement that God is being-itself is a non-symbolic statement. However, after this has been said, nothing else can be said about God as God which is not symbolic." In his introduction to vol. 2, however, Tillich wrote: "The question arises (and has arisen in public discussion) as to whether there is a point at which a non-symbolic assertion about God can be made. There is such a point, namely, the statement that everything we say about God is symbolic." *Systematic Theology*, vol. 2, 10.

[23] Gilkey, *Gilkey on Tillich*, esp. 73–8.

of the Christian faith through existential questions and theological answers in mutual interdependence."[24] Systematic theological work thus involves two interrelated tasks: it "formulates" the questions implied in human existence or "the human predicament" and it expounds the "answers" implied in the divine self-manifestation.[25]

Tillich's approach to theology calls, then, for analysis of two sorts of datum. On the one side, theology addresses the existential concerns of human life. These appear in many forms, such as our quest for freedom, our experiences of fear, anxiety, hope, and so on. This analysis of experience is not, however, a psychological or sociological study. It is made "under the impact of revelation," so that what theology is seeking is the "depth" or ontological significance of these aspects of experience and culture. Thus theology sees in these experiential concerns deeper questions about the nature of being and the reality on which our lives are founded. Here we see the continuation of Tillich's quest for a theology of culture.[26]

On the other side of the correlation, theology must offer an analysis of the meaning of Christian concepts and doctrines, such as "revelation," and biblical terms such as "Lord" and "salvation," etc. It is the purpose of Tillich's theology to show the correlation between these biblical and doctrinal ideas and the existential questions expressed in our common experience of life. In this way, as Gilkey suggests, Tillich saw himself as expounding the contemporary meaning of the Christian witness to divine revelation in Jesus Christ.

In our study of Tillich's approach to doubt and faith, we will not be concentrating on his major work, *Systematic Theology*, where this method is developed most fully. We will turn instead to those particular works in which he dealt directly with our theme. It is interesting to note, however, that in a section of volume three where Tillich discusses the process of sanctification, he identifies what he sees as two special problems of faith.

---

[24] Tillich, *Systematic Theology*, vol. 1, 68.

[25] Ibid., vol. 1, 70–2.

[26] For a detailed study of Tillich's notion of ontology and its significance in his theology, see Adrian Thatcher, *The Ontology of Paul Tillich* (Oxford: Oxford University Press, 1978); Gilkey, *Gilkey on Tillich*, chs. 5 and 6; and Newport, *Paul Tillich*, ch. 7. A less sympathetic study of Tillich's ontology is Alistair M. Macleod, *Tillich: An Essay on the Role of Ontology in His Philosophical Theology* (London: George Allen & Unwin, 1973). An earlier critique of Tillich's ontology is that by John H. Randall, "The Ontology of Paul Tillich," *The Theology of Paul Tillich*, ed. Kegley and Bretall, 132–61.

The first is "the question of doubt in relation to the increase of faith," while the second is "the question of the relation of the *eros*-quality of love to the increase of its *agape*-quality."[27] There is reason to believe that each of these presented particular difficulties for Tillich himself.[28]

Tillich chose these subjects for special consideration in various series of public lectures and in a number of subsequent books.[29] It is only the former of these questions which concerns us here, though a full treatment of Tillich's understanding of the life of faith would require a consideration of both.

The Dynamics of Faith and Doubt

Tillich's positive account of the nature of faith and its relation to doubt can be summarized under three key points: (1) faith is the state of being ultimately concerned; (2) doubt is a structural element in all faith; and (3) doubt is overcome through an act of courage. We will examine each of these points in turn.

In his book *Dynamics of Faith,* Tillich begins with the bold assertion that faith is the state of being ultimately concerned. He goes on to explain that there are subjective and objective aspects to this state, though both are "centered" in the immediate experience of the believer.[30] The objective dimension of faith is that reality or object toward which all acts of faith are directed. This reality, which we might call the genuinely ultimate, the real and proper object of all faith, is God. In immediate experience, however, people conceive of God in many different ways, or they may believe there is no God. So the subjective aspect of the state of being ultimately concerned refers to whatever people believe to be the primary focus, purpose, and source of their existence. This is what

---

[27] Tillich, *Systematic Theology,* vol. 3, 253.

[28] Of particular value here is May, *Paulus,* chs. 5 and 6.

[29] On the subject of love as *eros* and *agape,* see Paul Tillich, *Love, Power and Justice: Ontological Analyses and Ethical Applications,* the Firth Foundation Lectures at Nottingham 1952 (London: Oxford University Press, 1954); and Paul Tillich, *Morality and Beyond* (London: Routledge and Kegan Paul, 1964). The three works on doubt and faith are: Paul Tillich, *Biblical Religion and the Search for Ultimate Reality,* the James W. Richard Lectures in the University of Virginia, 1951 (Chicago: University of Chicago Press, 1955); Paul Tillich, *The Courage to Be,* the Terry Foundation Lectures at Yale University, 1952 (London: Nisbet, 1952; my references will be to the Fontana edition, London: Collins 1962); and Tillich, *Dynamics of Faith.*

[30] Tillich, *Dynamics of Faith,* 4–8.

functions for them as God. It might be their own immediate self-gratification, in work or sex or possessions; it might be family, nation, or even church. Our ultimate concern might also be directed toward the spiritual encounter with the one who truly is God.

Few of Tillich's critics have recognized that the concept "ultimate concern" is intentionally ambiguous, in order to accommodate these two aspects of faith. It refers both to an "object"—a reality which grasps the individual as being the holy, the ultimate reality—and to the subjective state in which the individual person is "concerned." In this subjective state, people are committed to what they perceive as ultimate reality. Something takes hold of them and they respond to that reality with a definite commitment, which Tillich calls an act of faith. These two aspects of the state of being ultimately concerned can be distinguished analytically but are united in experience, in the "centered act" of faith. The subject-object distinction is overcome through what Tillich calls the "ecstatic union" of faith. In this centered act all aspects of the human personality are involved. Faith includes cognitive apprehension, that is, some cognitive content, as well as the emotions and the will.[31]

Having outlined the way the centered act of faith includes all aspects of personal life, Tillich briefly identifies various distorted understandings of faith. The most important of these, for our purposes, he calls the intellectualist distortion, which identifies faith with believing. Faith cannot be limited to assent or belief, both because faith involves more than a cognitive state and because, at least at times, faith may express itself in dissent or doubt rather than assent.

All through his life Tillich rejected the idea that doctrinal orthodoxy could be used as a criterion of faith. He once wrote that "orthodoxy is intellectual pharisaism."[32] Much later, when discussing the nature and value of dogma, he argued that ordination candidates should not be required to accept unreservedly a series of dogmas, as such a requirement drives them into dishonesty. A more appropriate requirement is to be able to say that "this whole set of doctrines represents one's own ultimate concern and that one desires to serve in this group which has this basis as its ultimate concern."[33] For Tillich, then, the "criterion" of faith is not unqualified assent to doctrines, but the state of being ultimately concerned.

[31] Ibid., 7, 10.

[32] Tillich, "Author's Introduction," *The Protestant Era*, x.

[33] Paul Tillich, *A History of Christian Thought*, 2d ed., rev. and ed. Carl Braaten (London: SCM Press, 1967) xvi.

Tillich identified idolatry as another possible distortion of faith. Inherent in the dual structure of faith as ultimate concern is the possibility that what we subjectively regard as our ultimate concern is not in fact the genuinely ultimate. We can mistake our ultimate concern and can focus our lives on lesser things. In idolatrous faith some finite thing takes the place of the ultimate in a false ultimacy. That is to say, something finite, such as a political ideology, is mistakenly perceived as being of infinite importance for our lives. Yet idolatrous faith is still faith, Tillich claims, because in such a state we are (subjectively) ultimately concerned, even though we have in reality mistaken the proper object of faith.

Tillich stresses that idolatrous faith may have disastrous consequences for personal and social life. Here he is reflecting on his own experience in Germany; the example he uses repeatedly is that of "extreme nationalism," where "the nation as a God proves to be a demon."[34] Though the risk of idolatrous faith is always present Tillich is, perhaps unduly, confident that idolatry eventually breaks down. This is one point of distinction, then, between idolatry and genuine faith. The more idolatrous a faith, the less it is able to overcome the "cleavage" between subject and object and thus to convince people that its object is indeed ultimate. Idolatrous faith breaks down, while faith in the genuinely ultimate succeeds in "relating" us to our ultimate concern.

For Tillich the risk of idolatry is inherent in the structure of all faith and cannot be avoided. It follows from this element of risk that doubt is part of the structure of faith.

Since faith is the act or state in which a finite being is grasped by the infinite or "ultimate" reality, it will have "all the limitations of a finite act," including uncertainty.[35] This means that faith is uncertain or dubitable. Faith is uncertain precisely because it is the state in which the infinite is "received" by a finite being. Tillich's claim here is very similar to Barth's view of the objective certainty and subjective uncertainty of theology.

To explain the sense in which uncertainty and doubt are inherent in the nature of faith, Tillich distinguishes three types of doubt: methodological, skeptical, and existential.[36] Methodological doubt is that testing and questioning of facts, conclusions, and theories which

---

[34] Tillich, *Dynamics of Faith*, 1, 2, 17, 44.
[35] Ibid., 16.
[36] Ibid., 19–22.

is essential to scientific investigation and logical deduction and which serves as a stimulus to further inquiry. Skeptical doubt is an attitude toward all human beliefs and knowledge. Such an attitude often in fact degenerates into the intrinsically incoherent assertion that there is no possible truth.

The doubt which is implicit in faith is not either of these kinds of doubt. "It is not the permanent doubt of the scientist, and it is not the transitory doubt of the skeptic, but it is the doubt of him who is ultimately concerned about a concrete content. One could call it . . . existential doubt."[37] Existential doubt is an awareness of the "insecurity" of all our concrete knowledge.

To examine the precise nature of this doubt which is inherent in all faith, we must return to Tillich's statement that faith is subject to the limitations of our existence as finite beings. Even when, to the best of our abilities, our faith is focused upon God, the genuinely ultimate reality, still the limitations of our finitude obtain. As a result there are, I suggest, two elements in this existential doubt. First, we may doubt whether what we perceive as our ultimate concern is ultimate. Second, while we may be certain that we have rightly identified our ultimate concern, we may nonetheless question whether the symbols and concepts through which we apprehend that reality are appropriate to its nature. In the first aspect of existential doubt we are uncertain about what is the object of our ultimate concern, while in the second we are uncertain about the adequacy of our apprehension of that reality. Both aspects of uncertainty are inherent in the "existential" character of faith as the state of being ultimately concerned and must, if raised to consciousness, be accepted by an act of courage. That is to say, we must commit ourselves to that which concerns us ultimately in spite of this doubt.[38]

At this point one very important implication of Tillich's approach can be identified. For Tillich doubt does not signify a loss of faith.[39] If existential doubt does appear openly, as it does in specific individual or social circumstances, we should not regard that doubt as a sign of the "denial" of faith but as "an element which was always and will always be present in the act of faith." Indeed, Tillich adds, serious doubt should be seen as a confirmation of faith, that is, as an indication of the seriousness of that person's concern for the ultimate.

---

[37] Ibid., 20.
[38] Ibid., 16–17, 102–4.
[39] Ibid., 22.

It is important to stress that Tillich's claim that doubt is an essential element in faith is not a description of the "everyday experience" of faith. In fact, existential doubt is usually "overcome" in the centered act of faith, through our commitment to that which is for us the holy, our ultimate concern. In this state we may experience serenity and certitude. What should not be concluded from these aspects of the experience of faith, however, is that when these feelings break down we have "lost" our faith.

These observations raise the critical question of truth in faith. If all faith is subject to existential doubt, at least implicitly, how can we know that our faith is true?

Since faith as the state of ultimate concern itself includes both subjective and objective aspects of ultimacy, for Tillich the question of the truth of faith also has these aspects: "From the subjective side one must say that faith is true if it adequately expresses an ultimate concern. From the objective side one must say that faith is true if its content is the really ultimate."[40]

Clearly these criteria of true faith relate directly to the two forms of existential doubt identified above. It would seem, that is, that on the "objective side" faith may be said to be true when its object or content is the proper object of our ultimate concern—"the really ultimate." On the "subjective side" our faith is true when the complex of symbols, ideas, and rituals in which it is expressed are effective in mediating to us the reality we believe to be our ultimate concern. We might say that these ideas "work" for us, they "ring true."

The critical issues here take us back to Tillich's concept of religious symbols and the possibility that they "relate us" to our ultimate concern. It might appear that Tillich's argument about the inescapable insecurity in every concrete belief about God or our ultimate concern now contradicts the possibility of such symbols ever being completely effective. If doubt is always present, does this not mean that our symbols always fail, to some degree, and thus we are aware of doubt; or, if we are not aware of doubt, that our symbols are to some extent illusory? How then can we ever know that our faith is true?

Tillich addresses both sides of this dilemma. On the subjective side he holds that faith is true if the symbols in which that faith is expressed are "living."[41] Living symbols are those which are effective in evoking

---

[40] Ibid., 96.
[41] Ibid., 97.

"reply, action, communication," while dead symbols no longer have this impact. The subjective criterion of the truth of faith is, then, whether or not the religious concepts and rituals of that faith succeed in evoking in us or expressing what is for us the state of ultimate concern. This statement is equivalent to saying that in true faith those who believe are assured or convinced that their faith is true, that the object of their faith is the ultimate reality, genuinely God. In the state of faith, to use Newman's words, "you know that you know," or, to recall Barth's argument, we participate in the certainty of faith through our obedience, service, worship, etc.

Unlike Newman and Barth, however, Tillich did not regard the experience of such certitude or assurance as a sufficient guarantee that our faith is objectively true, for a faith which is subjectively alive may nonetheless be misguided and untrue. True faith, as against idolatry, is not only alive: it also expresses and participates in the really ultimate.

Here Tillich's argument seems to have reached an impasse. Since existential doubt is a necessary element in faith it would seem that we cannot know that the object which, subjectively, we believe is our ultimate concern is "the really ultimate." Tillich seems to be committed to a position of relativism.[42]

At this point Tillich's argument takes an important turn, giving rise to a quite original contribution to theology, I believe. Tillich contends that faith can be known to be objectively true if the symbols of that faith are self-negating.[43] Here Tillich introduces the concrete norm of his theology, the symbol of the cross of Christ. It is vital to our understanding of Tillich's theology to remember here that for Tillich a religious symbol does not merely express the object of our ultimate concern, it also participates in that reality.

Now the best symbols are those which make plain their own character as symbols, i.e., they participate in the reality they signify, yet also clearly point beyond themselves to that reality, thus transcending or "negating" themselves. In Tillich's theology the cross is the norm of faith and theology because this symbol perfectly indicates its own character as a symbol. In the symbol of the cross of Jesus we see that the ul-

---

[42] A clear and very incisive statement of Tillich's response to the problem of relativism can be seen in Mary Ann Stenger, "Paul Tillich's Theory of Theological Norms and the Problems of Relativism and Subjectivism," *Journal of Religion* 62 (1982) 359–75.

[43] Tillich, *Dynamics of Faith*, 97–8. Cf. Tillich, *Systematic Theology*, vol. 1, 150–2.

timate concern of Christian faith is not Jesus but "the Christ Jesus who is manifest as the crucified," or, in Tillich's shorthand, Jesus-as-the-Christ.[44] In other words, the cross of Jesus shows us Jesus is the Christ because it points beyond the dying man to Jesus as the Christ.

If faith is to be true and if a system of religious symbols is to be effective, there must be some way in which we can go "beyond" symbols to the reality itself. As we noted above, Tillich's philosophical critics asked for some logical explanation of how symbols are related to the non-symbolic. For Tillich, however, this "relating" comes about through the effective operation of a definitive—that is, self-negating—symbol. Tillich's assertion is that the cross of Jesus is this symbol. The norm of Christianity is also the criterion of the objective truth of faith. "The event which has created this symbol has given the criterion by which the truth of Christianity, as well as any other religion, must be judged."[45]

At its heart, Tillich's theology is dependent upon the self-revealing activity of God in the cross of Jesus Christ. Christian faith is true insofar as and because its central and defining symbol transcends itself in this way, effectively "relating" us to our ultimate concern, Jesus the Christ.

It is precisely here that we see the fullest implications of Tillich's claim that doubt is an essential element in the structure of faith. For Tillich no system of faith can genuinely express the ultimate unless it is subject to self-negation in the way that the symbol of the cross involves its own self-negation. Only faith which can and does incorporate this aspect, which Tillich calls the "Yes" and "No," can be true. Faith which seeks to avoid this element of existential insecurity, preferring a supposedly "clear-cut" if not literal expression of its ultimate concern, inevitably falls into idolatry, for its object is not the truly ultimate.

It is here, too, that we see what kind of doubt Tillich considers to be inherent in the structure of faith as ultimate concern. This doubt is not indecision or a withholding of assent. For Tillich doubt does not mean unbelief or the lack of a firm conviction in one's religious opinions. It is rather a characteristic of the symbols of faith and of the individual's participation in those symbols and thus in the reality they signify.

We can conclude that when Tillich says that doubt is an element in the structure of faith he means that the very symbols of faith must

[44] Tillich, *Dynamics of Faith*, 98.
[45] Ibid., 98.

incorporate this character of self-negation—a "No" as well as a "Yes." Tillich's own claim, though, is that the relativity of our knowledge is not absolute. Christian faith can be true, in the sense that the symbols of the Christian religion may be effective in relating us to the proper object of ultimate concern. It was toward this end, the experience of true faith in this sense, that Tillich's own theology and preaching were directed. That is to say, he was encouraging people to see the element of doubt in faith, but in so doing to affirm their faith. This affirmation of faith and doubt Tillich called an act of courage.

Faith and Courage

It follows from Tillich's argument concerning the truth of faith that the more aware we are of the symbolic nature of our religious concepts, the more aware we will be of the element of risk inherent in our faith. The element of doubt inherent in the structure of faith will at times be an existential experience. If the symbols of our faith are truly effective religious symbols they will not only relate us to the divine reality, they will also "negate themselves," and so we shall see beyond them to the reality they symbolize but which infinitely transcends them. In so doing we shall become aware of the inadequacy of all our religious concepts. As a consequence we shall become aware of the "No" inherent in our concrete faith and will experience existential doubt. Paradoxically this experience of doubt is not an indication that our faith is "weak" or that we have misunderstood the nature of God. Nor does it mean that the religious life in which we participate is in some sense inadequate. On the contrary, this experience of doubt is an indication that our religious symbols and practices have been effective in relating us to that which is truly our ultimate concern, and thus have demonstrated both their power and their limitation as symbols. Precisely because we have been enabled to know or relate to God, we feel the deep inadequacy of all our ideas and response to that reality. This doubt is an unavoidable element in genuine faith and must be met not by repression but by an act of courage. "Courage does not deny that there is doubt, but it takes the doubt into itself as an expression of its own finitude and affirms the content of an ultimate concern."[46] Such courage, Tillich adds, does not need the safety of unquestionable conviction.

[46] Ibid., 101.

For Tillich, then, the life of faith may involve times of certainty and serenity, but it may also include times when one must take the risk of faith upon oneself, believing "in spite of" doubt. Thus for Tillich faith is not to be seen as inconsistent with genuine doubt. Rather, without such doubt—at least as an implicit or structural element—faith ceases to be genuine faith, a state of ultimate concern.

In his book *The Courage to Be*, Tillich took this argument a stage further, arguing that faith can take the form of courage in the face of radical despair. Tillich has stated that he wrote *The Courage to Be* for people who are "possessed by radical doubt," in order to show what kind of faith can endure such doubt and meaninglessness, and so what kind of faith is possible for them today.[47] Tillich's argument in this book must be seen as a later development of his early concept of the "justification" of the doubter, though here he does not speak of the "law" of truth which has gripped the doubter but of the anxiety of "non-being."

In the central chapters of the book Tillich discusses several forms of anxiety which appear as threats to our existence: the anxieties of fate and death, of emptiness and meaninglessness, and of guilt and condemnation. Anxiety is the awareness of "non-being," that which threatens our being. Yet non-being is a form of being, for the "power" of being includes the various forms of non-being.[48] Tillich then considers the contemporary phenomenon of despair, in which all three anxieties are interwoven.[49] In despair, "Non-being is felt as absolutely victorious. But there is a limit to this victory; non-being is felt as victorious, and feeling presupposes being."[50]

The pain of despair is precisely the overwhelming awareness of non-being. We have lost all sense of what is true and meaningful in our lives. This is the "victory" of non-being. Tillich's claim, though, is that this victory is paradoxical, for such despair itself presupposes the power of being. Tillich goes on to argue that the acceptance of such despair is a form of courage and faith.[51]

[47] This comment is reported in Heinz Zahrnt, *The Question of God: Protestant Theology in the Twentieth Century*, trans. R. A. Wilson (London: SCM Press, 1969) 344.

[48] Tillich, *The Courage to Be*, 43–4.

[49] Ibid., 61–8.

[50] Ibid., 61. The distinction Tillich makes here between the immediate experience of despair and its ontological significance is materially equivalent to the distinction made between an analysis of structure and the description of a state of things, *Dynamics of Faith*, 21.

[51] Tillich, *The Courage to Be*, 152–66.

Tillich's contention is that in every act of self-affirmation a person is related to the divine reality, the "ground" of all being. It is an act of courage, expressing the (divine) power of being within human life. When we affirm ourselves, living and acting in spite of the anxiety of non-being, we participate in the divine reality, the power of "being-itself."

The next step of the argument involves the idea of acceptance of the situation of radical anxiety. To accept despair is itself an act of self-affirmation, Tillich claims. To accept the loss of meaning is an act of "absolute" faith, for it is faith without any concrete content. In the nature of the case all such content or meaning has been lost, in the anxiety of radical doubt and meaninglessness. Here faith takes the form of courage in spite of the apparent and total victory of meaninglessness.

Tillich's description of such absolute faith is very brief, indeed he says it is "indefinable, since everything defined is dissolved by doubt and meaninglessness."[52] Absolute faith is inherently paradoxical. In this state one is unable to believe anything, to "affirm oneself" through any positive meaning. Yet the sheer acceptance of this state can itself be seen and found to be a kind of self-affirmation and, in that sense, an act of faith. In everyday language, we use the expressions "just holding on" or "hanging in there" to describe such an act of self-affirmation.

In the final move, Tillich introduces a directly religious element into his account of the courage of despair. Though a person in such a state may not realize it, they are nonetheless grasped by a form of faith as ultimate concern. This faith, however, transcends theistic belief. Its object is "the God above the God of theism."[53] This God is not *a* being, but is the power of being inherent in every act of courage. This God appears most clearly, though, when the God of theism—we might say the symbolic-religious "face" of God—has disappeared in the anxiety of doubt. When our belief in the God of theism collapses, in despair, the God above God may "appear." The courage to be is grounded in this God.[54] Tillich's claim, then, is that the courage of despair may have revelatory power. It may enable doubters to see that despite their doubt God is with them and accepts them.

Rollo May has observed that the idea of the God above God was critically important for Tillich personally.[55] I suggest that this idea of

---

[52] Ibid., 171.
[53] Ibid., 180–1.
[54] Ibid., 183.
[55] May, *Paulus,* ch. 7, esp. 86–90.

God, which Tillich first described during World War I as "the paradox of faith without God" and soon after as the God of those who have no God, underlies all Tillich's thought about the nature of faith and its relation to doubt. For Tillich the reality of God—that ultimate, unconditioned reality which is experienced as the holy—cannot and must not be limited to the concepts of an individual personality, one being beside others.[56] God is at least personal, but God also transcends all our concepts and may appear to us as the accepting power of being, "the God above the God of theism."

What is expressed in the conclusion to *The Courage to Be* is Tillich's deep personal conviction that the state of radical doubt, including doubt about God, does not separate us from the reality of God. On the contrary, he claims that the situation of radical doubt reveals to us the nature of faith at its most fundamental level. Those whose doubt leads them to a point where the God of theism and every other positive religious concept has been "lost" in meaninglessness, but who affirm or accept this situation with courage, are, in that act, in the state of faith. They are grasped by the power of being and to them God "appears."

The use of passive terms to symbolize absolute faith is vital to Tillich's purpose. We cannot liberate ourselves from the grip of doubt.[57] We cannot find or grasp the God above God. We must accept the situation of the loss of the God of theism and in so doing affirm ourselves in the "courage of despair." Yet precisely this acceptance may lead us to the discovery or realization that we are "accepted in spite of being unacceptable."[58] Those who are able to conceive of this accepting reality as God will sense that they have been accepted. Presumably such absolute faith will lead on to a renewed experience of faith with some more positive and joyful content.[59]

We now turn to a critical appraisal of Tillich's approach to doubt and faith. One obvious strength is that it is so closely related to his own life experiences. It is interesting to note that many of these experiences are recorded in the form of negations: the idea of the absence or "loss" of God; the sense of the inadequacy of all concepts of God, the sense of

---

[56] Tillich, *Systematic Theology*, vol. 1, ch. 10, 261–79, esp. 268–73.

[57] Tillich, *The Courage to Be*, 170.

[58] Ibid., 160–1. Compare also Tillich's sermon "You Are Accepted," *The Shaking of the Foundations* (London: SCM Press, 1949 and London: Pelican Books, 1962) 155–65.

[59] Tillich, *The Courage to Be*, 175–6.

the "abyss" in all things, even within God; the paradox of faith without God; and, finally, the idea of the truth inherent in the experience of the loss of truth, the meaning within meaninglessness, the justification of the doubter. Tillich's theology seeks to deal comprehensively with all dimensions of life. He writes "under the impact of revelation" but in dialogue with life and culture as he experiences them. In so doing, Tillich has consistently maintained his purpose of seeking theological meaning in all dimensions of life.

A second major achievement in Tillich's theology is his dual concept of faith, "the state of being ultimately concerned." Tillich rejected the view that faith can be defined objectively, as Barth attempted to do, in terms of the self-revealing activity of God. Nor can it be defined in terms of a subjective state alone, whether the experience of certitude or as assent to orthodox doctrines. Rather, Tillich maintained that both sides of the dialectic are essential to faith.

The concept of ultimate concern is intentionally ambiguous in order to reflect the fact that faith itself is ambiguous. That is to say, by describing faith as ultimate concern Tillich enables us to say that the one object of all faith is that which is ultimate. All faith is faith in God, as perceived by the individuals concerned. On the other hand, the structural ambiguity of the concept of ultimate concern also enables us to say that much of what is, subjectively, "faith in God" does not in fact have God as its object but is, rather, centered upon some less than ultimate reality. It is the very nature of faith that it can be directed toward what we believe is God and yet that object of faith can be something other than God.

This dual concept of faith allowed Tillich to draw a number of important insights about the positive significance of doubt. Doubt is not a loss of faith; it is part of faith and is religiously significant. In particular, Tillich explains how it is possible to be "related" to God despite the experience of deep despair. The "appearance" of the "God above God" enabled Tillich to distinguish the ways we think of God—theism— from the being of God.

Another important implication of Tillich's dual concept of faith is that orthodox religious belief does not necessarily indicate faith at all. Such belief may be of less than ultimate concern to the individual person. A person may conform fully to the social and religious patterns of belief and worship, yet may do so only as part of another "concern"— perhaps to achieve popularity or public respect, or perhaps because they are afraid of God. As a consequence, orthodox belief cannot be used as a criterion of genuine faith because such faith may be idolatrous. Here is perhaps the most radical implication of Tillich's concept of faith as ulti-mate concern. Only when faith centers upon symbols and beliefs which effectively relate us to what is ultimate can such faith be true.

We must question, however, whether Tillich has given a sufficiently clear account of the positive nature of faith. What does it mean, both in terms of the content of belief and the experience of faith, to say that we are "effectively related" to our ultimate concern? While we may ac-cept that there can be no unambiguous description of faith, nonethe-less it would be helpful to have some more detail of what Tillich thinks faith is actually about.

Some idea of how Tillich would respond to this criticism can be gained from his book *Biblical Religion and the Search for Ultimate Reality*, in which he argues that the philosophical quest for "ultimate reality" reflects the same interest or concern as those who express their faith in more recognizably biblical terms.[60] "The man who asks the question of ultimate reality and the man who is in the state of faith are equal with respect to the unconditional nature of their concern."[61] In the final chapters of that book, Tillich describes a form of "philosophical faith," in which the biblical-personal and the philosophical-ontological "con-cerns" are combined. This possibility, Tillich argues, involves both an intellectual and a personal conversion, in which "the eyes of reason" are opened to divine revelation. In his *Systematic Theology*, Tillich describes the process of "receiving" revelation as "ecstatic reason." Through ecsta-tic reason a particular person is enabled to apprehend an original reve-latory event (such as the life of Jesus) as having ultimate significance, and is thus "grasped" by the divine reality and brought into the state of being ultimately concerned.[62]

Tillich's theology was dedicated to this purpose. He sought to be both a philosopher and a theologian, exercising "philosophical faith." As

---

[60] The criticism that Tillich's theological system and especially his concept of God as being-itself is fundamentally inconsistent with biblical faith is most strongly stated by Kenneth Hamilton, *The System and the Gospel: A Critique of Paul Tillich* (London: SCM Press, 1963) and by Alexander J. McKelway, *The Systematic Theology of Paul Tillich: A Review and Analysis* (London: Lutterworth Press, 1964). Even Tillich's friend Rein-hold Niebuhr criticized Tillich's theology, asking whether his "ontological speculations have not . . . falsified the picture of man as the Bible portrays it." Reinhold Niebuhr, "Biblical Thought and Ontological Speculation," *The Theology of Paul Tillich*, ed. Keg-ley and Bretall, 216–27.

[61] Tillich, *Biblical Religion and the Search for Ultimate Reality*, 58.

[62] Tillich, *Systematic Theology*, vol. 1, 120–31.

a consequence his theology, especially as expressed in his sermons and public lectures, has something of the character of a declarative performance or demonstration of this kind of faith. The final passages of many of his books develop a sense of climax. In particular the concluding sentences of *The Courage to Be* and of *Biblical Religion and the Search for Ultimate Reality* must be seen as declarations, made with power and joy, a proclamation of Tillich's faith in the victory of being over non-being. This is not simply a matter of style. These sentences express what Tillich described as the ecstasy of revelation. For Tillich "philosophical faith" can and does lead to a sense of encounter with the God of the Bible.

Another problem with the concept of faith as ultimate concern is that it appears that for Tillich it is impossible to be without faith; all people have faith. His concept of faith, he wrote, "is basic and universal. It refutes the idea that world history is the battlefield between faith and un-faith."[63]

We may question whether the word "faith" can reasonably be used in this way. Should we describe, for example, the obsession of the drug addict as an ultimate concern and therefore faith? Can we seriously describe Hitler's megalomania, his ultimate concern, "faith"? Perhaps these are extreme instances. They serve, though, to raise the question of whether it is finally justifiable to define faith in terms of its "structure" as ultimate concern and without reference to the content of its belief and the consequences of its practices. We might also question Tillich's assumption that all people do in fact have something which is for them of life-or-death significance, an ultimate concern. Tillich's idea of faith appears to be so universal in its scope that it is difficult to determine when the concept applies and when it does not.

Tillich might defend his analysis of faith along the following lines. First, he could argue that while the idea of the universality of faith does involve some anomalies such as those suggested, it also has a number of crucial benefits. Not the least of these is the implication that the person who doubts may nonetheless be said to have faith, still. Furthermore, to have faith is not the same as to have true faith. It is certainly inappropriate to describe the faith of the addict or the dictatorial aggressor as true faith. There are benefits, though, in allowing that even such idolatrous faith is still faith, for such a "universal" concept of faith emphasizes that all faith is subject to existential uncertainty. There can be no hard-and-fast division, furthermore, between the contents of true and

---

[63] Ibid., vol. 3, 139.

of idolatrous faiths. All contents of belief may become idolatrous. The truth of faith cannot be determined from the subjective side alone, in terms of the state of complete certitude or assurance. All faith involves this ultimate ambiguity: it may be true, though it is dubitable; and though it is subjectively certain, it may be false. To allow for this essential ambiguity in the nature of faith is not therefore a weakness, but a strength of the concept of faith as ultimate concern.

In evaluating these arguments, it is necessary to hold the "universality" of faith in tension with Tillich's strong warnings against idolatrous faith and to give due recognition to his positive and insightful theological statement of faith in Jesus Christ as the one who most effectively relates us to the accepting, redeeming God.

A further difficulty concerns Tillich's claim that doubt is a necessary element in faith. While we may accept the value of his argument as an analysis of the "structure" of faith, we might also object that Tillich does not take sufficient account of the negative, if not destructive, aspects of doubt. Tillich does not seem to recognize that religious doubt can undermine faith, destroying all sense of God and even the most elementary sense of meaning and confidence in daily life. In doubt, people sometimes say that they don't know what to believe about anything any more: nothing makes sense to them.

Tillich suggests that doubt must be accepted by an act of courage. The question is whether such an "act" is possible in the state of doubt, particularly in its radical forms. Doubt may debilitate a person to such an extent that "courage" seems impossible. How then is it possible, or appropriate, to speak of the courage of despair and of faith affirming itself in spite of doubt? Does this indicate that Tillich does not, in fact, take doubt seriously?

Several comments seem apposite. First, we must remember Tillich's distinction between the experience of doubt and the dubitability of faith. Though doubt may be a "structural element" in all faith, clearly Tillich is not suggesting that all people actually experience doubt or that any person experiences it all the time. Nonetheless it is possible to gain the impression from Tillich's arguments that doubt is always a benign experience, when in reality it can be deeply disturbing and may cause people great anguish.

These comments lead to a final question about both the content and method of Tillich's thought. I have argued that Tillich was able to derive a number of valuable insights into the relationship between faith and doubt through his analysis of what might be called "negative" aspects. By considering the religious significance of doubt, despair, and existential anxiety, Tillich has been able to show how faith and doubt are compatible as elements of the "structure" of faith. In this way Tillich has not only given a realistic account of the vulnerability of faith, he has also added to the credibility of his view by suggesting that these negative aspects of our experience are not inherently meaningless but may indeed have positive significance for faith and theology. Yet Tillich tended to deal with all these aspects of faith in a highly metaphysical way. For example, the human experience of guilt is seen as the awareness of a form of "non-being." This kind of analysis tends, though, to avoid the immediate and pressing question raised by that experience—namely, are we in some sense guilty and under threat of condemnation?

It might be argued that Tillich fails to deal with doubt and despair at the level at which they occur in the concrete circumstances of individual human lives. Perhaps his concern with ontology and his life-long desire to construct a system of philosophical theology in which the polarized elements of human existence are "unified" represents a theological-metaphysical escape from the genuine and immediate ambiguities of individual human lives and particular situations. Doubt and the ambiguities of life are not overcome by imaginative analysis and theological speculation. They are dealt with in the precarious finitude of daily living.

Tillich's thought may be seen as a metaphysical-theological "retreat" from the anxieties and distortions it purports to analyze. On the other hand, Tillich claimed that the theology he developed, and the lectures and sermons he based on it, were attempts to express, in his particular historical-cultural situation, the existential truth of faith. My own judgment is that in a number of helpful and incisive ways, Tillich succeeded in this objective.

These final considerations suggest to us, though, several further directions in which we might pursue our study of doubt and its relation to faith. Tillich's major contribution, I contend, has been to provide the methodological breakthrough in the theological understanding of doubt, that is, to show that doubt may have positive significance for our understanding of faith itself. What is now required, though, is an investigation of this possibility, a study of real experiences of doubt, in the lives of particular persons, to see if indeed doubt has the significance which Tillich suggests it may have. In the next two chapters we will examine two such life stories and the theological reflections derived from the lived experience of doubt and faith.

5

Doubt and the Religious Self

In the preceding chapters we considered three theological frameworks which seek to explain the nature of doubt and its relation to faith. We have found that an adequate view of faith and doubt needs to include logical, personal, and theological elements. Whereas we found Tillich's approach most helpful in combining these dimensions in his concept of faith as ultimate concern, we identified the need to examine how these dynamics are actually worked out in people's lives.

In this chapter we will consider the first of two life stories which explore the relationship of doubt and faith. In each of these stories the specific focus or object of doubt is a particular aspect of religious experience. The stories are valuable in themselves because they provide living expressions of the issues and dynamics discussed in our preceding chapters, but even more so because they indicate exactly how doubt can challenge and enrich the life of faith.

James W. McClendon has pioneered the use of biographical studies as a basis for contemporary theological reflection. In his work *Biography as Theology*, McClendon explains that he is not suggesting that theologians can usefully draw upon biographies to illustrate or demonstrate the meanings and implications of previously established doctrines—though this may be a beneficial use of biography. McClendon's purpose is more radical. He sees biography *as* theology. Life stories can be the means of knowing God and of discovering how we should speak of God, Christ, humanity, sin, grace, and so on.[1]

McClendon has outlined his method in the book already mentioned, as well as in his *Ethics*.[2] In each he uses life stories to explore the nature and meaning of Christian faith. His method involves searching for the "vision" or defining ideal which has guided the life being studied. In his study of Martin Luther King, for example, he tests out the significance of King's much quoted "dream." What was the basis of King's hope, and what does this teach us about the nature of Christian hope? McClendon's method shows that theology can usefully derive knowledge of God from human life stories—at least in some cases. Whether every life story has this significance is a question we will not consider here.

In this chapter we will examine the life and work of Harry Williams, whose theological work is deeply influenced by his personal struggle with doubt. Drawing upon his autobiography and other theological works, we will see that the specific focus of Williams' doubt was what he called "the religious self." In a sense, his doubt was self-doubt, but equally his quest for faith has been a quest for his true self. Indeed Williams has come to the conclusion that God is his truest self, which he calls "the final me." In the introduction to his autobiography, *Some Day I'll Find You*, Williams explains that much of his life has been a struggle between two opposing realities which were often confused with one another. Through psychoanalysis over a period of fourteen years, Williams gradually came to identify his central difficulty: "For years on end I mixed up God and the Devil, not knowing which was which."[3] It was only when these confusions were recognized that Williams was able to deal with "the religious self" and its crippling pretensions and enter into a joyful life of faith. It was through this same process that he came to see doubt as an essential ingredient in the life of faith.

Born in Rochester, England, in 1919, Harry Williams spent part of his early childhood in France, then returned to England for schooling. After studying at Oxford, he trained for the Anglican priesthood. He

---

[1] James W. McClendon, *Biography as Theology: How Life Stories Can Remake Today's Theology*, 2d ed. (Philadelphia: Trinity Press International, 1990).

[2] James W. McClendon, *Systematic Theology*, vol. 1: *Ethics* (Nashville: Abingdon Press, 1986).

[3] H. A. Williams, *Some Day I'll Find You: An Autobiography* (London: Mitchell Beazley, 1982) ix.

was a parish priest in London during World War II and until his appointment in 1948 to teach at Westcott. He moved to Trinity College, Cambridge, in 1951, initially as lecturer in theology, and was dean of chapel from 1958 until 1969. He then moved to Mirfield in Yorkshire to become a member of the monastic Community of the Resurrection. Most of Williams' books were written during his life at Mirfield. It is within this life of ministry and study that the polarities of life and faith have emerged.

Our study of Williams' life will focus on three aspects of his struggle: his confrontation with conventional religion, his mental breakdown, and the discovery of God as "the final me." In considering each of these dimensions of Williams' experience, we will also see how doubt played a pivotal role in the emergence of a life of genuine faith.

Confronting the Religious Self

It is clear that Williams' mother was a crucial influence upon his religious formation. She was a highly volatile woman, emotionally involved with evangelical religion. She adopted the attitude of being "out-and-out for Jesus."[4] Despite this fervor, during much of Williams' childhood and youth his mother conducted an extramarital love affair with a younger man, also an evangelical Christian and later a clergyman. Williams' analysis of his mother's religion is particularly important. It was, he suggests, a means of coping with guilt, "to protect herself against sin," against the possibility or actuality of indiscretion.[5] Perhaps because of this double-standard and self-deception, his mother's religion created a guilt-ridden atmosphere in the home, a regime of "moral and religious blackmail."[6] Many of Williams' childhood interests, such as the circus, cinema, and theater, were prohibited on religious grounds.[7] All this suggests an early and perhaps unrecognized sense of religion as a threat, as a force against his life and interests.

Overtly, however, during his childhood Williams regarded religion itself as theater and church services as a form of visual entertainment.[8] At one time he obtained a mail-order catalogue of ecclesiastical equipment

---

[4] Ibid., 15–16.
[5] Ibid., 38 and 44.
[6] Ibid., 51.
[7] Ibid., 57 and 58.
[8] Ibid., 72–5.

and with a few small purchases set up an altar in his room, to play Mass![9] On another occasion, while on a visit to Oxford, he heard William Temple preach and decided then that he would become a priest, for the glamour attached to that role.[10] In these actions, Williams later saw, he was identifying unconsciously with the aggressor in his life. The priest was not only an important and glamorous figure on the stage of religious theater, he was also the supreme representative of the "God" of his mother's guilt-laden religion. Williams was both attracted to and fearful of this God.

At school Williams experienced a different kind of religion, in the liberal Anglicanism of the principal, David Loveday.[11] Loveday believed in giving people a second chance rather than imposing guilt upon them. As a consequence, though, Williams left school "religiously divided." He had been deeply impressed by Loveday's accepting attitude, but still had "a sneaking feeling that only people out and out for Jesus were really Christians."[12]

At Oxford Williams studied theology, which he liked academically but it didn't affect him personally.[13] He still wanted to be ordained, although he didn't know why and attended only the minimum of religious observances.

When he moved to Cuddesdon for ministerial training he encountered an intense Anglo-Catholicism, which he experienced as very similar to the extreme evangelical religion of his home environment. Although there were obvious contrasts, these were only cosmetic. Both were systems of guilt and moral blackmail. "What I mean is that it was still the same old apparatus for producing religious results by whipping up guilt feelings and branding people for life with neurotic compulsions, sold as the voice of God."[14] In response to what he describes as an elaborate system of taboos, guilt-induced confessions, and other religious fanaticisms, Williams tried to create an "ideal self," a religiously acceptable self, which in fact excluded three-quarters of his real self. In his subsequent career as a priest Williams tried to be this "ideal self."

[9] Ibid., 63–4.
[10] Ibid., 56.
[11] Ibid., 81–6.
[12] Ibid., 85.
[13] Ibid., 86–7
[14] Ibid., 93.

From 1943 to 1948 Williams served as a curate in inner London. He described his religious life during this period in terms of a "pact" between himself and God. The contract required "nothing of self"—no self-assertion and especially no sex.[15] Williams later saw that the God of this "contract" was a neurotic projection of himself. He was attributing to God his own refusal of parts of his life which he could not acknowledge or did not know how to integrate into his life as a priest.

Two aspects of his life as a minister disturbed him especially. First, he realized that he did not want to change people, even though his religious ideas seemed to imply that he ought to do so. He did not even urge them to go to Church. He found that people were inherently good, sometimes in spite of, rather than because of, their religious beliefs. Indeed, he often found more joy and real caring among agnostics than among believers.[16]

A second aspect of his pastoral work also began to undermine his religious "self" and his pact with God. He began to realize through his counseling work that his theological "answers" to moral difficulties did not really resolve these problems at all. On the contrary, he saw how clear-cut moral definitions created guilt in the lives of people whom he secretly believed were good people, not bad. He began to wonder whether these priestly rules were not de-humanizing, both to himself and to others.[17] This "creeping awareness" and moral-theological doubt also caused him to feel guilty.

Williams describes these initial disturbances in his life as a priest as the beginning of "the revolt of the self" in which the true God was breaking through.[18] What is critically important here for our understanding of his theology is Williams' claim that God was attempting to reach him through his humanity, including through his doubt and uneasiness and, later, through his illness. Before Williams could develop that constructive theological understanding of his experience, however, it was necessary to work through some of the factors which were integral to his sense of crisis. Two of these were his sense of self and his attitude to conventional religion. It is clear that in fact Williams' struggle arose from the deep entanglement of his self-identity with the demands of his public position as an Anglican priest, and so to find himself it was necessary

---

[15] Ibid., 129–32.
[16] Ibid., 134.
[17] Ibid., 126–8.
[18] Ibid., 132.

to engage in a critique of conventional religion. The "target" of his criticism was sufficiently external to himself to permit this initial protest but, as we shall see, it did not finally resolve the deeply personal issues which had led to his predicament. One specific target of Williams' critique was the conventional view of doubt and its relation to faith, while another was the loss of personal autonomy and responsibility for one's life and actions which are induced by that inadequate view of faith.

Williams describes the view of faith and doubt he wishes to oppose very succinctly: "People sometimes confuse faith with sight as though if faith were perfect it would consist of complete certainty, that absolute inability to doubt which belongs to sight alone."[19] This is the popular idea of "strong faith," which implies never doubting or questioning. It means being certain. According to this idea, faith requires the exclusion of all doubt from the believer's consciousness. It requires the positive attempt not to doubt—in Newman's language, to "put down" doubts with a heavy hand. Believing is thus an intellectual activity, undertaken as a voluntary act, resisting doubts and questions. As a consequence people think that to grow in faith means to grow in certainty. Such growth comes about through the effective anaesthetizing of our critical intelligence, Williams argues. It is implied in this view of faith that people who ask awkward questions and who express doubts have not yet grown in faith. On this assumption, Williams observes, the Middle Ages are regarded as an age of faith, whereas in fact what we find there is "faith confused with sight so that in the cause of certainty doubt was repressed."[20] For Williams it is false and misleading to identify faith with "sight" or certainty.

In a number of his earlier works Williams describes what he sees as the psychological processes involved in this false identification of faith and certainty (or rather certitude). His purpose is to show how many consciously religious attitudes and feelings in fact result from the repression of doubt. Psychoanalysis can help us to see that often what we think we believe about God is not necessarily about God at all. The proper object of these beliefs and feelings may well be a part of ourselves which we call "God."[21] Often what purports to be Christian service is in reality self-centeredness masquerading as virtue and fre-

---

[19] H. A. Williams, *Tensions: Necessary Conflicts in Life and Love* (London: Mitchell Beazley, 1976) 42.

[20] Ibid., 42.

[21] H. A. Williams, "Theology and Self-Awareness," *Soundings: Essays Concerning Human Understanding*, ed. A. R. Vidler (Cambridge: Cambridge University Press) 1963.

quently leaves its recipients without comfort, while the care-giver is rewarded with feelings of self-satisfaction.[22]

At the foundation of these inauthentic attitudes, Williams argues, is a fundamental concern not with God but with ourselves, a desire to maintain as far as possible the image of ourselves as Christ-like. In a number of his sermons published in *The True Wilderness,* Williams spoke about "the religiously-acceptable pretending self."[23] This is an image of oneself which conforms to the demands of conventional religion. It is modeled on an image of Christ. This "pretending self" is the person I must try to be, the person I present to others as who I really am. The real purpose of much "religious behavior" is to project this image of ourselves, but in so doing to preserve a limited self-awareness. That is, it is crucial that we never acknowledge to ourselves or to others what we are really like, especially the ways in which we are not like this Christ image. In a statement clearly reflecting his own experience Williams remarks, "I go to Church, I read the Bible, I say my prayers, I do good works, I become a clergyman, in order to keep what I am at arms length."[24] On this basis he concludes that, psychologically, much that appears to be faith and virtue is in reality self-centeredness and avoidance of authentic faith.

In a later discussion of faith and doubt in his book *Tensions,* Williams argues that much religious belief has a similar inauthentic character.[25] Such faith requires a "created" certainty. Doubt must be repressed by enthusiasm or zeal, perhaps to the point of fanaticism: "Repressed doubt can make us into yelling zealots, fascists of the spirit who think that the noise they make is designed to persuade others while it is really designed to persuade themselves."[26] Such a reaction to opposition is explained by the fact that the persons concerned are in reality defending themselves, or rather the Christ-like self they pretend to be. The "opposition" here is not really a contrary opinion but is, rather, the true self, the self "locked away" from awareness. What is being opposed is the revelation of the truth about the real self and about the pretense maintained in conventional religious practices.

[22] H. A. Williams, "Psychological Objections to Christian Belief," *Objections to Christian Belief,* ed. A. R. Vidler (London: Constable, 1963) 43.
[23] H. A. Williams, *The True Wilderness: A Selection of Addresses* (London: Collins, 1976).
[24] Williams, "Psychological Objections to Christian Belief," 47.
[25] Williams, *Tensions,* 42–55, esp. 43–5 and 49–51.
[26] Ibid., 43.

For Williams himself, however, the resolution of these issues involved a much more profound personal crisis and the discovery of different ways of knowing both himself and God. It was through this crisis that he came also to articulate more comprehensively a new approach to faith and its relation to doubt.

Breakdown and Breakthrough

Williams' personality breakdown took place early in his time at Trinity College, Cambridge. He suffered an acute mental and social paralysis in which he became terrified by virtually any human contact. For quite some time he hardly ventured from his rooms.[27]

Through psychoanalysis he came to see that he only responded to the neurotic in his dealings with God.[28] The God with whom he had made a pact was a "no-God," or rather the true God and this neurotic "no-God" were so completely mixed together that he never knew where he stood. For some time this was literally true: he lost the use of his legs and could not move.

As he began to recover Williams was able to resume academic teaching but was as yet unable to participate in any religious life. His description of this aspect of his experience is particularly important for our understanding of his view of faith and doubt. Williams explains that he had "had enough" of God for the time being and stayed away as much as he was able from Church and all religious practices, public and private. It was, he says, "an indescribable relief not to have this ghastly figure breathing with disapproval down my neck."[29] It was necessary, for a time, to throw the "baby" of the true God out with the "bath water" of the neurotic idol. Years later he came upon Yeats' line, "Hatred of God may bring the soul to God," and saw this as a description of what had happened in his own life. In fact, though, there was faith in his unbelief. True faith involves a genuine relationship with God and every such relationship requires an assertion of one's autonomy from the other. One of the life-giving tensions of faith, Williams later argued, is that between autonomy from God and dependence upon God. We must in one sense rebel against God, as a child or adolescent must rebel against its

[27] Williams, *Some Day I'll Find You*, 166–75.
[28] Ibid., 177.
[29] Ibid., 176–7.

parents, in order truly to relate to God in open and genuine trust.[30] Williams' claim, then, is that his unbelief during this time was an expression of genuine faith, a making way for the real God.

This insight into the way in which the struggle of faith may involve unbelief and doubt was possible, though, only through the realization of another aspect of the Christian faith, the notion that sufferings are a medium of God's presence. They are an invitation "to join in Christ's sufferings . . . to help bring life and light and healing and liberty to mankind." The cruel and destructive aspects of suffering may be "charged with positive and creative possibilities."[31] Working through these insights, Williams came to a new understanding of faith and of the nature of God.

Two apparently contradictory elements of his experience, his "hatred" of God and the idea that sufferings may be an occasion of God's creative presence with us, came to be welded together in a new form of faith, a new sense of God's presence within his own life. Over some time Williams experienced moments of mystical awareness, visions of the presence of God in a field of snow or in the sea, or simply a state of bliss while riding on a bus.[32] What was focused in these experiences was also, though, the hard-fought struggle of many weeks and years, the struggle to find and accept his real self and to acknowledge God within that self rather than as a tyrannical opponent to his very existence. Williams puts it like this: "The idol whose slave I had been was being rung out, the true God was being rung in. And in place of my former narrow and destructive moralism I had begun a search for integrity."[33] The break-down became a break-through and Williams found that he was able to articulate a different view of faith and the knowledge of God.

Faith as "Inside Knowledge"

For Williams, faith is a kind of knowledge, a form of cognition. But the nature of this knowledge has been seriously misunderstood, even (or perhaps especially) within religion itself. Williams maintains that it is vital to explain the sense in which faith is knowledge. It is vital, in the sense of life-giving, for it may lead to release from false and destructive

---

[30] Williams, *Tensions*, 28–9, 32–4.
[31] Williams, *Some Day I'll Find You*, 177.
[32] Ibid., 178, 241, 246, 248, 249.
[33] Ibid., 199.

forms of faith, thus enabling people to be truly themselves and to discover the joy of God within the mystery of their own humanity.

To explain these possibilities Williams developed the terms "inside knowing" and "outside knowing."[34] In his book *The Joy of God*, Williams explains that what he is trying to distinguish are not so much two categories of knowledge or truth as two modes of knowing.[35] One such way of obtaining knowledge is *intellectus*, or intelligence, which involves "an intuitive apprehension of reality." The other mode of knowing is *ratio*, which involves thought or deliberation, reasoning from premises to conclusions. Like Newman before him, Williams insists that genuine knowledge can be obtained through *intellectus* and thus that it is not necessary to restrict the term "knowledge" to those beliefs and conclusions which are derived by formal reasoning alone.

For Williams the crucial point of this distinction is the personal element in *intellectus*. In this kind of knowledge we are personally involved as "insiders." Intelligence

> does not inspect its object from the outside. It enters into its object, delves deep into its object's innermost reality, clothes itself with its object, puts on its object as part of itself, and hence in the end abolishes the distinction between itself as perceiving subject and the object as object perceived.[36]

From this string of descriptive phrases and images we can see that "intelligence" here has something like the sense of military intelligence—it is knowledge derived from within the enemy camp, by involvement in the life of the "other." Sexual knowledge is another possible example of such knowledge. "Inside" knowing involves a union or communion with its object. In such knowledge we are not "outsiders," we are personally involved.

By contrast, in "outside" knowledge the knower remains objective and personally uninvolved. The means of such knowing can be clearly defined: a conclusion can be proved by logical inference, an experimen-

[34] An initial statement of this distinction between two kinds of knowledge can be found in Williams' sermon "Into All Truth," *The True Wilderness*, 15–20. A far more detailed epistemological analysis is to be found in H. A. Williams, *True Resurrection* (London: Mitchell Beazley, 1972); see esp. chs. 2 and 3, and in H. A. Williams, *The Joy of God* (London: Mitchell Beazley, 1979) esp. 50–7.

[35] Ibid., 51–2.

[36] Ibid., 52.

tal result demonstrated and repeated by any "competent" person. The agent of such knowing does not affect or influence the content of the knowledge as such. Outside knowledge in this sense remains "outside" the knower. It is for this reason that outside knowledge can be said to be certain. The truth of such knowledge is independent of the person who apprehends it. It is said to be "objective truth."

One of the themes of Williams' books is his concern to demonstrate the difference between these two kinds of knowledge and the implications of this distinction for faith and theology. In so doing Williams seeks to indicate some of the disastrous consequences which arise when these different ways of knowing are confused and particularly when people reject the possibility of inside knowledge altogether. In these circumstances, people try to obtain outside knowledge in matters where that form of knowing is inappropriate. The outside approach to knowledge is appropriate to certain aspects of life, such as scientific investigation, but where this mode of knowing is imposed upon the whole of our lives it has what Williams calls "death-dealing" consequences. Williams' own ministry and theology seek to challenge and redress what he sees as an undue preoccupation with outside knowledge, in society generally but especially in matters of faith and morality.

Many of Williams' sermons and reflections argue that in religion outside knowledge is "death-dealing," while inside knowledge is the way to resurrection, a new life of faith. This thesis is developed in considerable detail in his book *True Resurrection.* In successive chapters Williams describes these possibilities—the resurrection of the body, of the mind, and of morality, and finally the resurrection through suffering and death. In each case there are two stages to his argument. He begins by explaining the "death-dealing" effects of remaining "outsiders" in these aspects of our lives, when we try to remain objective and uninvolved in these elements of our personal existence. The second stage of Williams' argument is a description of the joyful, though often also painful, process of accepting all of oneself and accepting the risk of being an "insider." Here Williams uses stories from his counseling ministry to describe the process of "resurrection."

In his chapter on resurrection and mind, we see most clearly the basis of Williams' view of faith and its relation to doubt. He describes the state of living deadness which results when the methods of scientific objectivity are regarded as the only legitimate means to knowledge and where technical information is considered the only valuable knowledge.[37] Personhood becomes equated with mind and mind with machine. Knowledge becomes a form of possession and control. But this kind of knowing never satisfies us. Indeed it is death-dealing: "It kills the living reality in order to analyse it."[38] Williams calls for a different understanding of knowledge, involving a personal communion with its object, such as our knowledge of the place we call "home," our knowledge of other people, our knowledge of a piece of music or of a literary work. All these examples have one thing in common, Williams observes: "the absence of intellectual certainty."[39] There is no objective certainty about "inside" truth. It is not something which can be demonstrated or proved. If we are to have life-enhancing knowledge in these aspects of our lives, rather than living deadness, we must accept doubt and intellectual uncertainty. This does not mean that what we know in this way is false or illusory, only that it cannot be proved incontrovertibly by "objective" means. For Williams, then, if we are to enter into the joyful experience of such inside knowledge we must abandon our concern for "controlling" reality through objective knowledge.

Williams' theology is based upon his conviction that God cannot be known through "outside" knowing. Genuine faith involves the knowledge of God through the most profound form of inside knowing.

It is important to note that Williams sees a *positive role of doubt* in this transition from "objective religion" to faith as self-awareness. If we are to abandon faith as outside knowledge, this content of faith must be subjected to doubt. This doubt will focus upon the objectified content of faith, that reality which is believed to be God or the ultimate truth of faith. In some instances, for example, this content of faith will be what we believe is the message of the Bible, regarded as "the revealed Word of God." In others it may be the historic "deposit" of faith expressed in the creeds, or perhaps it will be the Church itself which is seen as the immediate object of faith. The reason such mediating structures or objects of faith must be "abandoned," according to Williams' argument, is that they function psychologically as idols, which help us to avoid the truth about ourselves. "Objective religion" helps us to avoid the risk of genuine faith. We can even make Jesus into such an idol. If we are to come to knowledge of God through self-awareness, then, we must reject these idols and abandon this form of faith and the content of such "belief."

---

[37] Williams, *True Resurrection*, ch. 3, esp. 61–71.
[38] Ibid., 65.
[39] Ibid., 92.

What we have been describing in psychological terms, however, cannot be experienced in this way. The doubt which is necessary for the transition from "objectifying" religion to faith as self-awareness must be experienced as real doubt, for it is the undermining and shattering of beliefs about God, held sometimes with fanatical zeal. Williams' lectures and sermons about faith and self-awareness must be seen as attempts to induce this kind of doubt. His purpose, at least initially, is to strip away the hypocritical pretensions of what he sees as false religiosity, to expose such "faith" as self-centeredness and the God of objective religion as an idol of the defensive, false self. That is to say, *Williams' purpose is to encourage people to doubt,* to accept that, for all their orthodox belief, they do not in fact know God with certainty and perhaps they do not know God at all.

Furthermore, if we accept Williams' arguments in this its negative strand, we are likely to feel that we do not know ourselves at all. We may realize that we have not understood our true motives and feelings—and so we shall not know whether we have faith or not. At this point we shall indeed be in doubt. But we shall also be on the verge of, if not already entering into, faith as self-awareness and the discovery of the mystery of God within ourselves.

Discovering God as the Final Me

The outside or objective way of knowledge is, Williams contends, inappropriate to the knowledge of God: "objectivity is a funk-hole."[40] Those who assert that there is such "objective" knowledge of God do so, often with great vehemence, out of fear of personal involvements and the self-knowledge which is essential to all genuine faith. Here we see the basis of Williams' claim that the knowledge of God requires self-awareness. His argument is that objectifying religion or "outside" knowledge of God arises not from real faith in God but from fear of the self. As already noted, such religion and the knowledge of God it claims is in fact a form of self-deception and self-evasion. It is inherently defensive for it is fundamentally intended—albeit unconsciously—to protect us from awareness of our true selves. We depend upon the God of objective faith to "save" us from what we really are in the depths of our being.

---

[40] Williams, *The True Wilderness,* 17.

In his autobiography Williams describes the process by which, in his own life, such objective religion was broken down. The exact means of this "cross and resurrection" experience is of particular importance for our understanding of his view of doubt and its relation to faith. For Williams it was not a matter of changing his "theology," i.e., substituting one set of ideas about God for another less adequate set. The means by which Williams came to a new form of faith was the process of self-awareness: by discovering, that is, the false and self-deceptive nature of his previous religious life and by receiving into awareness those aspects of his personality which this religion was seeking to conceal.[41] In this way Williams came not only to personal wholeness but also to discover what he regarded as the reality of God within himself. For Williams, then, the "inside" knowledge of God begins with genuine knowledge of self.[42]

Williams describes his own struggle to know God in terms of the discovery of various kinds of "me": the me I present to others—the person I want them to think I am; the me I present to myself—the person I like to think I am; the me I am really, "locked away out of sight" but which still exercises an influence on the other me's. There is, however, yet another me: "the me in which there is something infinite, the me where God and fullness dwell, and dwell not as a stranger or a visitor or a permanent guest but as far more fully myself than the other me's."[43] This "me" Williams calls "the final me." I can go on living as if there is no final me, but the superficial me's are often attracted by this final me, knowing intuitively that there must be such an ultimate reality. The prospect of such "fullness," of discovering the final me, is also frightening; for the final me is a threat to the self-sufficiency of the superficial me's I pretend to be. It is, therefore, more comforting to think of myself as these more finite me's and of God as an "outside" reality, something quite other than me.

The center of Williams' theology is his concept of the relationship between the final me and God, and thus the relationship of self-knowledge and the knowledge of God. For Williams, *God is the final me.*

---

[41] Williams explored the relationship between psychological insights and theological understanding in a number of essays and lectures published during this time: Williams, "Theology and Self-Awareness," 69–101; H. A. Williams, "Psychological Objections to Christian Belief," *Objections to Christian Belief,* ed. A. R. Vidler (London: Constable, 1963); and Williams' contribution to James Mitchell, ed., *The God I Want* (London: Constable, 1967) 161–90.

[42] Williams, *Some Day I'll Find You,* 347–9.

[43] Ibid., 353.

He is the me which, using the unavoidable spatial metaphor, we can say lies beneath the more superficial me's. God is the final me, and is present and at work in the other me's when they have become organically part of the final me, though we must also think of Him as infinitely transcending the final me.[44]

While we must think of God as something other than ourselves, in objectifying language, and while indeed God is a reality which infinitely transcends us, it is also true that God must be known through discovering "the final me."

We are confronted here by a paradox, Williams suggests. In thought, this is a contradiction: God is both me and is infinitely other than me. In prayer, too, God is the One we address, yet God is also within us as the spirit which expresses itself in prayer.[45] This is the paradox and mystery of "inside knowledge," which is also the essence of faith. He concludes that if we are to have knowledge of God we must learn to see the infinite within the finite, the divine within the human, God within ourselves.

For Williams, then, the life of genuine faith requires the struggle to find the infinite reality of God within the finitude of oneself. This process will involve the "death" of the religiously-acceptable pretending self and will also involve the loss of that false certainty which is inherent in objectified religion. But faith as self-awareness also involves a resurrection: though God as the final me destroys my false or pretending self, God raises me up to experience the joy of God *within* my finite, personal existence. In the loss of the pretending self, I find who I truly am. This resurrection is not a single event or experience, though, but is "God's continuous creative act."[46]

It is important at this point to be clear about what Williams is advocating about self-awareness. While it is true that psychoanalysis was a crucial element in his own growth toward self-awareness and genuine faith, he is not suggesting that psychological processes as such are a substitute for or alternative to the spiritual quest for God. Psychoanalysis cannot create faith, Williams insists. Faith is the gift of God, the discovery of the potential of the self as the "final me," through participation in our relationship with God.[47] Williams' sermons encourage

[44] Ibid., 359.
[45] Ibid., 358–9. See also H. A. Williams, *Becoming What I Am: A Discussion of the Methods and Results of Christian Prayer* (London: Darton, Longman & Todd) 1977.
[46] Williams, *The Joy of God*, 66.
[47] Williams, "Theology and Self-Awareness," 78.

his hearers and readers to engage in honest self-examination. Clearly his counseling and teaching were other means to the same objective. Through caring relationships and rigorous honesty, we may abandon those pretensions which prevent a genuine encounter with our true selves and thus with God. For Williams prayer is a particularly powerful means of discovering who we truly are.[48]

Another crucial element in the life of genuine faith and the discovery of God as the "final me" is doubt.

Doubt as an Essential Element in the Life of Faith

Williams' positive account of the necessity of doubt as an element in genuine faith is best stated in his book *Tensions: Necessary Conflicts in Life and Love*. The theme of this book is that conflict is life, while the avoidance of intellectual uncertainty and personal tension is deadening.[49]

The first conflict Williams describes is that between autonomy and dependence. We have already noted Williams' argument that faith in God may involve a kind of defiance or opposition toward God. The argument is taken a step further with the suggestion that growth in faith may involve periods of atheism, when we disbelieve in God. In a memorable passage Williams writes:

> I suspect that to love God with all our heart will sometimes, perhaps often, involve us in being atheists. We must not evade the conflict of our atheism. We must be ready to accept the tension of our discovery at certain times that we think the whole Christian bundle of tricks is a lot of bloody nonsense.[50]

Williams is saying here that the ongoing life of faith can include periods of deep frustration with God and with our religion. But these can be honestly acknowledged and should be included in our understanding of faith itself. In subsequent chapters Williams describes the role of doubt and "unknowing" as elements in the life of faith, in prayer, action, and hope. Having expressed his opposition to the view that faith

---

[48] The title of Williams' book on prayer, *Becoming What I Am*, clearly indicates the close connection between prayer and self-awareness.

[49] Williams, *Tensions*, 14 and 15.

[50] Ibid., 32.

necessarily excludes doubt, Williams positively declares that doubt must be accepted as "the healthy and inevitable concomitant" of faith.[51]

Here Williams uses a number of metaphors which help to explain how faith and doubt can be compatible. First he suggests that for most people the "crisis" of doubt does not occur as a catastrophic event. Rather, they experience doubt "over the length and breadth of their lives, though generally in dozens of uneven heaps." In this sense the life of faith may be "peppered" by doubt. Faith and doubt are elements of an on-going tension. This image helps to explain how faith and doubt are compatible even though, intellectually and logically, belief and doubt are incompatible. For Williams the life of faith includes both belief and unbelief, held in tension with one another. Accepting and affirming this tension *is* faith.

Williams' use of the time-frame of an individual's life is important here. He wants to break the idea that faith is a state of unquestioning belief which is to be maintained continuously, at least ideally, throughout one's life. This perfectionist, all-or-nothing image is simply inaccurate. Rather, he sees the life of faith as including periods of doubt or even outright disbelief, other periods of serene belief, and still other periods when all these elements are mixed together in creative conflict or tension.

In a second image Williams suggests that doubt and faith must live in the same house, not as enemies but as friends. Doubt must be seen as an element which enriches the household of faith.[52] Expanding on this image we might add that as friends or partners who live together over a period of time tend to become like one another, each taking on some of the characteristics of the other's personality, so it is with doubt and faith. Faith may accept doubt "into itself" as Tillich has suggested, and doubt may itself imply faith. Williams' subsequent exploration of the positive benefits of accepting the tension of faith and doubt can be seen as a description of these possibilities. Here he is seeking to explain what it means to say that faith may involve or include doubt.

He begins by mentioning briefly a number of the common causes of religious doubt, such as the reality of evil and suffering in the world.[53] While in some respects the universe may be held to reveal God to us, in other respects it also seems to deny God's reality. Williams does not seek to "answer" this problem. He suggests rather that religious conviction,

[51] Ibid., 44.
[52] Ibid., 45.
[53] Ibid., 45–9.

if it is an honest expression of our life in the world, must be "laced" by doubt. Paradoxically such faith will find its primary expression in the cry from the cross, "My God, my God, why have you forsaken me?"[54] Here a cry is addressed to the God who is experienced as absent, yet is still known as *God.*

Faith involves both a "Yes" and a "No," Williams argues. It is not a state of continuous, doubt-free conviction and assurance. In the life of faith our experience will only be partially coherent. We may feel compelled to say, as it were in the same breath, "Yes, it is true," and "No, it is not so." This apparently paradoxical statement serves to indicate the *dialectical* element in Williams' view of faith and doubt, and which he claims is essential to all genuine faith. This "No" is not outright denial or disbelief, even though at times it may seem to take this form. The "No" of faith, the doubt which is part of faith, is a "No" held in tension with a "Yes." This element of dialectic, between the "No" and the "Yes," serves to indicate the very nature of faith.

Thus for Williams the life of faith includes the acceptance of the tension between knowing and unknowing, between belief and unbelief. He describes the way doubt influences the character of prayer and Christian service. A more profound humility makes possible a quality of love which is not present when faith is seen as the possession of objective religious truth.

Another crucial implication of Williams' view of faith and doubt relates to the doctrinal content of faith—our beliefs about God. In stark contrast to Newman, he argues that *commitment* in faith must be held in tension with *inquiry.* He speaks of "the cross of theological understanding," which today includes the realization that all our knowledge, including our understanding of God, is "not a matter of seeing with clear, innocent and unconditioned eyes," but is essentially a product of our culture and history.[55] Our concepts and images of God are themselves socially and historically conditioned. We can accept the inherent relativity of what we say and know of God when we realize that "unknowing" is an essential part of our knowledge of and relationship with God. In an argument reminiscent of Tillich's theology, Williams argues that our doctrines are models, partial and inadequate descriptions of God, which serve to symbolize that which is not directly accessible to us.[56] This is

---

[54] Ibid., 47.
[55] Ibid., 63 and 64.
[56] Ibid., 69.

not to say that we must not take the truths so expressed seriously, but rather that they must not be understood literally. Theological understanding will thus involve acceptance of how little we know of God, of how inadequate our doctrinal formulations are, while also affirming these expressions as indicators of the nature and object of our faith.

Finally, we note two interesting observations Williams has made about his quest for theological understanding. First, he remarks that as he learned to find and receive more and more of God as "the infinite" within his own life and personality, *doctrinal belief as such became less and less important* in his religious experience.[57] His knowledge of God became more and more knowledge *of* God, as an "insider," and less a matter of belief *about* God, as an "outsider." But Williams also found that as he pursued this way of encountering God, particularly through the disciplined prayer of his religious life, the *realities* symbolized by Christian doctrines—such as grace, forgiveness, resurrection—*came to be elements of his everyday experience.*[58] For Williams, then, the acceptance of the "cross of theological understanding" has led to a positive enrichment of his religious life. Through the cross of doubt and the tension of knowing and unknowing, there is also a resurrection of faith and an experience of the joy of God.[59]

Harry Williams' theology makes a particularly valuable contribution to our understanding of the nature of both doubt and faith. A first major achievement is his description of the actual experience of faith. Rather than analyzing faith as a propositional attitude, through the logic of belief, or in terms of its doctrinal content, Williams has given an incisive personal account, explaining in numerous ways what it actually means for an individual person to be a Christian. One of the strengths of this approach is his clear and practical demonstration of the falsehood of the concept of faith as objective certainty. Williams has shown that the object of this kind of faith, at least in extreme forms, is not God at all. Combining theological and psycho-analytic insights, he relentlessly pursues the self-deceptive character of objectifying faith. In reality the "outside" approach to knowing God keeps God at arms length, as well as protecting ourselves from genuine self-awareness.

Two specific benefits flow from this analysis. First, Williams' argument helps to explain some of the apparent incongruities in religious

[57] Williams, *Some Day I'll Find You,* 367 and 368.
[58] Ibid., 373.
[59] Williams, *The Joy of God, inter alia* but esp. 19 and 20, 45–50, 104–7.

experience. One of these concerns the ideas of "strong" and "weak" faith. Williams has shown that fervor and vehemence are not necessarily indications of strong faith, but perhaps the opposite. If people devote their lives to an objective form of faith but avoid accepting themselves, they fail to receive the joy and "nourishment" of God's presence within themselves. The "riches" they have stored up through their religious commitment are likely to fail them when they encounter times of personal suffering or struggle. Others, however, who know their spiritual poverty and consider their faith weak may find that in their "weakness" they are strong. These are practical, and indeed biblical, insights into crucial aspects of Christian experience.

Another strength of Williams' analysis here is its ability to explain why there is often such vehement opposition to the expression of doubt within religious communities. Those whose faith is characterized by what Williams calls "outside knowledge," and whose religious commitment requires a created certainty, must oppose doubt, for the expression of doubt constitutes a fundamental threat to the very basis of their faith. As Williams explained in regard to his own case, opposing opinions can be seen as a menacing threat—a murderous attack upon the self.[60] From this insight we can see why doubt is sometimes so vigorously opposed, but also that much supposed "defense" of faith, in apologetic and dogmatic theology, is not so much defense of the truth of God, as it purports to be, but is in reality religious self-defense. It follows from this argument that such opposition to doubt often cannot be resolved or negated by "objective" argument. If we are to encourage people to engage in the "inside knowledge" of authentic faith it may be necessary, as Williams has done, to seek to break down the religious pretenses of objectifying religion and to offer, through our personal testimony and the faith we practice, a viable though vulnerable alternative.

Williams' detailed insights into the dynamics of doubt in the life of faith are the direct outcome of his concept of "inside knowledge." One of the interesting implications of this approach is the positive role of doubt in the transition from objective religion to faith as self-awareness. Williams recognizes the difficulty of this transition, using the metaphor of cross and resurrection to explain the cost and the transformation involved. He has helpfully shown that very often what people experience as religious doubt is in fact *self-doubt*. In doubt people feel a loss of con-

---

[60] Williams, *Some Day I'll Find You*, 143–4.

fidence, or that they have lost something quite central to their lives. They may feel lost, as if they do not know how to live in this changed situation. Williams' arguments help to explain that these intuitions are correct, but he also helps us to see that in the loss or death of our "religious self" we have not lost God or ourselves. These arguments are highly illuminating and carry considerable credibility.

By pursuing the implications of faith as "inside knowledge," first in his own experience and later in his writing, Williams has been able to indicate the sense in which faith and doubt are compatible. What Williams has shown is that the compatibility of faith and doubt can be understood, accepted, and (even) enjoyed only if we recognize that faith is not primarily a state of intellectual belief. It is rather a "journey" in which we must engage with the mystery of God and ourselves, at times in belief and at times in doubt. Such faith is a dimension of life, or rather it *is* a life, a style or way of living which embraces both believing and doubting, in contrast to which, Williams suggests, other styles of life are not life at all but are "living deadness." For Williams, then, to explain the relationship between faith and doubt is to recount the story of his own struggle to find himself and the true God. The knowledge of God through faith and doubt is the journey of "becoming what I am." The idea of journey is crucial here, because it overcomes the concept of faith as a static, all-or-nothing situation to be achieved and maintained despite all the challenges and changes that arise during one's life. Williams' view of faith allows for us to grow and to change, in short to be alive.

Williams' use of autobiography and the many other personal stories derived from his pastoral experience is not, therefore, simply a matter of style. It is quite essential that faith be understood in this way. Faith is the living process by which I "become who I am" in a dynamic relationship with "the final me." This journey of faith, involving struggle and growth, belief and doubt, suffering and joy, is made possible through "inside knowing" and involves necessarily the risk of uncertainty. Through this detailed account of doubt as an essential element in faith, Williams has given much greater content and credibility to Tillich's assertion that doubt must be "accepted" as part of faith, by an act of courage. He has also given further proof of the value of biography as a source for theology.

There are, however, some difficulties which have to be considered as limitations to the achievements just outlined. One set of problems relates to Williams' understanding of faith. It could be argued that his emphasis on self-awareness and the knowledge of God through self effectively replaces the Christian doctrine of salvation with concepts of psychological health. Christian spirituality has been superseded by "personal growth." This objection, baldly stated, serves to indicate several limitations in Williams' idea of faith.

Lord Hailsham has argued that Williams has not given adequate weight to the role of *conviction* in faith. Though we do not have complete knowledge of God, nonetheless we believe so much of the truth as we can grasp. We live and act upon our convictions.[61]

This objection serves to clarify Williams' understanding of the role of doubt in relation to faith. In Williams' view, faith is like a journey undertaken in hope rather than immediate, present certainty. This is clearly the point of the last chapter of *Tensions* where Williams speaks of the "final resolution" of conflict in a "joyous celebration." In this sense there may be an assurance or conviction that tensions and uncertainty are not ultimate. We may also at times enjoy a preliminary awareness of this final state, a glimpse of the celestial city from "the delectable mountains," particularly through our experience of laughter.[62] It is crucial to Williams' theology, though, that such hope and assurance cannot be achieved through the repression of doubt and attempts to avoid tension and ambiguity. We cannot make ourselves certain. It is therefore essential to faith that we travel in hope, accepting doubt, conflict, and tension as well as whatever conviction and assurance are given to us.

Another limitation of Williams' view of faith is his strong emphasis on the individual. His critique of "objective" religion seems to suggest that all Christian service for others is unworthy because it is secretly self-serving. This would lead to a view of faith which abandons social responsibility until we all find our true selves. Clearly this would not be Williams' intent. In his own life he continued in both sacramental ministry and pastoral care. We could, however, reasonably ask for a more socially critical view of Christian faith and discipleship than Williams offers. While he is critical of the many aspects of organized religion, he seems essentially to assume both the credal and ecclesiastical structures of the established Church as "given." His theology encourages individuals to find their own faith and life in God, almost despite the Church and society. The failure to offer a more integrated view of the wider implications of faith is a serious limitation.

---

[61] Lord Hailsham, "Review of H. A. Williams' *Tensions*," *Theology* 79 (1976) 310–2.
[62] Williams, *Tensions*, 109–15.

These questions lead to the broader issue of our assessment of Williams' theology as such. The question of whether Williams has reduced faith to psychology ultimately rests on the adequacy of his concept of God as "the final me." In a critical appraisal of *True Resurrection,* A. E. Harvey argues that Williams has effectively abandoned the essential core of the Christian message of resurrection, reducing the notion of resurrection to a way of living, "a set of values, a style of living," produced by the "miracle" of human beings just being themselves. Harvey rejects what he sees as the underlying assumption of Williams' theology, namely that the "Eternal Word" of divine truth is inherent in human beings and need only be discovered by self-awareness.[63]

Harvey's somewhat acerbic criticism drives right to the heart of Williams' theology with its fundamental conviction of the inherent goodness of all people and all reality. Williams implies through all his works that when people engage in the kind of self-awareness which he enjoins, through the inward journey of prayer and the quest for that "something infinite" which he describes as the "final me," they will discover the "glory" of their humanity *and* they may see the transcendence of God. Like Tillich, Williams operates with a strong sense of God's revelatory activity immanent in personal experience.

Against this position Harvey argues that we cannot find truth within ourselves but must look to God, especially in God's Word, Jesus Christ. Williams has replied briefly to this criticism.[64] He argues first that the purpose of his theology has been no more than to convey the living reality he has himself experienced. He does not therefore claim to present objective truths of the kinds that Harvey seems to suggest can be apprehended in the doctrines of the Christian religion. On the contrary, Williams' point is exactly that the living reality of God can be apprehended only through one's immediate experience. On the specific point of Harvey's objection, Williams argues that it is thoroughly appropriate to describe the experiences of life being made new as "resurrection." Wherever there is such renewal in people's lives the Creator is present.

In another context Williams further defended his approach by distinguishing it from Don Cupitt's theology of "spirit," as expressed in

---

[63] A. E. Harvey, "Untrue Resurrection," *Theology* 76 (1973) 28–31.

[64] H. A. Williams, "Resurrection: True or Untrue," reply to A. E. Harvey, *Theology* 76 (1973) 96 and 97.

his book *Taking Leave of God.*[65] Williams rejects the idea that faith as self-awareness implies that there is no objective reality denoted by the term "God." Whereas for Cupitt "becoming spirit" does not imply any ontological claims about the existence of a transcendent reality, "God," Williams insists on making such a claim. This argument helpfully elucidates the logical force of Williams' approach. As already suggested, his work actually assumes the credal structure of the Church's faith. He implies that God is known through Jesus Christ. His concern is to explain what such faith means and more exactly to expound how we can truly know this God. Williams' theology is, then, offering us more of an *epistemology* than a theology as such. "God as the final me" is not so much a description of God as a way of expressing how God is to be known.

If this is so, we do not need to resort to the polarization implied in Harvey's Barth-like rejection of human experience as a source of revelation. Nor can we accept Williams' insistence that we must find God within ourselves or not at all. These are not genuine opposites. Williams has insisted that the reality of God is not ourselves as we are. When we seek God through self-awareness, it is the transcendent reality of God we are seeking, not ourselves as such. Williams' point is that we cannot know God without also knowing ourselves in truth and depth, and he has made a strong case for this thesis.

Acceptance of Williams' view of faith does not require the claim that "objective" knowledge of God—for example, through critical study of the Bible or of the history of Christian doctrine—provides no knowledge of God. True, objective knowledge is not the same thing as a personally engaged faith. Nonetheless, it can provide a sense of who God is and how God has and does relate to human history. Williams' own earlier life, when he tried to maintain an objective form of faith, involved some knowledge of God. Even if he confused God and the devil, this did not mean he had no awareness of God at all. To this extent it is necessary to moderate the claim that God can only be known through self-awareness. This claim seems to imply an "all-or-nothing" situation which does not fit the reality of human experience of life and faith as a continuing process of growth and discovery.

---

[65] H. A. Williams, *Whither Theology?* The Second Basil Hetherington Memorial Lecture delivered at St. Peter's House Church and Chaplaincy, University of Manchester, October 22, 1981. The text of this lecture is available in duplicated form from St. Peter's House. Cf. Don Cupitt, *Taking Leave of God* (London: SCM Press, 1980).

If we were to evaluate Williams' thought as a "system" of Christian doctrine, there are other critical points we would raise. For example, although much of his thought makes use of the images of cross and resurrection, there is no clear Christology as such. It might also be argued that Williams does not offer a sufficient doctrine of atonement, nor of the missionary purpose of the Church. While a systematic theology as such was not his purpose, the one area where his theology is clearly focused is on the cross and resurrection, yet he has not adequately shown how our present experiences of suffering and healing are related to Jesus' death and resurrection and how all these aspects express the character and life of God. In the end, Williams' theology needs a more developed doctrine of God.

In this chapter we have found value in exploring the life-story theology of Harry Williams, which offers a clear account of how faith can relate to and include doubt, as well as belief or conviction. Williams' approach is immensely fruitful, as it offers valuable insights into the nature of faith, as well as suggesting new ways of thinking and speaking about God. In the next chapter we will examine another such life story which also raises critical issues about how God is known, through faith and doubt.

6

A Celebration of Doubt

In this chapter we will consider the work of Val Webb, in which the dynamic relationship of doubt and faith is used as the basis for theological reflection. In her book *In Defense of Doubt*, Webb provides many insights into the negative impact on her own life when doubt was suppressed. But she also offers an alternative and more positive response, a celebration of healthy doubt as the essential ingredient in faith.[1]

Webb's work is significant for our present study for two particular reasons. The first relates to her identity as a woman who came to theology later in life. Unlike the other thinkers we have studied, she has not been a professional theologian or an ordained minister, but had a career in science before she studied theology. *In Defense of Doubt* is her first theological book. In this work she gathers much of her own life experience into the theological conversation. Her book includes a number of anecdotes and other personal reflections, along with brief outlines of different theological approaches, concepts, and issues. As a work of theology it is far more personal than most theological books. It makes use of a narrative style, though it is not simply a personal story. She gathers insights from her scientific background, as well as her own journey and struggles, and uses these as a basis for wider reflection. She also makes use of the feminist "hermeneutic of suspicion" to critique the way

---

[1] Val Webb, *In Defense of Doubt: An Invitation to Adventure* (St. Louis, Mo.: Chalice Press, 1995). Since we will be making frequent reference to this one source, in this chapter I shall simply indicate page numbers in Webb's book in parenthesis within the text.

doubt and doubters have been dealt with in the past. Here too her own experiences provide the basis for her approach. Finally, she moves toward a new paradigm, which issues in proposals for living the insights she has sketched and celebrates.

Val Webb's book is also important because she explores the significance of doubt in its own right. Unlike most theological discussion of doubt, which begins with a concept of faith and then discusses doubt in the light of that concept, Val Webb deals with doubt as an experience with its own inherent significance. She offers a firsthand account of negative experiences of doubt, and then describes a more positive or constructive perspective. Through allowing these experiences to speak for themselves, she is able to offer a fresh evaluation of the nature and meaning of doubt.

In the following pages I will use a specific method to frame and present Webb's experiences and ideas. This framework is not used in the book itself but is my own interpolation from it. Webb says that theological study enabled her to *give voice* to her doubts, when previously they were suppressed. They had to be kept to herself, and they made her feel guilty. I will use this dynamic of experiences being given voice to present the "messages," some spoken and some unspoken, which were part of Webb's experience of doubt and will then describe features of Webb's theology which answer those messages. In this way, I will collate the various elements in Webb's book which amount to a phenomenology of doubt.

Val Webb's experiences and characterization of doubt can be described within a paradigm of faith dominated by the idea of *authority*. I shall describe a number of "statements" made about, or sometimes to, the person who doubts. Each of these statements reflects an aspect of the paradigm of authority. Though Webb herself does not use the idea of "the voice of authority," she does clearly recount that she received these "messages" from the churches of her upbringing.

She grew up in Queensland, Australia, and participated in the conservative form of Christian congregational life of that time. It was a form of Christianity which emphasized strong personal commitment, the need for the forgiveness of sins, offering "testimonies" in the gathered worship service, and the idea that faith is essentially about believing the doctrines taught from the pulpit and said to be derived from Scripture. It was made clear that genuine Christians never question these beliefs or practices. Strong faith never doubts. Webb notes also many other elements which were intermeshed with this faith-perspective, such as the implication that ordained ministry is for men only. A Christian woman may seek an education but will in due course inevitably marry and raise a family (40–1, 68–71). Webb herself imbibed this entire faith perspective, except that privately she had many questions to ask. There were many things which did not cohere with all that she as an intelligent young woman was learning about the world and life in general. This forced a separation between "faith" and "reality" as she knew it to be. While at university she had done some critical study of the Christian faith and discovered that many other people had experienced similar difficulties to her own, and that there were other faithful and biblically grounded ways of understanding Christian faith. But these ideas were repudiated by her church.

Then, well into adult life, she moved with her family to the United States and had the opportunity to study theology. As her studies progressed she found ways of articulating and understanding her faith that were more appropriate to her own experience. There no longer needed to be the separation of "faith" and "reality." All this to her was a liberating and transforming experience.

The Voice of Authority

There are three central aspects of Webb's experience of doubt in the earlier part of her life: isolation, exclusion, and repudiation. These experiences are closely interrelated, and can be seen over against the dominant position of the authority figures of her church and what she saw as its unified belief system. I will describe these experiences in terms of three statements of the "voice of authority."

You are alone because you do not have faith. The first feature of the paradigm of authority is the implicit statement that everyone agrees upon the truth of Christian doctrine, except for that isolated individual who doubts. She or he is alone in their doubts. Thus Webb has written:

> When I recall the struggles I personally had with doubts in a theological environment where doctrines could not be questioned, the enforced isolation comes most vividly to mind. I could spot so many inconsistencies in the dogma, but no one else seemed to see the problems, or if they did, they too were suppressing their doubts in order to be accepted by the group (41).

The sense of isolation here is but one feature of Webb's use of the category of abuse to describe the situation of a person who doubts, parallel to sexual abuse and domestic violence. So often the victims of such violence are blamed by society for their plight, and the persons themselves may accept this view, believing the violation to be their own fault and that they are alone in their situation. Only they believe their abuser to be such. Meanwhile other people cannot understand why they put up with the situation. Webb describes her own history of doubt in these terms: "Those who have not been subjected to a theology that victimizes by blaming the doubter for doubting cannot understand why one does not challenge the authority, and refuse to take the blame" (37). The paradigm of authority thus regards anyone who questions the prevailing doctrine and teaching as unusual, out of step with everyone else. That person is likely, then, to consider that there is something wrong with herself or himself. If they are isolated and feel rejected, it is their own fault. It is because they have doubts and do not have faith.

Whereas in most areas of human knowledge it is essential to question prevailing theories and ideas, Webb has found that "somehow when doubt rears its head in religious conversation, there are many who insist we abandon all creative questioning and give blind acquiescence like the emperor's loyal subjects." She goes on, "Since the day poor Thomas was labeled for refusing to believe without seeing the physical evidence, doubt has scored a negative vote in religion" (2). Where are the "little boys," she asks, who will protest that the emperor has no clothes, and verbalize the inconsistencies between their experience and the doctrinal teaching of their church? In Christian communities there seems to be an inherent resistance to and rejection of questioning and doubt.

It is implied here that faith is identical with believing the doctrines of the Church as taught by the authority figures of a particular community. As a consequence, a person who questions and doubts that system of belief is said not to have faith.

From her subsequent study of doubt, Webb has found that the *naming* of doubt is a powerful element. The doubter is alone, and the voice of authority says so—with all the authority of God. This naming implies that to doubt is abnormal and therefore not a part of the common experience and tradition of faith. I think Webb speaks for very many people when she suggests that those who have disturbing questions about their faith feel that it is they, and they alone, who have these questions.

You do not belong, and you have nothing to contribute. This statement reflects another essential feature of the view of faith which centers on authoritative teaching. Here the experience of ordinary people, perhaps especially women, is not seen as a resource for theological understanding. The "truth" is derived from other sources—notably the Bible, as interpreted by (male) authority figures. It is assumed that there is one source of authority and only one authoritative interpretation. Other people are to listen to the teaching of that voice, to learn and believe. They do not of themselves have a contribution to make to the understanding of faith. Their part is intellectually passive. In this model, the ordinary people of the church contribute through their practical efforts, in many different areas. But they do not contribute to the understanding of faith, and especially not through questioning and inquiry. Such questioning is seen as disruptive to the life of the community and a challenge to the authoritative teachings of the leaders.

In her chapter "Tales from the Survivors," Webb relates the experiences of William Cowper, Harry Emerson Fosdick, and John Hick, all of whom report being regarded as a disturbing intruder in the church community because of their awkward and unwelcome questions. Fosdick, for example, during his early years as a theological student, could not go to church because there his questioning mind was considered a disturbing intrusion (51–3).

Many churches, Webb argues, are united by a common viewpoint (which is natural, she recognizes) and by *fear of* and resistance to other perspectives. Where the defining basis of a church's fellowship is doctrinal conformity and a shared system of belief, doubt will be seen as a challenge to the faith and will be experienced as a threat to the community itself. As a result those who question that system of belief will sense that they do not belong and have nothing to contribute.

The third message of the paradigm of authority to those who doubt is: *You are wrong because you do not know God.* The implication here is that the official teaching of the church is truth and any questioning of it is therefore wrong. Another "tale from a survivors" is that of Carl Jung, who doubted the God of his father's Calvinist preaching. Initially he believed that to surrender to doubt was an unforgivable sin. Later he came to believe that it was in fact God who was calling him into a new freedom of thought and being.

Within this paradigm of authority, Webb observes, doubt is seen as "the result of an inadequate, false or failed conversion attempt, something that 'didn't take properly'" (57). Though she doesn't mention Guinness here, the approach she describes can be seen clearly in Os Guinness's book *Doubt: Faith in Two Minds,* where a pathology of doubt is offered. Guinness explains the causes of doubt, each indicating some failure in the development or understanding of belief.[2] Doubt is caused by "inadequate foundations" in faith.

The suggestion that in some way the doubter is wrong has two meanings or aspects. In the examples we have mentioned so far, the "fault" has to do with the intellectual content of faith. According to the paradigm of authority, faith is essentially a matter of right belief. To question the authoritative teaching of the church is to be wrong, and thus to espouse a view which is incorrect. In addition, however, Webb's use of the idea of abuse enables her to show that many people who question and doubt also come to think that there is something wrong with them. Being told that they are alone and do not belong leads people to blame themselves for their "faults." Webb relates at some length the struggle of Mary Jo Meadows, quoting from her book *A Time to Weep, A Time to Sing.* Even when she could no longer believe, she blamed herself: her faith in God was not deep enough. She asked what flaw in her life made her unable to believe what "everyone" did, while she was filled with doubts and questions.[3] Webb describes Meadows' constant attempts to overcome her "faults," and suggests that she represents "the epitome of a victim of theological abuse" (64–6).

In the paradigm of authority, the fault or failing of the doubter is taken to have a theological basis. Since God is understood through the definitive teachings of the church or group, those who question that teaching may be said not to know God. A clear illustration of this implication can be seen in the story of Mary Jo Meadows referred to above. When she acknowledged her doubts, even becoming angry with God, she quickly "backed off" and threw herself into "finding faith" again, through "acceptable" forms of Christian service such as teaching Sunday school and having another child. The implication Webb sees in Meadows' story is that her doubts were taken as a clear sign that she did not know God, or had become separated from God, so she needed to find her way back to faith.

Webb's approach to faith and doubt has undergone what she identifies as a paradigm shift. Her thought here draws directly from Thomas

[2] Os Guinness, *Doubt: Faith in Two Minds* (Berkhamsted: Lion Publishing, 1976).

[3] The reference is to Mary Jo Meadows and Carole A. Rayburn, *A Time to Weep, A Time to Sing: Faith Journeys of Women Scholars of Religion* (Minneapolis: Winston Press, 1985) 239.

Kuhn's book *The Structure of Scientific Revolutions*.[4] Kuhn posits that major breakthroughs in scientific research often require more than the discovery of new information. They require a new interpretative framework—or paradigm—within which existing information and theory is re-cast, to provide a shift in focus or perspective. In Webb's experience the paradigm of authority has been replaced by a paradigm of love, with a consequent change in her understanding of doubt and faith. The intermediate stage in her theological development has been the discovery of the creative potential of doubt. This has included the recognition of a large cast of doubters, both in the Bible and in the history of the church.

Discovering Doubt: Invitation to Adventure

One of the critical elements in the emergence of a new paradigm of thinking is the recognition of new or previously ignored information. Through her theological studies, Webb discovered "a great tradition of doubters" in the life of faith. Far from being alone in her questions and struggles, she found herself in the company of many great figures of faith. She invokes a long list of "struggling saints," from Athanasius to Rosemary Radford Ruether, suggesting that their autobiographies are "alive with doubt." These people were all urged toward new apprehensions of God, through the creative persuasion of doubt.

Beginning with the Bible, she notes that Sarah laughed at the promise of a son, a "normal reaction" for which God did not condemn her. The element of protest and doubt in the Psalms and in Job is also mentioned. Jesus also doubted the "human constructs" of the Pharisees and the religious rules which locked people into oppressive situations, and he did not condemn those who questioned and doubted but was "always ready to encourage the genuine doubter" (15). Webb's argument here seems to conflate all protest and questioning of established religious ideas into one category, which she calls doubt. All such protests are assumed to have a positive outcome, approved by Jesus.

Similar difficulties occur in the treatment of figures in the early Church, such as Augustine. The *Confessions* are said to "loudly acknowledge his companion doubt" (17). Augustine's doubts, which

---

[4] Thomas S. Kuhn, *The Structure of Scientific Revolutions*, 2d ed. (Chicago: University of Chicago Press, 1970). In theology, a major symposium on the notion of paradigm shift not mentioned by Webb is Hans Küng and David Tracy, eds., *Paradigm Change in Theology: A Symposium for the Future*, trans. Margaret Köhl (Edinburgh: T & T Clark, 1989).

drove him to study and search for a faith in which he could rest, were "the fingers of God." All his life he confronted new questions and responded to newly emerging heresies. While these statements are true, Webb does not distinguish Augustine's earlier doubts, which preceded his conversion, from the later questionings, which were raised by others. This suggests that simply to represent all questions as doubt is confusing. Augustine's arguments against heretical ideas are anything but doubtful.

Similarly Kierkegaard's writing is characterized as "doubting in the face of the complacency of the Danish church" (18). This again seems to ignore the fact that while Kierkegaard attacked and protested against "Christendom," he also saw faith as a way of living and believing in the face of doubt and thus overcoming it. Many of the other figures mentioned, such as Bonhoeffer and Küng, really fit into the category of protest.

Nonetheless there is something to be said for representing these theological protesters as doubting. They are people who challenged what was believed to be the truth about God, and as such their doubt challenged what was said to be orthodox Christian belief.

These questions lead us to issues of definition and it is here that Webb makes a quite important contribution. The "problem" of doubt is generated by the identification of faith with belief. "The thesaurus lists *doubt* as the antonym of *faith* and *belief.* Herein lies the problem to be corrected if doubt is to get a fair hearing" (3). That is to say, because faith has been identified with belief, there has been confusion about doubt, and those who have doubted have been regarded as people who have lost their faith.

For Webb, faith is the response of an individual or group to what they experience as the reality of God. It is not to be identified with a set of dogmas or belief statements. Such statements may be subsequent articulations of that religious experience or faith, and they may adequately express that experience for a time. But the statements as such are not identical with the faith which has given rise to those beliefs. As a consequence, it may be that the experience of faith can give rise to doubts about those very belief statements, indicating that they no longer adequately represent the content of that particular stream of religious experience for the people concerned.

Thus Webb argues that doubt is not the antonym of either faith or belief. The opposite of faith, she asserts, is to be without the experience of faith, while unbelief is the opposite of belief. Doubt is not the opposite of faith, it is the awareness of difficulties or questions about the content of belief or the meaning of faith.

> Perhaps the best way to talk of doubt in relation to "faith" and "belief" is to see doubt as the awareness of *discrepancy* between "faith" and "belief." Doubts appear in religion, as in any system of learning, where there is difference between what we are told to believe—taught as "truth"—and what we experience or intuit (4).

From these initial indications, Webb moves to open out her subject. She suggests that the emergence of doubt may indicate that a belief system has become "static, stale, or insipid, bogged down by unhelpful dogma or inadequate instruction." In such situations it is God's grace which nudges or prods people toward a faith which is alive and relevant (8). It is God who evokes doubt as a way of calling forth more genuine faith.

Thus in the second main phase of her argument, Webb introduces the notion of "healthy doubt." Healthy doubt, Webb suggests, represents the "nudging" of God calling us to choose different "authorities" and different ways of seeing our situation (79, 83). In contrast, to deny or resist doubt is to cling to an old authority. I will outline the major steps by which Webb develops this argument, as it forms the basis of an alternative concept of faith.

Webb argues that healthy doubt enables continuous growth toward new possibilities, new understandings of life with God. But this requires, as one element in a new paradigm, a developmental view of faith. Webb devotes a chapter to describing James Fowler's schema of faith-development—or at least a simplified version of Fowler's stages of faith. We will not recapitulate those ideas here. She is critical of faith-development thinking, however, to the extent that it implies an "end stage" or a linear progression "ever upward" (92–4). She rejects the notion of a hierarchy of stages, preferring to see Fowler's stages as forms of experience which we may encounter during our life's journey.

In place of the "stage" emphasis, Webb proceeds to her second major theoretical source, the idea of *process*. The way she moves to process thinking, however, is particularly insightful and is also quite crucial to her theology; for it is in the idea of a God who participates in the process of our lives that Webb finds her ultimate "defense" of doubt.

The difficulty Webb sees with some uses of the "journey" image of faith and "stage" or developmental models is their focus on an *end or goal, where God is presumed to be.* The question of where we imagine God to be, in relation to our journey, is a key defining element which largely determines the way we understand and respond to doubt (96–7). Much Christian thinking implies a dualism in which we are engaged in a spiritual journey toward God, who is not with us in the present. Webb posits a different perspective, drawing upon elements of process theology.

In process theology, God is understood as being with us in the present, as well as in the myriad of possible futures. God is both immanent in every element of the created order as well as infinitely transcendent. God has not determined the course of human history, but is affected by what happens within history. God's "initial aim" in creating does not determine the outcome of history, but seeks to evoke loving, creative choices from us and with us. God's action and creativity involve bringing into being the moments of our existence and the possibilities of our choices and actions. God creates possibilities for us and responds to the actions we take.

Every event and every moment in time, according to process metaphysics, is related not only to every other moment but also to the possibilities of that moment, seen or unforeseen. Every moment "feels" those other moments, as Webb puts it, and is responsive to the interconnectedness of all reality. God also knows and feels all these moments and choices. God is *in* the process and God is in process. God's own life is evolving with us, even as our lives too are in process.

Human beings, however, have much more limited awareness and imaginations. We can choose what God "aims" in our present situations, but often we do not, because we cling to past descriptions, interpretations, and simply because we have limited awareness of how things are and how they relate to each other. To grow in awareness of creative possibilities and to make more loving choices is to become more like God.[5] It is here that Webb sees the role of creative doubt. When we are dissatisfied with older ways of thinking, or when we find they no longer fit our changed situation, God is "nudging" us to question those fixed interpretations and inviting us to new paradigms, new

---

[5] The preceding paragraphs are a brief summary of some of the key ideas of process theology, drawing upon Webb's summary, at 98–104, and my own study of process thought. Webb cites as a useful introduction to process theology Robert B. Mellert, *What Is Process Theology? An Introduction to the Philosophy of Alfred North Whitehead, and How It Is Being Applied to Christian Thought Today* (New York: Paulist Press, 1975). Another valuable introduction is John Cobb, *God and the World* (Philadelphia: Westminster Press, 1969).

courses of action, and new commitments. Webb envisages a constant, creative flow of reflection, interpretation, and choice. "Doubt emerges at the interface of every becoming moment, when the possibilities for richness that God presents challenge our temptation to repeat the past. Doubt surfaces with this 'suggestion' that there is a richer way to think and act than previously" (102). As such, doubt is not a sign of weakness but of maturity. Doubt is not the opposite of faith, but part of the activity of healthy faith; it is a sign of engagement with reality and commitment to living with God.

These ideas are developed in a chapter called "A Certain Richness of Experience Now." Here Webb reflects her own sense of discovery in faith, which allows her permission both to doubt (without guilt) and to explore new possibilities in theological understanding (without fear). A crucial element for her is the emphasis on *process or journeying* rather than the idea of God as the final truth to be believed and held onto as a goal to be reached. Faith for her is a continuous process of responding to God's nudges and lures; it involves the freedom to choose the new and different—with God. Such living is "not about answers" or winning a heavenly prize, but is about "abundant living" here and now (105–6). She describes this process as a spiral rather than a linear progress: "A spiral, winding in widening circles of questions and answers, but still advancing to a certain richness" (108). God is with us in this journeying, encouraging and provoking. Prayer involves a conversation of openness, attuning ourselves to choose the richness offered in each moment.

A Living Faith

From the preceding outline we can see that for Webb healthy doubt is an essential element in a living faith. Doubt which is suppressed or which emerges in protest against an authoritarian belief system is unhealthy in the sense that it is not the ideal (though it may be justified and perhaps even inevitable). On the other hand, doubt which arises when faith itself is an exploration of life, possibilities, new opportunities, is healthy. I suggest that when Webb speaks of "healthy doubt" she is intending an attitude of intellectual and personal freedom, an openness to different perspectives which welcomes what is new or different, and is always willing to learn and respond to those opportunities. This attitude is rightly described in Webb's title as an "adventure."

We can also see now the ways in which Webb's new paradigm would respond to the earlier "statements" we called "the voice of authority."

Webb's view of faith clearly involves that faith includes doubt, necessarily. Her developmental and process view of faith implies that doubt is a continuous element in the growth of faith, not a threat to faith. Thus the response of the new paradigm to the statement "You do not have faith" is to assert that doubting is not an absence of faith, but is in fact clear evidence of faith, as a response to the "nudging" of God and an exploration of new possibilities and directions for believing and acting.

As Webb has rightly seen, at the heart of both paradigms is the question of God and how God is to be understood and known. Webb's new paradigm offers a view of God as inherently involved in the changing processes of the universe itself, as well as in the lives of all people. As a consequence, Webb asserts quite clearly *that to know God is precisely to engage in creative doubt.* Contrary to the view that doubt separates us from God, Webb sees doubt as a response to God. "Doubt emerges at the interface of each becoming moment, when the possibilities for richness that God presents challenge our temptation to repeat the past" (102).

In the concluding chapters of her book, Webb develops the theme of "growing together through love and understanding." Here I think Val Webb makes a very strong contribution to Christian thought, through her description of the kind of church in which doubt is welcomed and included as integral to the life of the community. Each succeeding chapter widens the circle of relationship. Initially Webb discusses the ways in which we grow in faith and doubt through our individual experiences and relationships. She emphasizes the place of *feelings* and *experiences* as well as beliefs and ideas. She goes on to critique fundamentalism as a form of religion which seems to emphasize experiencing salvation in Christ, but in fact is rationalist in its concerns. But she is also critical of an exclusive emphasis on feeling states as evidence of "possessing the Holy Spirit" (117–20). In contrast to these approaches, she explains that in process theology feelings and experiences, even our bodily states, are forms of response to God's presence in every moment and its creative potential.

Webb then goes on to consider what things stimulate such creative "feeling" and exploration. She recognizes that for some people nature may be the primary stimulus, while for her it has been the printed word. Conversation can also be a medium of God's prompting to doubt. Here Webb emphasizes the element of *attention* or openness. To receive such doubt we must be sensitive to God's nudging and be in the habit of recognizing God's activity in the events of our lives (129).

When she turns to "Doubt and the Faith Community," Webb draws on many of her earlier experiences, seeking now to articulate positive directions for a community growing in faith through doubt. She argues that Jesus' ministry "preached relationship rather than dogma" (138). This becomes the foundation for her approach: it is only through relationships of authenticity and love that a Christian community can acknowledge doubt and can grow in faith. The difficulty for such a community is to accept and tolerate diversity amongst its members.

In place of conformity to a code of belief, Webb argues for a church "glued together" by love. If love and welcoming of others is the basis of a community's life together, rather than allegiance to a set of doctrines, people can affirm that they are at different "stages" or points in their journeys and can affirm, encourage, and support each other despite their differences. Indeed their differences become valued elements in their life together. New metaphors for such a community emerge. Webb suggests the idea of a "base camp," in which the faith community functions as a resource for climbers who go out to different peaks and challenges and return to share their pursuits and failings, affirming one another's efforts.

In such a community, creating "space" for doubt is crucial to growth. "Providing this hospitality for the sharing of doubts as well as triumphs would be the greatest step a church community could take toward unity and unconditional love" (145). To explain how this might occur in a church, Webb draws on the image of a scientific conference, where researchers report on their work, including negative results, perhaps years of "unfruitful" experimentation, and *all* reports are valued and respected. She longs to hear a preacher acknowledge doubt and perplexity about some item of doctrine. This could only occur if churches abandon the charade in which doubt is denied and clergy are considered (and pretend) to be people who have "all the answers."

What is needed is a recovery of the idea of the church as a community of fellow-searchers (146–50). There is indeed a good biblical and theological concept on which Webb might have drawn here, the notion of a pilgrim people of God, which resonates well with her emphasis on journey and process. This concept was affirmed, for example, in the Second Vatican Council's *Lumen gentium*, Dogmatic Constitution on the Church.[6]

---

[6] *Lumen gentium*, Dogmatic Constitution on the Church, *Documents of Vatican II*, ed. Austin P. Flannery (Grand Rapids, Mich.: Eerdmans, 1975) ch. 7: "The Pilgrim Church."

In her final chapter Webb extends the notion of hospitable love to address the question of interfaith dialogue. The central question and source of doubt here, as she expresses it, is whether "Jesus is the only Way." Her approach again centers upon the idea of doubts as the "nudges" of God. If doubt has this meaning, "is it unreasonable to think that the question of 'truth' in other religions may also be God, nudging us to think beyond our limited doctrines?" (161). Just as love, respect, and compassion are the basis for genuine unity in the Christian community, these same attitudes are essential to genuine interfaith dialogue in which people may sense further the "nudges" of God, calling their beliefs into doubt and thus calling them toward more creative freedom, celebration of life and love, in partnership with God and with all God's people. Webb sees her Christian commitment as enabling her to engage in such dialogue, rather than as a barrier to acceptance and respect of other faiths.

Before concluding this chapter, we shall briefly consider the contribution made by Webb's "defense of doubt" for our own study of the relation of doubt and faith. On the positive side, Val Webb's study is immensely valuable because it provides personal insights into the relationship between doubt and faith. Hers is not a theoretical argument, but a personal story of the dynamics of faith emerging through pain and struggle, study and discovery. It is a story told from the hard-won position of a "survivor" of abuse, yet with understanding and a concern for those who have yet to find the freedom she celebrates. As such, like Harry Williams' theology of self, this account rings true with personal integrity and authenticity. Many people who have struggled with doubt and have known similar condemnation will find themselves identifying with her account and grateful for her insights. Her description of the relationship between doubt and a form of faith centered upon authority is particularly helpful.

Another strength of Webb's approach is her implied recognition of the ambiguity of doubt. In the first part of her story she tells of the painful aspects of doubt, while later she represents doubt as a wonder-filled exploration of new possibilities in life and faith. Unfortunately she does not actually identify this contrast in her treatment of her subject. Nonetheless we can see from her account that doubt, questioning, and exploration in faith have a dual potential. They can be a source of personal alienation and isolation, or they can indicate a positive, adventurous situation. It is interesting to ask what makes the difference here. If we follow Webb's analysis, it seems *that the response of the church community is a major determining factor*. If, as she found, the church sees questioning and doubt as an unwelcome, rebellious, and intrusive element, then doubt will be experienced as a real threat to faith. The person who experiences such doubt may accept this "naming" and may think therefore that they do not have faith. It seems likely that many people have left the Church, thinking that because of their doubts they are not people of faith. On the other hand, where doubt is welcomed as an expression of freedom, even as an intimation of God's presence, there is no such anguish. Here, the same questioning attitude is affirmed as an expression or form of faith. This positive response may actually elicit further exploration and growth in faith. Val Webb's personal account of doubt and faith has demonstrated the ambiguous potential of doubt.

While it is clear that the church community has a significant role in responding to expressions of protest or questioning, this is surely not the only factor influencing the experience of doubt and its eventual outcome. It seems likely that other factors are at work as well. One of these is the concept of faith operative within the church community. Where faith is identified with the attitude of belief, or with the content of specific belief statements, there too doubt is seen as the absence of faith. On the other hand, where faith is seen in a more dynamic way, allowing growth and exploration, as well as affirmation and commitment, doubt is not seen as the absence of faith. It is a major achievement of Webb's approach that she has identified these sources of difficulty and confusion.

When we turn to consider her alternative account of doubt and faith we find a number of strengths and weaknesses. We begin with her constructive idea of faith. At one point Webb explains that a life of responsiveness to God is faith. "The way of living that concentrates on God's relational activity in our present, and trusts the future, whatever it might be, is called 'faith'" (106). Here we see several crucial elements in Webb's new paradigm, which indicate both strengths and weaknesses. First, it seems for her that faith and doubt have become indistinguishable. The way of living she calls faith is the way of continuous responsiveness to God. In this she is surely right. In its broadest sense, faith includes our life of prayer, worship, service and trust, as well as such things as belief or questioning. But for Webb, the life-stance of faith means being continuously responsive to new and creative possibilities as they are presented to us by God, in each moment and situation, and this responsiveness is what she has also called "healthy doubt."

I see several difficulties here. It is not clear why Webb assumes that every new situation and possibility is to be preferred to whatever previously exists. What is the basis for seeing the novel as more desirable to the customary, and for asserting that to be with God we should always reject the old and choose the new? Sometimes the new may indicate the break-down and disintegration of good things, perhaps as a result of neglect or failure to care for those things and the values inherent in them. Second, Webb gives no indication of how we are faithfully to choose amongst the possibilities in every situation, sometimes very many possibilities. How are we to recognize the lure of God within our choices and potentialities, and to distinguish God's "nudging" from temptations, delusions, or the mere entertainment value of the different? This question leads to the third difficulty, concerning this conception of God. While it is not Webb's purpose to offer a systematic theology as such, the difficulties we have noted come down to questions about the adequacy of her account of who God is and how we know God. She has rightly identified this as the central issue in any understanding of faith and doubt.

In her own model Webb asserts, "'God is with us' is now" (103). The journey of faith involves choosing freedom and greater richness as God continuously offers these to us. Exactly how this activity of God relates to the life of God, as seen in the witness of the Bible and especially in the person of Jesus Christ, is a crucial issue here, as it is for process theology more generally. Again we note a major weakness in Christology. In what way does the life, death, and resurrection of Jesus Christ characterize Webb's understanding of the presence and activity of God? Jesus seems to be no more than a model of faithful responsiveness to God, in the distant past.

Another factor significantly missing from her account of God and of faith as responsiveness to God is the element of *sin*. Webb seems not to recognize that while God is active in the processes of life, calling us toward new possibilities, so too there is a dimension of reality which drags us down, toward destructiveness and evil. It is a major weakness of her process concept of God that she offers no basis on which to distinguish the nudges of God from the temptations toward evil.

Another significant question about Webb's view of faith and doubt concerns the role of *belief* and doctrinal understanding, within the ongoing life of faith. Here Webb offers her own experience as the basis of an answer. She acknowledges that some people find belief easy, while she needed a long process of study, talking with others, thinking, and debating issues to work through doctrines and beliefs. In some cases she has come to "comfortable conclusions," while in others she has taken a "step of faith"—but not blind faith. She describes how she came to this belief and how it is different from "blind faith." "Belief is the final product in each case, but the path to belief is different. For some, the authority of another is sufficient for imitation. For me, belief came after I personally worked through the pregnancy, confinement, and labor to 'give birth' to new understanding" (109).

For Webb, then, the kind of doubt and faith she has described can lead to belief, even through an "act of faith." Unfortunately, she does not explain what she means by this phrase, though we can infer that it contrasts with other beliefs where she has come to "comfortable conclusions." Presumably an act of faith means something like the classical notion of assent to a proposition or doctrine she cannot entirely comprehend or prove. If she had explored what she means here, and how this act of faith and her other beliefs relate to doubt, her account of doubt and its relation to faith would have been even more helpful and insightful. She does not, however, deal with this crucial question. Neither does she explain what role beliefs might have in the actual *living* of our faith, informing our actions, choices, and commitments, as clearly they must. Webb's interest is in emphasizing the journey as a process. This is a valuable emphasis, but the question of how we are to make choices and how our understanding of God and beliefs about God are involved in making those choices is a crucial issue which needs to be explored further. For example, from Webb's account of faith it is difficult to see just what faith actually means, as a way of living. What content, for example, would she give to the concept of *mission*? What is the content of the "transformation" God seeks? Webb seems to presume that all movement forward, all change from an old or familiar commitment to a different perspective, is inherently desirable. All change is progress. But are all our journeys equally appropriate, in the process of God's transformation?

While Webb is right to emphasize the value of our journeying as such—against an exclusively goal-directed view of life and faith—she rejects the idea of a goal or direction toward which the process is moving. It may be true that we are continually in process, but it is questionable whether a Christian theology can entirely jettison all sense of eschatological consummation. The journey of faith includes the hope that in some way God is the end and goal of our journey, as well as a participant with us in the process. This is one dimension of God's being which distinguishes our lives from the divine life. God is both immanent in time and transcends our time. God is both the one who journeys with us and the one who lures us from "beyond," toward God's ultimate rest and fulfilment. Webb has articulated well the Christian virtues of faith and love, but has not adequately included the dimension of hope.

Finally, we come to Webb's account of doubt itself. Her description of doubt as the recognition of a discrepancy, between one's experience and official doctrines or accepted explanations of how things are or should be, is a very helpful insight. This idea enables us to see how religious doubt is similar to the kinds of doubt exercised in other quests for knowledge, such as the physical sciences. It is precisely when the data of experience do not "fit" the expectations arising from current theory that doubt emerges, and new investigations and learning follow. Webb's interpretation of religious doubt thus has the potential for helping people to a more integrated understanding of their religious experience, as part of their lives as a whole.

On the other hand, she seems to have ignored other aspects of the experience of doubt. Not everyone's doubts lead to the well-informed and creative outcomes Val Webb has enjoyed. And not every limitation on peoples' awareness is caused by authoritarian, male preachers. For some people, doubt is simply perplexing and paralyzing. Some people have enough intelligence to recognize the problems or inconsistencies in doctrines they have been taught, but do not have the ability to grasp complex ideas or the disposition to live with ambiguities. For these people, doubt creates great and sometimes lasting perplexity. In her enthusiasm for creative freedom, Webb seems unable to countenance these negative and limiting aspects of doubt. Furthermore, if we are *always* doubting, we cannot act and we cannot live. Faith, love, and life are possible only when we have affirmation as well as critical questioning.

This in turn brings us to the relation of doubt to belief. As we have seen, at a key point in her book Webb acknowledges what she calls "an act of faith," in which she has accepted or affirmed some articles of doctrinal belief. But she does not explain how this act relates to doubt. Here I suggest is a crucial weakness in her account. Whereas she is right to distinguish faith from belief, in the sense of the intellectual ideas through which faith is expressed, nonetheless some element of believing is an essential ingredient in faith. Loving action and creative choices, even if they are not arrived at through a process of reasoning, imply beliefs about what is good and true.

Webb has not explored these philosophical implications of her vision of faith and its relation to doubt. Though she argues against the thesaurus, we cannot in fact deny the structure of our language. In common usage, doubt is the antonym of both belief and faith. The linguistic and conceptual problem Webb actually wants to deal with is quite crucial: whereas we have in English two nouns, belief and faith, we generally use only one verb, to believe. To have faith is to believe, in common usage; and so doubting, as the verbal opposite of believing, "slides" into being the opposite of faith. Only as we expose these philosophical and linguistic difficulties can we negate the confusions which result. Perhaps there is a case for us to take up the suggestion of John H. Westerhoff that we use "faithing" as a verb for the entire activity of faith, of which believing is but one part.[7] In so doing, however, it will be necessary to show how faithing can include, in many different ways for individuals during their lives, and in varying ways within the faith community, both belief and doubt, as well as those other creative elements such as hospitality and love. Val Webb's book has in fact gone a long way toward offering us such an account.

Once again we have found, both through the strengths and weaknesses of Webb's account, that the central element in understanding the relationship of faith and doubt is an understanding of God. Webb's more creative view of faith and her "defense" of doubt are made possible through theological exploration, toward a view of God who actively participates in our life of faith. To speak of a God who nudges and prompts us, in doubt and faith, is to imply a very active, immanent, and responsive God. This much Webb makes clear, but she does not develop this understanding of God further. I suggest there are valuable indications here for the further *theological* exploration of the significance of doubt as part of the Christian experience of faith. In our next chapters we will turn specifically to explore in more detail a doctrine of God which is consistent with a positive appreciation of doubt and its relation to faith.

---

[7] John H. Westerhoff, *Will Our Children Have Faith?* (New York: Seabury Press, 1976) esp. 99–103.

7

The Context of Doubt: Divine Conversation

One of the consistent themes emerging from our study thus far has been the need to understand faith in a dynamic way. As Newman showed, faith must be understood in personal terms, as part of our lives as human persons. It is we who respond to an apprehension of God with that affirmation we call faith. Barth, Tillich, Williams, and Webb all speak of faith in terms of our personal engagement with God.

In this chapter I will take up these insights, to press them further toward a more comprehensive, theological understanding of the relationship of doubt and faith. The *theological* issue which has arisen persistently through the preceding chapters is the question of the nature of God: If faith is understood as created by God, bringing us into a dynamic engagement with God, then an appropriate concept of God is both implied in and required by that understanding of faith. Such a concept of God must allow for human response, in a dynamic and mutual engagement with God. This leads us to an issue we found at the heart of all three theological frameworks considered, the question of God's revelation to us. For all their differences, Newman, Barth, and Tillich all see faith as responsive to the revelation of God. The various difficulties we found with their theological understandings of faith and doubt center upon the ways in which God's approach to us is apprehended and thus upon the nature of our involvement with that revelation.

In order to explore these issues further and to identify a different way of framing them, we will begin with the metaphor of God's speech or address to us—God's Word—as a dominant metaphor for God's self-revelation. I shall argue that the nature of God's approach to us needs to be rethought, in such a way as to encompass more comprehensively the biblical witness to God's engagement with people. Furthermore, if we do reshape our understanding of God and God's self-revealing life with us, in the ways I propose, we shall also find in this reconfiguration a much more appropriate understanding of doubt and its relation to faith. Doubt, belief, and faith, I shall argue, need to be understood within the context of *divine conversation.*[1]

In this chapter I shall sketch the outline of a theology of divine conversation. In the next two chapters I shall indicate how this theology is consistently witnessed in the Scriptures of the Old and New Testaments. Then, in the final chapter, I will describe the situation of faith beyond the modern dichotomies of belief and doubt, as the divine conversation continues.

Divine Speech: Reconsidering the Categories

The idea of talking to God is a popular understanding of prayer. The Bible suggests that we should let our requests be made known to God, with supplication and thanksgiving (Phil 4:6). We also speak commonly of listening to what God has to say to us, through our reading of the Bible and attending to the teaching and preaching of the Church. It is interesting, however, that we have not generally brought these two ideas together, to think of a conversation in which we speak with and listen to God. It is this possibility I want to explore here, as it offers not only a more integrated and holistic spirituality, but a theological framework which makes greater sense of doubt and its role within the life of faith.

The theological issue to be addressed here is this: What kind of God do we imply when we suggest that we can live our lives in "conversation" with God? When we speak of listening to God, or ask God to listen to us, what does this mean for our understanding of the nature of God? I want to suggest that our common experience of God implies that God is not only one who speaks to us, and not only one who listens to us, but that God invites us and draws us into an ongoing con-

---

[1] An earlier version of some elements of the argument of this chapter can be found in Frank Rees, "The Word in Question: Barth and Divine Conversation," *Pacifica* 12 (October 1999) 313–32.

versation. God is a conversationalist. This dimension of our life with God is well attested in the Bible. Unfortunately, these elements of biblical faith are frequently overlooked or pushed aside by the more formal and philosophical categories through which theology has attempted to describe the nature of divinity.

In order to explore the idea of God the conversationalist, in this chapter I will sketch a broad account of the activity of God inviting us into conversation, embodying a conversation with humanity in Christ, and continuing that conversation through the Spirit, in the life of the Church and toward the ultimate involvement of the entire creation in divine conversation. I suggest that it is in this context that we should understand the relationship of doubt and faith. My contention, however, is that we do not have to invent or construct a theology of divine conversation *ex nihilo,* out of nothing. On the contrary, there is much in the biblical witness which suggests a continuing conversation of belief and doubt, a conversation between God and the people of Israel or between God and the Christian believers.

A theology of divine conversation is the theme of Walter Brueggemann's recent *Theology of the Old Testament.*[2] His approach is foreshadowed in an earlier essay in which he suggests that reading and interpreting the Old Testament is nothing less than participation in a conversation with God.[3] We should note the idea of "reading and interpreting" as the medium of engagement with God. This hermeneutical perspective we will need to consider in more detail shortly. At this point Brueggemann observes that the conversation with God is not a simple process. On the contrary, "the theological substance of Hebrew scripture is essentially a theological process of vexed, open-ended interaction and dialogue with the Holy One and all those other than the Holy One."[4] The documents of the Old Testament are multi-vocal. There is not just one testimony to YHWH but many, and sometimes the voices contradict each other. The experience of God is varied and sometimes "vexed"; the conversation is often strained. It is for this reason that Brueggemann's major work is subtitled "Testimony, Dispute, Advocacy." Because his development of the theme of divine conversation is so original and so

---

[2] Walter Brueggemann, *Theology of the Old Testament: Testimony, Dispute, Advocacy* (Minneapolis: Fortress Press, 1997).

[3] Walter Brueggemann, "Biblical Theology Appropriately Postmodern," *Biblical Theology Bulletin* 27 (1997) 4–9.

[4] Ibid., 5.

comprehensive, in relation to the Old Testament at least, I want to outline Brueggemann's approach in a little detail, before suggesting some
directions in which I think it can be developed further.

Brueggemann argues that we should understand the Old Testament
as rhetoric, a form of speech in which God is immediately known. Far
from sophistry or empty words, rhetoric in the Old Testament "constitutes reality."[5] Following Barth, Brueggemann accepts the authority of
the text and its "speech" as constituting "the reality to be studied."[6] He
resists the reductionist moves which interpret the experiences of Old
Testament figures and groups in psychological or sociological terms.
The rhetoric of the Old Testament is "originating theological data." In
Israel's testimony we encounter the God of the Old Testament. We
might say, following a Barthian way of speaking, that for Brueggemann
God is what God says in the Old Testament. Thus the book describes
three major blocks of material or bodies of rhetoric: Israel's core testimony to YHWH, its counter-testimony, and its unsolicited testimony. In
each of these voices, and through their counter-play, readers are drawn
into the conversation with the God of the Old Testament.

It is in the first main section that Brueggemann develops and sub-
stantiates his idea of rhetoric and conversation as the basis of his theology. The core idea is testimony. Israel offers, as if in a courtroom, its
testimony to YHWH, and the heart of its testimony is verbal sentences.
These sentences have active verbs, with God as their subject: God has
said or done these things to us, me, or to Israel. The core testimony of
Israel centers on verbal sentences which reveal God as one who creates,
who makes promises, who delivers, commands, and leads. Then follows a
description of the adjectives and nouns which also play a part in the
rhetoric of testimony. We will not attempt to summarize Brueggemann's
incisive exposition here. Our purpose is only to grasp the theological
argument developed from it. Brueggemann insists that "theological argument does not go behind this witness with questions of ontology,
wondering 'what is real.' What is real, so our 'verdict' is, is what these
witnesses say is real."[7] Accepting the rhetorical framework of testimony
to a courtroom, Brueggemann reads the Old Testament as testimony and
therefore sees theology as the content of that testimony. God is what the
testimony discloses.

[5] Brueggemann, *Theology of the Old Testament,* 65.
[6] Ibid., 18, n. 47; 118; 119, n. 6.
[7] Ibid., 206.

The conversation within the text is, however, multi-vocal. There are other voices which lead us into Israel's counter-testimony. Here Brueggemann sees a "cross-examination" of Israel's core testimony, challenging and testing the God who creates, promises, commands, etc. In this mode, the rhetoric addresses three core issues: YHWH's hiddenness, ambiguity or instability, and negativity. Protest is the dominant element, expressed very powerfully in the psalms, through a number of questions addressed to God. How long must the people suffer? Why do they experience such senseless and unjustified suffering? And where is God? The God of fidelity, who promises salvation, is hidden or absent entirely. Indeed in Exodus 17 the question arises whether the Lord is amongst the people at all.

In addition to his superb exposition of texts in this section, there are two crucial elements Brueggemann draws out. The first is the radical commitment of the Hebrew Scriptures to the truth. They insist in including these "vexatious" elements in their God-talk.[8] The biblical conversation is not always easy or happy. Furthermore, the clear implication is that YHWH is the cause of these complications and tensions: "The root cause of such theological disputatiousness arises from and is sustained by the Subject of the conversation, namely Yahweh, who prizes candor and rejects all deceiving denial."[9] Here we may recall in passing the verdict of the text that it was Job and not the soothsayers who spoke the truth about God. While it is at times true that Israel's disputes with God arise from their unfaithfulness, at other times their protest and anguish have no such grounding. YHWH is found to be capable of fury, violence, and neglect and the question arises whether the covenant promises have been abandoned from God's side. In the face of YHWH's silence Israel is not silent, but maintains its testimony, holding in tension its core witness and its counter-testimony.

The third element in Brueggemann's theology is the "unsolicited" testimony of Israel, in which it offers on its own behalf its understanding and praise of YHWH. Here there is not so much a synthesis of the previous positions as the development of a framework within which each can be held in tension. The central theme, again reminiscent of Barth's theology, is that of partnership. Israel sees itself as YHWH's partner. On the basis of this partnership, the human person, the nations,

---

[8] Ibid., 379.
[9] Ibid., 325.

and the entire creation are also called into a partnership with YHWH, in which each has a contribution to make to a continuous conversation. The crucial theological insight here is that God the conversationalist is interactive. God creates "space" for the freedom of human life and indeed the whole created order to have its own existence and thus to stand over against and with God. God insists on their right to such independent being, Brueggemann asserts. Human beings are most fully human when we have both the "courage to assert" and the "confidence to yield." As genuine partners with YHWH, we have the right to our own testimony and to abandon ourselves to the trustworthiness of our Creator. Without either of these elements, our humanity is lost. In Israel's testimony we find that the people were "emboldened" to take initiatives and to make their own assertions, to voice their protests and to offer their "unsolicited" testimony. Israel's life in faithful conversation with YHWH included all these elements.

Brueggemann's massive work offers a very substantial exposition of theology of divine conversation, which has the great benefit of being deeply grounded in the Bible and in so doing helps us to make much greater sense of the plurality and complexity of the texts and the experiences to which they bear witness. These fruits arise from his insistence that we read the texts as testimony and engage with them as such, without attempting to go "behind" them into questions of ontology. It needs to be emphasized, however, that the biblical text is making ontological claims. What Brueggemann is wanting to assert is that ontological questions are not to be seen as "deeper" or prior questions; rather they are addressed "within" the reading. In so doing, Brueggemann is adopting an "intra-textual" approach to the Bible, which may not be acceptable to all his readers. His case for this approach is his reading of the texts.[10]

There are, however, several critical issues we do need to raise before moving to our own elaboration of a theology of divine conversation. It is questionable whether Brueggemann's use of the courtroom metaphor, as the over-arching context within which Israel's testimony to YHWH is to be understood, is appropriate. It is true that some passages, such as Isa 41:21-22; 45:20-21, and perhaps the disputations in Job, evoke this

---

[10] Brueggemann offers a very extensive discussion of the hermeneutical questions surrounding his approach to the biblical texts in the opening chapters of his book. For a concise explanation of "intratextuality," see Mark Brett, "Intratextuality," *A Dictionary of Biblical Interpretation,* ed. R. J. Coggins and J. L. Houlden (London: SCM Press, 1990) 320–1.

image. But whether all conversation with YHWH fits the idea of a court trial is less convincing. We can agree that the concept of justice is a crucial concern of the Hebrew Bible, including the celebration of God's justice, but that is something different from suggesting that the entire framework of our relationship and "conversation" with God is the specific mechanism by which a court seeks to establish a just finding.

A second and more significant criticism concerns Brueggemann's exposition of the active verbs in which Israel's core testimony is expressed. While one hesitates to critique the work of so eminent a scholar, my contention is that there is one form of divine speech which he has not included. Along with the divine promises, commands, and leading, God is also seen as a questioning God. My contention will be that Israel's testimony includes a witness to a God who asks questions. The questions we find in the Old Testament include not just questions Israel asks in its counter-testimony. There are also questions posed by God to the people and to various individuals. These too are crucial parts of the conversation.[11]

In accepting Brueggemann's contention that YHWH is an interactive God and that the disputatiousness of the text is itself provoked by YHWH, we can press this idea further to see that God asks genuine questions (not purely "rhetorical" questions) and invites the people to propose and explore answers. Or, to risk a confusing use of terms, God's questions are indeed part of the rhetoric: these are real questions God is asking. A brief survey of some of the questions God asks will enable us to develop further the image of a conversational God, into its wider biblical and theological implications.

The Questions God Asks

Ched Myers has raised the possibility of an "interrogatory theology."[12] His essay outlines a number of questions posed by Jesus, which

---

[11] Brueggemann does occasionally note a divine question, though he does not identify questioning as a distinctive form of YHWH's address. He refers, for example, to Jer 8:22 in which YHWH asks "the haunting question": "Is there no balm in Gilead? Is there no physician there? Why then has the health of my poor people not been restored?" Brueggemann, *Theology of the Old Testament*, 253.

[12] Ched Myers, "'I Will Ask You a Question': Interrogatory Theology," ch. 5 in *Theology without Foundations: Religious Practice and the Future of Theological Truth*, ed. Stanley Hauerwas, Nancey Murphy, and Mark Nation (Nashville: Abingdon Press, 1994). Myers

he argues represent challenges to the Church and to civil authorities in North America today. While I concur with his analysis, I think the character of the questions God asks is broader than those Myers considers. God not only challenges us with prophetic questions about the civil and economic order. God also invites us into a conversational lifestyle, a partnership of discovery in relationship and community.

The experience of a God who asks questions can be clearly seen throughout the Bible, challenging, opening up possibilities, raising issues, and questioning other approaches and previous statements. What is clear from many of these examples is that the questions posed are genuine questions. These are not like the questions many of us were asked in Sunday School, where there was a "correct answer" already known by the teacher asking the question. Here people are genuinely invited to consider what they will say and do in response to God's questions.

The first questions God asks within the Bible are found in the stories of creation and fall. In Genesis 3 we read that the man and the woman had eaten from the tree, and the Lord God came "walking in the garden at the time of the evening breeze" (v. 8) and called to the man, "Where are you?" (v. 9). In the subsequent dialogue, the man makes an excuse, explaining that he was afraid of the Lord because he was naked. God asks who told him he was naked, and then further asks if he has eaten the forbidden fruit. After the man tries to shift responsibility to the woman, the Lord asks her also what she has done.

Too easily, this story has been used to provide a historical or quasi-historical "explanation" of how sin and evil entered the world, which it clearly does not explain. What it tells us is that there is sin or alienation in the very structure of our relationship with God. Furthermore, to focus upon the human beings in this way, and thus to make sin the central reality in the story, is to miss what the story is telling us about God. Here God is presented to us as one who comes seeking the company of people, like a friend dropping in for a drink. God comes with the simple question, "Where are you?" This is the governing principle of the relationship. God does not come to check up on them, suspecting that they have done wrong. Rather, the story presents a God who genuinely—we might even say "innocently"—asks where they are.

---

has a superb exposition of the episode in Mark 11, where Jesus asks the chief priests and scribes whether the baptism of John came from heaven or was of human origin. Myers explores several other questions posed to the Church today by Mark's Gospel.

The first question God asks invites readers to think about where we are in relation to a God who comes seeking us. If we allow this question to stand in its own right, as "innocently" as I have suggested it is, this image of God sets a limit on some of the other inferences drawn about God from the later parts of this and subsequent stories. Certainly there is the image of God as law-giver and judge, but the judgment and laws of God must be seen within the context of God's seeking friendship, companionship, a stroll in the evening cool. Where are we? We exist within the context of a God who seeks our company.

A second episode in which God comes by and asks genuine questions is found in the following chapter, Genesis 4. God asks Cain, "Where is your brother Abel?" (v. 9), and again after Cain protests ignorance, we find the question, "What have you done?" (v. 10). This is a difficult story to comprehend, since it seems to suggest that the Lord is responsible for provoking Cain by having "no regard" for him and his offering (v. 5). Nonetheless, there is here a definite suggestion that God is interested in the way human beings relate to each other. Clearly the implied answer to Cain's question, "Am I my brother's keeper?" is "Yes."

Before God we are called to answer for each other. God is interested to know where we are and how things are between us. Again, it is important that we see these questions as something more than setting obligations. The image of God as judge can blind us to the underlying concern of God, who is the creator and who is later to be known as the covenant partner of human beings. Even the punishment of Cain has its limits. God acts to protect Cain from the cycles of retribution that so frequently flow from human acts of violence. In this story, the God who approaches Cain asks questions rather than makes demands. We are invited to answer for ourselves and for each other's well-being, in partnership with One who is genuinely interested in our livelihood and security.

A different example of the questions God asks is found in the prophetic literature. Isaiah 1:10-20, a prophetic oracle of judgment and invitation, addresses the people of Israel and challenges the religion of the temple. Essentially it argues that temple worship is worth nothing if the people will not do justice, particularly by caring for the widows and orphans. The Lord asks, "What to me is the multitude of your sacrifices?" (v. 11), and at the heart of the oracle, "When you come to appear before me, / who asked this from your hand?" (v. 12). The language of challenge is very powerful. These are not questions seeking information; here God's questions have the effect of challenging the priorities of the people and undermining the confident theology of the leaders.

It is important to note the irony in this passage and its questions. The prophetic saying challenges the temple worship and theology. It sets a huge question mark over the way people have understood God and their responsibilities toward God. It challenges them to rethink their priorities and invites them to "argue things out," to engage in a reconciling conversation with the Lord. But this book of prophecy is one of the books of Israel's Scriptures: it was read in the synagogues and places of worship. It was used to remind subsequent generations that their worship involves an encounter with a God who challenges their priorities. In worship, they meet with the God who asks such confronting questions, and they cannot seek to use the temple or any other ritual as a way of hiding from God or from what God calls them to do.

In a similar way the writer of the second part of Isaiah uses rhetorical questioning to invite the exiles to remember the acts of God in creation and in the exodus, and thus evokes hope of a further redemptive work of God to make a pathway for them through the desert. One of the recurring themes here is the question, "To whom then will you liken God?" Through the prophet's preaching, God invites the people to consider who God is and whether indeed there is anyone else like YHWH, any other God in all the world. As they sense the loss of their "nationalist" God, YHWH invites them to question that previous theology by remembering other experiences of God and seeing God's creativity and Lordship in different ways. Here the divine questioning actively uses and develops religious doubts in order to evoke a new and more appropriate form of faith.

Probably the clearest intimation of God's questioning approach to human beings in the Hebrew Bible is found in the story of Job. In chapter 38 we read of God answering Job from the whirlwind, repudiating Elihu and those who have gone before as people who "darken counsel by words without knowledge" (v. 2). Job is asked to gird his loins for God will question him. There is a translation difficulty here. In some renderings Job is asked to gird his loins "like a man," while in others he is to "answer as a man." The latter version is particularly evocative, suggesting that it is appropriate for a human being (not just a "manly" person) to wrestle with the questions God asks.

In the subsequent speeches, God asks Job about the creation, the elements, the life of the animal world, and many other aspects of the universe. God is responding to Job's own questions about the misfortune which has overtaken him. If Job wants to order the universe, can he account for the whole creation? Eventually Job acknowledges that

God's wisdom is more than he had understood. Before he had known these things by hearsay; now he really sees the Lord with his own eyes (42:1-6). But the outcome of this questioning and answering is a restored relationship. God declares that Job alone has spoken the truth about God, his family and wealth are restored to him, and his prayer for those who had spoken folly is accepted.

Though there are many difficult theological issues which arise from the story of Job, some of which we will consider in our next chapter, these last episodes make it clear that an attitude of questioning and struggle is welcomed by God. It is not necessary to draw the conclusion that God commends Job only after God has reduced him to silence. The Lord does not repudiate Job's questioning but rather welcomes it by responding in a similar way. The final chapters represent a mutual questioning. This indicates the way to wisdom. Those who claimed to have great knowledge about God but who did not enter into the struggle, preferring to stand apart and "theologize," are shown to know nothing of God. The person they condemn for his struggling with God is invited into a "debate," where God and Job question each other as equal partners. It is out of this genuine struggle and questioning that wisdom and good fortune emerge.

When we turn to the New Testament, we find also many intimations of the questions God asks. A number of crucial questions are posed by Jesus. These have been recorded in stories which were told in the earliest communities and which shaped their discipleship. As such, these stories and the questions they pose continue to challenge communities of disciples today. They are questions God asks us as well.

In Mark 6:30-44 we have the story of the feeding of the five thousand. When the question of food for the crowd is raised, Jesus challenges the disciples to feed them (v. 37). They protest that it would be too expensive, and then Jesus asks, "How many loaves have you? Go and see" (v. 38). It seems a very simple question and instruction. But in the context of Jesus' challenge to feed the hungry, it is significant. The disciples do not have the money to buy food, yet Jesus asks them to look for what resources they already have. This question remains with the Church today, to consider what resources we have, in contrast to the attitude which limits our concerns to what we think we can afford. There is a double challenge here. We are asked to be concerned for the hungry and to look to what resources we have to address their need. But there is also the challenge to see beyond physical hunger and our present financial resources. God questions our preoccupation with material things and invites us, through Jesus' question and action, to join in a discovery of how many "loaves" we do have, in the company of Jesus.

Probably the most important question posed within the New Testament, however, is that found in Mark 8:29 and the parallel stories. Having asked the disciples who other people say Jesus is, he now asks, "But who do you say that I am?" Peter responds on behalf of the group, "You are the Messiah." In the tradition of the Church, this story has functioned to define the foundational confession of the Church, that Jesus is the Christ. This feature of the story, though, should not blind us to the fact of the question itself. Jesus invites an answer, and here discipleship is defined not by the specific content of the answer so much as engagement with the question. It should not be forgotten that the person who gave this answer goes on to deny ever having known Jesus. The question "But who do you say I am?" is not asked once and then is answered definitively. It stands at the heart of the Gospel, as an invitation to every person and every community to give an appropriate answer. What we say and do in response to this question is a real determinant in how we engage with God's mission in the world. How we live is our answer to this question. The God who asks questions invites us to be part of the conversation in which we determine who Christ is.

Two further questions Jesus asks deserve to be mentioned because of their spiritual and missiological significance. In the story of Gethsemane (Mark 14:32-42), Jesus returns three times to the sleeping disciples, finally asking, "Are you still sleeping and taking your rest?" (v. 41). Though Simon in particular had protested his loyalty and determination to stay with Jesus, he was found asleep when his companionship and support were needed most. In this story, too, there is a challenge to those who purport to be followers of Jesus. Like the challenge to provide food, this story is not only about physical efforts and wakefulness but poses the figurative challenge to be alert to what God is doing and to where we may be called upon to struggle with Christ in our situations. To those who claim to be heirs to the apostles, the question of whether we are still sleeping and taking our rest is a definite challenge and perhaps also a rebuke. It invites a conversation about what it means to be awake to Jesus and to participate in his struggle.

Finally, in Luke 24:5 a question is posed from the empty tomb: "Why do you look for the living among the dead?" In the immediate context, the question is a rhetorical way of introducing the news of the resurrection, "He is not here, but has risen." But the question has more than this immediate rhetorical significance. The risen Christ cannot be contained, neither by the tomb nor by any form of experience or tradition which attempts to limit God's ways. The question, "Why do you look for the living among the dead?" is a challenge to the Church in every age to maintain a tradition of living faith. To do so, we need constantly the provocation of God's questioning and the courage to explore those questions in conversation with God.

There are numerous other questions posed in the preaching of Jesus and in the rest of the New Testament. My point has not been to offer an exhaustive list or even a comprehensive outline of the questions God asks. Rather, my purpose has been to give some detail to the idea that in the Bible God is not only presented as one who makes statements or issues "words," promises, or commands. God is also known as one who invites, even provokes, the responses and suggestions of humans as partners in a conversation.

God the Conversationalist

The image of a God encountered through questions is not entirely new to us. In Chapter 3 we considered briefly a lecture of Karl Barth in which he described the "miracle" of preaching. While the gathered people are seeking a response to their question "Is it true?" they find their own question called into question by God. We suggested that it was unfortunate that Barth's later theology of the word of God did not seem to include sufficient emphasis on this dynamic and interactive aspect of God's address to us. I now propose that we press the idea of a God who asks questions further, to explore the concept of God the conversationalist.

The image of God I am seeking to outline here is not derived from ontological considerations about the nature of God as three "persons," the character of their relationships one to the others, and other metaphysical issues within the classic debates about the doctrine of God as Holy Trinity. I am offering here a formulation of experience of God, which might inform further ontological thinking about God at a subsequent stage. To that extent I am following Brueggemann's proposal to "bracket" ontological questions while we proceed with an "intra-textual" theology. My objective is to indicate a way of thinking about God which is consistent with the biblical witness and is also credible for people seeking to live a Christian life in the contemporary world. One crucial element of this consistency and credibility is the capacity of this theology to make sense of our experience of doubt and faith. My contention is that doubt and belief exist and have theological significance within the context of God the conversationalist.

God the conversationalist encounters us in three distinctive ways, which we might call "movements" within the divine-human conversation. I will describe these as inviting, exploring, and gathering.

Invitation

God invites us into conversation. God's originating and continuous creative activity provides a context for conversation. Just as children are born into a home and relationships, where they quickly learn that some things happened before they were born, humanity exists in a context which is and was "prior" to us. But this statement is not so much about chronology as about origin. We did and do not create the context of our lives. We are responsive persons and to this extent we are "secondary" in our partnership with God. Our creativity and responsiveness exist within the context of God's originating and continuing creativity.

The world which is "before" us, however, is not experienced as entirely indifferent to us. Though there are some aspects of our environment which tower over us and make us aware of the insignificance and seeming futility of many of our efforts, we experience our world as an invitation to respond. We have the ability to imagine things otherwise, to analyze problems, and to construct plans to change things. We have the ability to reach out to others, in loving and creative ways. These aspects of human life are what Karl Rahner called "self-transcendence." In Rahner's thought they bring us also to experience of God.[13]

An important implication of this idea of God as inviting source is that God does not completely control or determine the direction of the conversation and thus of our relationship with God. This image of God recognizes God as a living being, a genuinely social being whose character is subject to the outcome of relationships. The God who asks questions does not know all the answers to the questions. The asking of questions is a genuine request, inviting someone else to contribute to the conversation. Furthermore, the answers we offer to God's questions impact upon God. We are invited to be responsive, just as God too is

[13] A helpful introduction to Karl Rahner's distinctive understanding of human experience as implying also relationship with God can be found in his essay "Experience of Self and Experience of God," *Theological Investigations*, vol. 13: *Theology, Anthropology, Christology*, trans. David Bourke (London: Darton, Longman and Todd, 1975) 122–32.

infinitely responsive and infinitely creative. Whereas we are often far from creative in our responses, sometimes seeking to close off options and avoid the challenges that might lead to our growth or to justice and opportunity for others, God does not respond in these ways. Where we close off options, God moves to open up still further opportunities.

In a genuinely free world, God does not know how we are going to respond to the questions and opportunities set before us. As a result, distortions, misunderstandings, and outright misuse of resources and opportunities arise. Evil is a reality in such a world, but it is not an intended dimension of God's inviting creativity. Evil is the distortion and misuse of opportunities and potentialities offered to us.

If we think of God as a conversation partner, we can see God as one who introduces suggestions, possibilities, and new directions into the conversation. Human beings also can make statements and proposals, as well as posing our own questions to God. It is sometimes necessary in asking questions to preface a question with a statement or an explanation of its background. In a similar way, the divine-human conversation involves more than the invitation to conversation. God contributes more than questions. Particularly through the life and mission of Jesus Christ, God introduces a new possibility for relationship between humankind and Godself. Here we see a second dimension of movement in the possibilities of divine-human conversation.

Exploring

In the life of Jesus, we can see God exploring the potential and direction of the divine-human conversation. In Christ, God joins us as a human participant in the conversation. God does not so much describe to us possibilities for our lives as demonstrate them for us, or perhaps even with us. There are several major aspects of Jesus' life and ministry which can be understood in this way and which can be appropriated into our own lives and the life of the Church.

First, as he is presented in the Gospels, Jesus' life explored the conversation with God. From the story of his questioning the teachers in the Temple onwards, we have the picture of a person who is dedicated to the purpose of God in his life. Jesus came to John for baptism and then was driven by the Spirit into the desert. Thus began his ministry of following the way of God, wherever it would lead him. He was tempted to pursue his own fame and well-being, but set this aside in a commitment to remain in open conversation with God.

When Jesus enthused about what God had made known to him (in Luke 10:21-22), he is not referring to information about God; rather, he is reflecting on the joy of God's saving presence with lepers who have been healed and with sinners who have found reconciliation. Jesus' attacks upon the religious were often based on their inability and unwillingness to see God's presence and purposes in the very ordinary circumstances of life. He was continually discovering what it means to be open and available to the surprising presence of God.

For Jesus, the exploration of life with God led to suffering. In the paradox of the cross, we see Jesus united with God's purpose of love for sinners, yet experiencing alienation from God. Here too, we are invited by the Scripture to see his life as an open exploration of conversation with God. His life is offered to God, even in his cry of dereliction. The response of God is to receive that offering, raising and exalting Jesus and thus bringing to fulfilment Jesus' life of exploration with God.

In this way, we can understand the life of Jesus as an indicative statement introduced into the divine-human conversation. But what is astonishingly new in this turn in the conversation is that the statement of God is embodied in a particular human life. Here God is offering us a sketch of how things might be, an indication of how a human life could be lived in continuous consciousness of the divine presence and constant responsiveness to God's purposes.

From this initial dimension of Jesus' life as the embodiment of divine conversation, exploring relationship with God, several other significant features flow. Just as Jesus' life is consistently open to God, he is also open to people and to their needs. He is presented in the Gospels as being available to other people, who interrupted him with their requests, questioned his teaching, and tested his genuineness. Jesus' availability for others should not be seen only as a consequence of his exploration of relationship with God. Rather, it is one essential medium of that relationship. Jesus seeks conversation with God through encounter with God's people. His healings and miracles are part of his exploration of God's presence and purposes.

Another important feature of the divine conversation embodied in Jesus is the element of questioning. While Jesus is constantly available to other peoples' questioning and testing, he also challenges the prevailing views of God. His teaching and actions push back the boundaries of acceptable thinking about God's purposes and reign, about which people are "the people of God" and about what it means to be in right relationship with God. Often he refused to answer particular questions, instead reframing an issue with his own challenge to the questioners.[14]

The divine invitation to life as conversation with God is embodied in Jesus. His life is also an invitation to others to participate in the same conversation and exploration of life with God. Jesus is constantly evoking a community, a life together with God. Just as Jesus invited people to become his followers, his life itself became a medium of invitation. In the resurrection, Jesus' entire life is taken up by God and is no longer bound by the limitations of time and place. Whereas in the historical life of Jesus the divine conversation was embodied in one person, now that life and conversation continue through many persons and groups. His works and deeds continue to impact sinners and lepers, in many places, even though he is not physically present as a human being. Despised people find acceptance and the religious are confronted by his disturbing questions still. Furthermore, in experiences of suffering and alienation, people discover—as Paul testified (Rom 8:37-38)—that there is nothing that separates us from this living, inviting God. The experience of suffering may itself be a medium of the conversation, as it was for Jesus. Here too God is embodying proposals and possibilities for our lives, in continuing the divine conversation. The question, "Why do you seek the living among the dead?" thus becomes an invitation to further exploration of what it means to be with God, in the face of change and insecurity as well as our actual death.

The conversation embodied became a further source of embodiment. Telling the story of Jesus became a further expression of Jesus' own life with God. Other people, such as the apostles, pursued the conversation further, through evangelical witness and theological exploration well beyond the physical and religious context of Jesus' own life. For them and for all who have followed, Jesus' life opened up new possibilities of life with God. It was for this reason that they used the term "gospel" to speak of Jesus. Here is a form of divine speech, a life that is inviting news.

Our capacity to engage in such Christ-like conversation with God is, however, dependent upon a further creative dimension of the life of God. In a third movement of the divine conversation, through the presence of the Spirit, God is bringing the whole creation into consensus, a new awareness of itself and its life in God.

---

[14] The question about the man born blind, in John 9, is a case in point.

Gathering

The doctrine of God as Holy Spirit is the distinctively Christian way of thinking of God's continuing creativity, by which God works within human beings, our society and culture, and the whole creation, raising awareness of God and seeking to draw all things toward God. As such, the life of the Spirit amongst us might be called a continuation of the conversation seen in Christ. Here too, though no longer in one specific human life, the possibilities of life fully available to God are explored and worked out in practice. The conversation continues and human beings may become aware that we are being drawn into this Christ-life. It is the specific mission of the Holy Spirit to evoke this possibility and thus to draw out from our lives and our world a consensus.

The notion of a consensus is generally used in political or decision-making contexts, where conflicting interests and viewpoints arise. A consensus here means arriving at a point where all agree to a course of action or a viewpoint. There are three distinctive features of a genuine and positive consensus. First, it contrasts strongly with an enforced solution, in which the strongest party imposes its interests or purposes upon others. In a consensus, all groups agree to the proposed direction or viewpoint. Second, a consensus is different from a compromise, though reaching consensus may require some element of compromise. To reach consensus involves finding a course of action which meets the needs and goals of all concerned. Politically, leaders speak of a "win-win" outcome, where all parties to a dispute recognize that they have gained what they really wanted to achieve—though not necessarily all that they originally claimed! This may require a changed understanding by the various participants of what they really want to achieve, a redefinition of goals and relationships. Third, reaching a consensus is rarely the end point, a termination of relationship or finalization of an "issue." A consensus is usually a decision to work together, to continue in relationship. This is one of the most distinctive features of consensus decisions. They are usually characterized by hope. The goal of consensus is not only the end of a dispute or the determination of a particular issue. It facilitates living together, with a heightened degree of awareness of each other's needs and contribution. A group or society which learns to relate in this way has a resource of experience to which it may return again and again. It gathers strength and learns how to avoid disputes, how to build and preserve peace. Consensus, then, is not just a way of resolving problems but is a way of living together.

We can use this concept of consensus to develop further the notion of God the conversationalist. As the inviting source of the conversation, and through offering and embodying possibilities to us in Christ, God is seeking to gather a consensus community. The divine conversation is open-ended. God has not determined the outcome and has not decided in advance of the conversation the "answers" to every question that emerges. The process is genuinely open. But that does not mean that the conversation is directionless. God's sovereignty does not have to be understood in terms of control and determination. It may be that God's sovereignty is exercised through infinitely creative responsiveness, allowing us genuine freedom, including the freedom to discover new ways of relating to God, to explore and "answer" God's questions. The consensus God seeks is not the termination of an issue but is a continuous process of living together, which involves all the participants by their choice and builds a dynamic life of peace and harmony. The specific means by which God is doing this is the activity of the Holy Spirit. It is the distinctive mission of the Spirit, as John Taylor has so effectively argued, to evoke from us a greater awareness of aspects of ourselves and our situation, so that we may see in them the presence and purposes of God. This awareness also brings us to recognize and make choices about how we shall live, in relation to God. This in turn requires from us, at least at times, costly sacrifice.[15]

Through the gentle invocation of the Spirit, God is seeking our responses, toward consensus as the way of life. In heightened awareness of our own real needs and values and a similar recognition of others and their desires, we reach out in hope of a new community. The idea of divine conversation as consensus-gathering recognizes that there are different perspectives, dissonant "voices" as Brueggemann suggests, and all have a legitimate place around the table. No one claim or voice overwhelms the others. On the contrary, the "Other" is welcomed and respected, with forbearance and love, for without the contribution of each and all the conversation is truncated and impoverished. Here there is a genuine acceptance of plurality, a community of difference.

In its fullest measure, the gathering consensus includes not only the human community but the life of the entire creation, creature with creature and creation with Creator. These ecological dimensions of the

---

[15] John V. Taylor, *The Go-Between God: The Holy Spirit and the Christian Mission* (London: SCM Press, 1972).

Spirit's mission also have theological significance. First, there is the possibility that God may be speaking to human beings, particularly, through the needs of the creation, our "environment," inviting us to learn more peaceful and creative ways of coexistence. The earth may be teaching us something about the nature of salvation—and sin. Even in its suffering, the earth may be a medium of divine conversation. Furthermore, in presenting us with these extended dimensions of sin and salvation, the cosmos may also be inviting us into a fuller, more holistic vision of the divine embodiment, in which the risen life of Christ is not just the "first-born" of the human dead but of the entire creation.[16] This greater vision of God's embodiment and gathering consensus calls forth still further exploration of the possibilities of life with God. The conversation continues.

The Context of Doubt

The idea of God the conversationalist provides a theological basis for understanding the relationship between doubt and faith. Doubt can be seen as a significant element within the divine-human conversation, having potential for enrichment of the conversation as well as for confusion or even abandonment of the relationship. As Brueggemann has found, dialectic tensions within the experience of God are a crucial part of the biblical testimony. God the conversationalist is not limited to a specific context, form, or content of expression. As a consequence, we can see within the biblical texts significant differences in the witness to God's approach and in the ways the people respond. In addition to word of promise and texts of hope, there are passages of protest and bitter dispute. Each can represent the word of God; each can express authentic faith.

An important feature of this metaphor of God the conversationalist is that it recognizes the place of human beings as genuine participants in the divine conversation. We have a contribution to make in response

---

[16] Jürgen Moltmann's theology has explored these implications most extensively in his "ecological doctrine of creation" and in his theology of the Holy Spirit as "the spirit of life." Jürgen Moltmann, *God in Creation*, trans. Margaret Kohl (London: SCM Press, 1985); and Jürgen Moltmann, *The Spirit of Life: A Universal Affirmation*, trans. Margaret Kohl (London: SCM Press, 1992). For a brief sketch of some of the ecological implications of his theology, see Jürgen Moltmann, "Reconciliation with Nature," *Pacifica* 5:3 (October 1992) 301–13.

to God, but we are also capable of initiating elements within the conversation. It also follows that no one party knows or can determine in advance how the conversation will proceed. By preserving the genuine freedom of human agents, while maintaining the freedom and creativity of God as well, this theology is both more credible and coherent.

This conception of God attributes positive significance to doubt as an element within the conversation. If we think of faith as participation in the divine conversation, then we can see that doubt—as well as belief and the constructive formulation of our understanding of God and the world—can have a crucial place within the life of faith. Indeed, within the context of divine conversation, we can speak of the activity of God causing us to doubt. The questions God asks can undermine the false certitudes humans build for themselves, including certitudes about God. In his autobiographical theology, Harry Williams described how God as the "final me" seeks to break through, undermining the false and pretending "me's" by which I may seek to avoid the truth about myself. Only as this doubt causes me to engage genuinely with myself can I enter into the joy of living with God. Val Webb's theology similarly sees God "nudging" us into doubt and thus into the adventure of life in process with God.

In the next chapters we will turn to the biblical witness to explore in some detail the significance of doubt within the divine conversation. In the Old Testament we find testimony to faithful doubt, as part of Israel's response to God's invitation. In the New Testament, faith in Jesus can include both belief and doubt, as means of exploring the potential of life in conversation with God. Finally, we shall gather these insights into a consideration of constructive aspects of doubt.

8

Faithful Doubt:
Participation in the Divine Conversation

All too easily, it is assumed that a faithful response to God always involves believing or obeying what has been said by God or about God. Yet this is clearly not the case in the Bible. There are other important and creative strands in which God is challenged by the people's protests and laments. Another strand involves the rejection—in the name of God—of what had previously been understood about God. In one sense, God is rejected in order that a richer and more appropriate response to God can emerge. These are the forms of faithful doubt evidenced in the Bible and they are vital elements in the divine conversation. Thus, while the Old Testament witnesses to a continuous conversation between YHWH and Israel, the conversation is of many forms. YHWH's approach, through invitation and promise, stricture and judgment, calls forth a plurality of responses.

Our specific interest in this chapter is to explore a number of passages and themes within the Old Testament which indicate that doubt, questioning, protest, and struggle can be expressions of *faithful* response to God. This does not mean that these are the only forms of faithful response. Clearly that would be an absurd claim. Nor does it mean that doubt or protest are the most appropriate response to God. Though sometimes this may be the case, in numerous other contexts faith expresses itself most appropriately in praise and celebration, or in positive trust in God's promises to the people.

Though the concept of doubt as such does not occur within the Old Testament, we will examine three strands within the Hebrew Bible in which we see a witness to faithful doubt. Here individuals and communities engage with God, questioning, protesting, and exploring what it means to have faith in "the Holy One of Israel." As we shall see, doubt is an intrinsic part of their faith and of the divine conversation.

Robert Davidson has explored the role of doubt within the Old Testament, finding many examples of faith challenging the prevailing beliefs or ideas about God, whether these are derived from other religions or from within Israel's own traditions. These expressions of faith he calls "the courage to doubt":

> Among the many traditions which found expression in worship in ancient Israel and were handed on to the future through worship, there was one which we might describe as "the courage to doubt," using doubt in the widest sense to indicate any questioning of, or protest against the adequacy of inherited faith.[1]

Implicit in Davidson's view is the suggestion that to continue with the inherited faith is inappropriate, though perhaps the more convenient response.

In an evocative paper on the theological significance of doubt in the Old Testament, Davidson indicates his understanding of doubt even more succinctly: "For our purposes doubt may be defined broadly as any serious questioning of, or uncertainty about, God and his purposes."[2] As we shall see, Davidson believes that at least some such doubt may be said to be inspired by God, and challenges the recognized "mediators" of God's word and will.

James Crenshaw has studied the development of what he calls skepticism in ancient Israel. This idea is similar to Davidson's notion of the courage to doubt, though Crenshaw presents it in different ways.[3]

---

[1] Robert Davidson, *The Courage to Doubt: Exploring an Old Testament Theme* (London: SCM Press, 1983) 12.

[2] Robert Davidson, "Some Aspects of the Theological Significance of Doubt in the Old Testament," *Annual of the Swedish Theological Institute*, no. 7 (1968–69), ed. Hans Kosmala (Leiden: E. J. Brill, 1970) 41–52.

[3] In an early article on this theme, Crenshaw refers to Davidson's ideas and identifies what he calls "a skeptic's mental outlook" with such doubting thoughts, recognizing that doubt may be grounded in profound faith. James L. Crenshaw, "The Birth of Skepticism in Ancient Israel," *The Divine Helmsman: Studies in God's Control of Human*

The skeptic in some way rejects the present reality or doubts the way things are presently understood, in the strength of a better understanding, albeit that the better way is not yet articulated fully. The skeptic seeks a better understanding and in this sense is hopeful in that skepticism. Crenshaw goes on to distinguish skepticism, pessimism, and cynicism. He sees a continuum, if not a progression, of ideas and experiences here. "Once the sceptic loses all hope of achieving the desired transformation, pessimism sets in, spawning sheer indifference to cherished convictions." This is a very important insight, for it emphasizes that the doubting person operates out of concern or engagement, rather than apathy. It is only when doubt or skepticism turns to pessimism and cynicism that hope is abandoned.

Crenshaw's study also shows that these experiences can lead in different directions. He describes skepticism as "the handmaid of religion," since it assists religion (we might say "faith") "in its endless struggle to prevent belief from becoming hollow testimony to a reality belonging only in the past."[4] Crenshaw's book *A Whirlpool of Torment: Israelite Traditions of God as an Oppressive Presence* shifts the emphasis from skepticism closer toward pessimism.[5] I will draw upon these studies of doubt in the Old Testament, to describe three specific ways in which faithful doubt is part of the divine human conversation.

Pleading and Protest

The faith of Israel's ancient leaders and teachers clearly included elements of protest, argumentation, and pleading with God. The collective impression is that, at least at times, faith involved a very lively conversation with God. Along with divine blessings and promises, many difficulties, tensions, and lasting ambiguities are evident in the stories of the ancient leaders such as Abraham and Moses.

For the people of Israel, as also for Paul and the writer to the Hebrews, Abraham is a paradigm of faith. What is this faith of Abraham which is reckoned to him as righteousness (Gen 15:6; Rom 4:9)?

Events, Presented to Lou H. Silberman, ed. James L. Crenshaw and Samuel Sandmel (New York: KTAV Publishing House, 1980) 1.

⁴ Ibid., 3.

⁵ James L. Crenshaw, *A Whirlpool of Torment: Israelite Traditions of God as an Oppressive Presence* (Philadelphia: Fortress Press, 1984).

The faith of which Abraham is a paradigm cannot be a matter of intellectual assent to confessional statements (as if such had evolved) for, as Davidson has noted, Abraham has a strong tendency to argue with God.[6] Rather than assent, Abraham's faith seems much more like a trust in God even though Abraham questions and challenges what he thinks God may be doing or saying to him. Within two verses of the identification of Abraham's faith, we find him questioning God: "O Lord GOD, how am I to know that I shall possess [the land]?" (Gen 15:8).

The particular incident in which these issues are most clearly seen is the story of Abraham's pleading with God for the people of Sodom and Gomorrah, whom God intends to visit and destroy (Gen 18:16-33). Abraham wrestles with the question of God's justice: Can the just God really act like this, to punish the good people along with the bad? His challenge is boldly expressed: Shall not the Judge of all the earth do what is just? (v. 25). Within this bold statement there are two elements. First there is the implicit belief about God—that the Lord God will act justly. But this belief was not easy to maintain, in the face of many appearances to the contrary. Abraham expresses his faith in a challenging way. He acknowledges that he is not God, he is but dust and ashes (v. 27). Even so he persists with his questioning, for in Abraham's faith there is a continuing tension between his own questioning and protest, on the one hand, and his acknowledgment of his own limitations and his obedience to God, on the other.

In an incisive exposition, Davidson argues that it is precisely Abraham's faith which leads him to argue with God and to challenge a concept of God which seems to contradict the facts of the situation. God who is said to be just seems to be acting unjustly. To acquiesce here would be an act of cowardice. To challenge God is an ultimate act of trust in God. On this basis Davidson rejects a common misconception of faith, which defines trust "in such a way that it eliminates questions and stills the voice of protest."[7] The contemporary Jewish writer Elie Wiesel has argued that God forgave Abraham his questioning, because it expressed his concern for others, not himself.[8] But if Abraham's

---

[6] Davidson, *The Courage to Doubt*, 39–53.

[7] Ibid., 43.

[8] The reference is to Elie Wiesel, *Messengers of God* (New York: Random House, 1977) 86. Davidson, *The Courage to Doubt*, 48.

pleading is a form of faith, challenging an inadequate conception of God, there is nothing to be forgiven, Davidson concludes. If anything what needs forgiveness is the refusal to ask the questions.

Before leaving the Abraham stories I want to consider the stories of Sarah's laughter, which can also be seen as a significant expression of doubt in the divine-human conversation. Genesis 18:1-15 tells a story of the Lord appearing to Abraham in the form of three men, bringing the promise that Abraham and Sarah will have a son. Sarah, listening behind the tent, laughed to herself. But "the Lord" asked Abraham why Sarah had laughed, posing another divine question. "Is anything too wonderful for the Lord?" (v. 14). Sarah denied that she laughed, because she was afraid, but the Lord said, "Oh yes, you did laugh" (v. 15).

This story has passed without comment in Davidson's exposition of doubt and faith in Abraham's story, continuing the patriarchal emphasis of the Abraham stories in which Sarah is left out of the conversation. She is excluded from the positive relationship which Abraham enjoys with God, who talks openly with Abraham while Sarah is shut away in the tent. Her laughter is "to herself."[9]

Commentators vary in their interpretations of Sarah's laughter. Mary Jo Cartledge-Hayes has written a brilliant first-person narrative of Sarah's bursting into laughter, here and again when her son is born.[10] Walter Brueggemann sees both Abraham and Sarah as models of disbelief. Both are bemused by God's promise. It is only when Isaac is born that Abraham's disbelief and Sarah's hidden sniggers are transformed to joyous laughter.[11]

Perhaps this story is genuinely ambiguous. Sarah's laughter is not pure derision, a disbelieving rejection of God's promise. Nor is it necessarily purely innocent, as Eileen Vennum seems to suggest. Laughter is not always univocal, signifying joy or derision, hope or cynicism. It can be the outburst of a completely non-plussed state in which we don't know what to make of things.

---

[9] The impact of Sarah's being "locked out" of the discussion is well articulated in Eileen Vennum, "Is She or Is She Not? Sarah a Hero of Faith," *Daughters of Sarah* 13:1 (January–February 1987) 4 and 5.

[10] Mary Jo Cartledge-Hayes, "Sarah, Laughing," *Daughters of Sarah* 13:1 (January–February 1987) 8 and 9.

[11] Walter Brueggemann, *Genesis: A Bible Commentary for Teaching and Preaching* (Atlanta: John Knox Press, 1982) 158–9. But cf. Walter Brueggemann, "Will Our Faith Have Children?" *Word and World* 3:3 (1983) 272–83.

Graeme Garrett has written of the theological significance of laughter, explaining that much humor takes the form of two reality-perspectives "colliding" in our minds or consciousness.[12] In the sudden realization of this collision, the absurd thought that both could be true, or both could happen at once, explodes into laughter. Perhaps Sarah's laughter is like this. She is an elderly woman who has lived half her life beyond child-bearing years and all of it in deep shame and disappointment. Now she contemplates joyously nursing her own child, a gift from the Lord. The clash of Sarah images evokes her laughter.

Sarah's laughter may be the laughter of doubt. Like another woman long after her, she asks herself, "How can this be?" Sadly, she must laugh to herself, just as for a lifetime she has held to herself the anguish and shame she felt in not having a child. Nonetheless, God knows what cannot be laughed out loud. But when she is invited to speak she denies it and speaks of *fear*. Perhaps here there is a basis for Brueggemann's negative judgment. But it is noticeable that in the text no comment is passed on this fear. She is rebuked but not punished, neither for her fear nor her laughter. She is simply left with the reality of the situation. The two sets of expectations are set before her, with the invitation to pursue the promise—until that day when she can indeed laugh out loud.

The story of Moses' call to be the leader of the people of Israel is another example in which we find a succession of objections which are countered and then finally dismissed (Exod 3:7–4:18). Within this call narrative we see a clear indication of Brueggemann's idea of dialectical tensions in Israelite theology: YHWH is known as their God and yet always remains unknown and elusive. The liberating God is a free God, who will be what God will be.

Davidson discusses the view, found in various commentaries, that Moses spoke "not befittingly." The subsequent signs are punishments for the sin of disbelief.[13] Yet the text itself makes no such inference. Moses' faith in God includes a profound loyalty to God, but this does not exclude questioning, doubt, and protest. This is not unbelief. This is precisely the commitment to God which asks: "What does this mean? How can this be right?" Moses insists on working through to a consistency in relationship

[12] Graeme Garrett, "'My Brother Esau Is a Hairy Man': An Encounter Between the Comedian and the Preacher," *Scottish Journal of Theology* 33 (1980) 239–56 and in Graeme Garrett, *God Matters: Conversations in Theology* (Collegeville: The Liturgical Press, 1999) ch. 2.

[13] Davidson, *The Courage to Doubt*, 64.

and understanding. This is not a "darker side" of Moses' greatness as leader. This is part of Moses' courageous knowledge of God. It is part of what is meant when it is said of Moses, in contrast to all others, "With him I speak face to face—clearly, not in riddles" (Num 12:8).

In another example in Exodus 5, Moses is sent to Pharaoh to demand the release of the Hebrew people. But the immediate effect is a worsening of their plight, which gives rise to objections from the people against Moses himself. He in turn takes this to God (v. 22): Why has God brought misfortune to the people, and perhaps it wasn't such a good idea to involve Moses in this in the first place! As Davidson notes, Moses' complaint is tantamount to accusing God of not keeping the promises which were the very basis of Moses' call. Again there has been a long history of commentary seeking to explain Moses' behavior. Calvin, for example, observed "how deep is the darkness which had taken possession of [his] mind."[14] Umberto Cassuto speaks of Moses daringly raising these issues "after he had overcome his doubts and completely dedicated his life to the fulfillment of his exalted mission."[15] But Davidson is surely right in arguing that Moses has not overcome his doubts: these protests express his continuing doubt. The question of real interest here is what is the meaning of his doubt, not to presume that Moses must have overcome his doubts in order to continue his role as leader. Moses does not doubt that the Lord is "in charge," as it were, but he cannot understand what is happening. He again doubts that he is the right person for the job, and protests that God is doing the wrong thing in allowing him to make such a mess of things![16] God's response, as with the initial call sequences, is to reaffirm the call and to assure him that God knows of the peoples' suffering and will redeem them.

In this short incident we see a faith that struggles with God, committed to God's purpose yet unsure what that purpose is. Obedience and doubt are mixed together as parts of the divine conversation.[17] Moses' faith is grounded in God's revelation of who God is and what God will do and be for the people. Within this certainty, however, there is much squirming, doubt, and protest, as well as a continuous

[14] Ibid., 69. Davidson's reference is to Calvin's *Harmony of the Pentateuch*, II, 124.

[15] Davidson's reference is to Umberto Cassuto, *A Commentary on the Book of Exodus*, trans. Israel Abrahams (Jerusalem: Magnes Press, Hebrew University, 1967) 744.

[16] Here we note, as we found with Williams' theology, the close association between doubt of God and self-doubt.

[17] Other incidents of complaint and protest can be seen in Exod 17:41; 19:12, 21.

stream of mutuality and prayer. All this is the story of Moses' faith and without any one part of it we distort the ancient story.

Lament

Another consistent part of the human response to God in the Hebrew Bible is lamentation. The clearest expression of such lament is in Israel's worship. In the psalms we find a complex compilation of experiences, ranging from triumphant praise to bitter remorse and despair, all addressed to God.

While the psalms of praise and confidence are perhaps the best known, in fact the largest group of psalms are laments, and of these the individual laments alone are more numerous than any other group of psalms.

Psalm 38 is a good example of how anguish is boldly expressed in worship. It begins with the utterance of a person who is not only in pain but whose distress is said to be at God's hand: the author is wounded by God's arrows and anger (vv. 1 and 2). Friends, family, and strength are gone, while enemies gloat. The psalmist calls to the Lord for salvation (vv. 21-22). It is not stated whether the person's distress is relieved. One reason this is a good example of the laments is precisely that the author so boldly addresses God both as the cause of the trouble and yet with trust in God as the one who will save. There is, here, a deep question about God, about why this is happening and why God does not quickly come to the psalmist's aid.

A similar dynamic can be seen in Psalm 109, with the additional element that the writer challenges God's silence (v. 1). The author laments his or her suffering, but what has God to say? The psalm urges God to speak a word of blessing and thus it expresses trust and hope in God, with a promise to praise the Lord should this transpire.

These elements can be seen, too, in the community laments, which tend to rehearse God's actions for the people in the past, e.g., Psalm 74. The lament articulates the concern and distress of the people in the present. Inherent in this act are two fundamental elements: a trust in God, at such depth that the people freely express their anguish, even resentment and bitterness, before the Lord; and a deep questioning of God. Why is it that God has acted like this in the past but not now? Why were they saved—these ancestors—but not us?

Following Sigmund Mowinckel, who speaks of worship as creating a world, and other scholars who posit the social construction of reality,

Brueggemann understands the psalms as "world-creating" or "world-ordering."[18] With our language, in this instance the language of Israel's praise, we create a world; that is, we order and shape our experience into what we might call "our world." If our experience is of the form Brueggemann calls "dis-orientation," however, our previous understanding of God and our world is broken up, disturbed, and undermined. In short, it is in doubt. A new understanding or formulation begins with the recognition and articulation of this fact.

In the lament psalms, the implicit "world" that has fallen apart is a world where "God is in his heaven and all is right with the world." But all is not right with the world, and if God is in heaven, what is God doing about the world? Two aspects of reorientation are taking place in the psalms of lament. First there is the recognition of what is no longer believed, no longer a reality. This is doubt about a *previous* view of God and the world. But the fact of this rejection or denial, expressed as lament, then clears the way for some new evocation of faith and relationship. Lament, then, is an important and theologically significant part of the faithful human response, within the divine conversation.

Lament is also a powerful element within the book of the prophet Jeremiah, especially in the "Confessions."[19] Crenshaw describes Jeremiah's experience of God as "seduction and rape." Davidson also finds in these passages evidence of the most profound suffering in the life of the prophet. Loneliness and bitterness, with an increasing sense of failure, are the hallmarks of these confessions until, as Davidson puts it, "Jeremiah went to the very brink of cognitive and spiritual collapse."[20]

Initially Jeremiah's laments are like those we have seen in the psalms: he doubts the worthwhileness of his ministry, since God seems

---

[18] Walter Brueggemann, *Israel's Praise: Doxology Against Idolatry and Ideology* (Philadelphia: Fortress Press, 1988). See esp. ch. 1, "Praise as a Constitutive Act." Elsewhere Brueggemann has suggested that the life of faith generally can be understood in terms of three directional ideas: becoming securely *oriented*, being painfully *disoriented*, and becoming surprisingly *reoriented*. These themes he finds central to the theological understanding of the psalms and they provide a helpful framework for the classification and exegesis of many psalms. See Walter Brueggemann, *Praying the Psalms* (Winona, Minn.: St. Mary's Press, 1982), and Walter Brueggemann, *The Message of the Psalms: A Theological Commentary* (Minneapolis: Augsburg, 1984).

[19] These passages are Jer 11:18–12:6; 15:10–21; 17:14–18; 18:18–23; 20:7-12, 14-18. Crenshaw has a valuable discussion of the critical issues regarding these passages, their literary form, and possible historical setting. Crenshaw, *A Whirlpool of Torment*, 31–8.

[20] Davidson, *The Courage to Doubt*, 127.

to allow the wicked to prosper, while he is in anguish (12:1 and 2). But in Jer 15:18 the prophet's doubt of God comes directly to the surface: "Truly, you are to me like a deceitful brook, / like waters that fail." Is God his enemy? This, then, is the basis for the allegations of deception and enticement in chapter 20. It is not by choice that Jeremiah is a prophet. God has called him and nurtured him, even before birth. As Crenshaw sees it, against the background of God's call for Jeremiah to remain celibate, the charge of seduction, which Jeremiah uses against God in 20:7 ("enticed" in the NRSV), is even more evocative. He is abandoned by God and a laughing-stock to others.[21]

Thrown into the most impossible doubt, Jeremiah does not know what to think, whom to trust, who is his friend and who is his enemy. The only thing he can do is quit. But the word of the Lord cannot be contained within him. Jeremiah *has* to believe it is real. His doubt has led him to an incontrovertible sense of reality. He has "been to the edge," and though the Lord seems to be his enemy, along with all the other mockers, this word must be spoken. This is Jeremiah's "Here I stand . . . ."

In this part of Jeremiah's story, then, we see a most excruciating experience of faith in God which leads to doubt at the most profound level, and *through* that doubt continues as faith. Were Jeremiah to have believed his opponents or abandoned his ministry, that would have been a negation of the divine call. But Jeremiah does not move along Crenshaw's continuum, from skepticism to pessimism and cynicism. For Jeremiah the road of doubt was the pathway of obedience. He doubted the prevailing theologies of his day, but he also doubted his own doubts, wrestling with the confusing reality of God until finally he must speak. All this is his faith.

In this part of his ministry, then, the dynamics of doubt and faith involve Jeremiah in a process where everyone else seems to have faith and only he has doubts, and this seems to be his weakness. But what he learned in this weakness later became a resource out of which he ministered to others in their time of great crisis. When all the external certainties were lost and he was at the point of quitting, it was then that his faith, in the form of lament and doubt, found a new certainty. The word of God became for him a reality on which he could depend, despite his mockers, despite the sense of disaster all around. Thus, when

---

[21] Crenshaw, *A Whirlpool of Torment*, 39.

the final destruction came, it was Jeremiah who could be "cool in the crisis." He had already learned to trust God in the absence of so many "tokens" of God's presence, in the Temple, the prophets, and the scribes. Out of this confidence, he was able to lead others to a new opportunity of faith, the beginning of a "new covenant," a new development in the divine conversation.

One further expression of lament, within the Old Testament response to God, is *Rachel's weeping*. In Jer 31:15 we read:

> A voice is heard in Ramah,
>   lamentation and bitter weeping.
> Rachel is weeping for her children;
>   she refuses to be comforted for her children,
>   because they are no more.

This weeping is the sound of what Christopher Morse has called "Rachel's Refusal." For Morse the figure of Rachel in Jeremiah "represents the suffering, not of one who dies in childbirth, or in what could be called a tragedy of nature, but of those who are deprived of their freedom by an oppressive power in history."[22] Morse notes that Jeremiah hears a word from the Lord, for Rachel and for those who suffer "within the sound of her voice," calling them to cease weeping, for there is hope for their future (Jer 31:16-17).

What is particularly significant in this example is the refusal to accept comfort. There are situations where only God can speak of hope. To be true to herself, Rachel must weep.[23] Rachel's refusal to be comforted by others is a refusal of every explanation and excuse, every attempt to pour words over the raw wound of her grief. Only God can answer this question.

Rachel's weeping must therefore be heard as a powerful resonance from the Hebrew Bible, calling into question every theology which seeks to "answer" her grief. The only appropriate theological response is to wait with her until the Lord gives new hope. Rachel's waiting and weeping are also parts of the divine-human conversation.

---

[22] Christopher Morse, *Not Every Spirit: A Dogmatics of Christian Disbelief* (Valley Forge, Pa.: Trinity Press, 1994) 9.

[23] In discussing Rachel's weeping, Brueggemann has referred to the propensity for religion to try to silence her grief. Brueggemann, "Will Our Faith Have Children?" 272–83.

Sifting the Silence

In the previous chapter we mentioned briefly the questions God asks in the book of Job. Now we turn to consider Job's own participation in the divine conversation. Here and in the book of Ecclesiastes, however, the dominant element in the conversation is God's apparent silence, or what Brueggemann calls God's hiddenness. The human responses might therefore be called *sifting the silence.*

These two books derive from the Wisdom literature, the best known of which is the book of Proverbs, offering many sayings and teachings about wise living and the ways of God. In Job and Ecclesiastes, however, we find a different perspective on God's wisdom. The current teachings about God are called into question.

Davidson sees the book of Job as a parable dealing with two rival theologies, inherent in Israel's tradition.[24] The dominant theology views the universe in terms of rewards and punishments. Those who follow the ways of the Lord will be rewarded, and the wicked will get their just deserts. Within this book another view emerges, however, for clearly Job is a righteous man, yet he now suffers deeply. Will he abandon his trust in God, or is it possible that a person might be righteous without rewards? The outcome of the parable seems to offer an alternative world view, in which the universe is ultimately mysterious, far less predictable, and probably more dangerous than the purported world of religiously interpreted rewards and punishments. Yet, for Job, such a world is also in the hands of a righteous God who, despite all appearances, can be depended on.

Crenshaw is surely right, though, to ask what kind of God this is.[25] Is the question of God's integrity adequately addressed by the final suggestion that God restores to Job all his fortune, family, and flocks? Is there not here the sense of God as "oppressive presence" and of faith as a "whirlpool of torment"? Perhaps indeed it is a dangerous thing to come too close to God, as Jacob discovered. What is the righteousness of this God and how might a person and a community live in the way of righteousness?

The story of Job is a profound assertion of the ultimate mystery of God. At the end, after God speaks, Job acknowledges this mystery overtly. Before that, his trust in God is muted. He knows that God is

---

[24] Davidson, *The Courage to Doubt,* ch. 9, "Rewrite or Rethink," esp. 178–81.
[25] Crenshaw, *A Whirlpool of Torment,* 74.

not as his friends say, but he can neither say nor show what God is truly like. We see here two crucial elements in Job's response to God. First, Job persists in refusing to believe the accepted ways of understanding God, which would imply that he has in some way deserved his plight, or that God is capriciously vicious. Job's faith in God here is largely characterized by what he does not believe, though it implies a profound trust which he cannot really explain. Then the second element to be noted is that God declares that Job has spoken the truth (42:7). The outcome, then, is not only the silence of worship, as Crenshaw suggests, but a definite assertion about Job and about God. It is an affirmation of the faith inherent in Job's refusal of the orthodox theology and its explanation of suffering. *Job's doubt is affirmed by God as theological truth.* Job's struggle to maintain faith in a righteous God, even as God seems to be his enemy, is found to be more faithful than the confident beliefs of the conventional theology.

There is here, I suggest, a different but important strand in the witness to divine conversation. In Job's instance, response to God has chiefly taken the form of denial of those "answers" which do not express his faith. He continues to protest his innocence before God. He does not know why he suffers, but will not speak falsely against the Lord. Though he waits upon God, the discourse is focused much more on what he denies than what he can affirm. Here there is faithful doubt—not doubt of God, but doubt of all that is said and accepted about God. The conversation reaches its affirmative stage only after God has spoken. Then Job's implicit affirmation of the mystery of God becomes overt.

This brings us finally to the book of Ecclesiastes, and the figure we call Qoheleth, the "Preacher." The life-situation in this work is more tranquil. No great drama has befallen Qoheleth. These chapters are the reflections of a scholar and sage who has "seen it all." According to Crenshaw, Qoheleth is a pessimist who has moved beyond skepticism to a definite pessimism.[26] In his discussion of Qoheleth's experience of God, Crenshaw speaks of "the silence of eternity." God is not present and knowledge of God is not accessible to human beings. This is the outcome of the Preacher's study of all the great traditions of his faith.[27] Other studies do not draw the inference of pessimism, however. Rabbi

---

[26] Crenshaw, "The Birth of Skepticism in Ancient Israel," 16, n. 5.

[27] Crenshaw, *A Whirlpool of Torment,* esp. 79–88.

Harold Kushner's reflections on Ecclesiastes, for example, are strongly life-affirming.[28] Here it seems that we have an example of the dialectical tensions within the Hebrew Bible, where God is both known and remains elusive, so different readers draw diverging theological inferences from the same text.

It is helpful here to reflect on the significance of the much-quoted line "all is vanity" (Eccl 12:8). Davidson has argued that the Hebrew *hebel* means something like "emptiness" or "devoid of any ultimate meaning."[29] This does not mean there is no functional worth in things, nor any pleasure in life. Indeed the opposite is the case, and much of Qoheleth's preaching is from the didactic Wisdom tradition, encouraging good living and wise policies. But in the end, life to him is an insoluble mystery. Thus a survey of the various strands of the Hebrew tradition, concerning creation, prophecy, the Torah, worship, and wisdom leads Qoheleth to conclude that while there may be meaning in it all, for God, we humans cannot know it. It is inaccessible to us; we cannot answer the ultimate questions.

Davidson reads the Preacher as offering us a positive form of faith, though it lacks specific content in the sense of belief statements. "Eat your bread with enjoyment, and drink your wine with a merry heart; for God has long ago approved what you do" (Eccl 9:7). This means we should just "take life as it comes to you day by day, live it to the full—that is God's gift."[30] Here there is no great anguish about life, nor is there any strong conviction of meaning. It is simply an affirmation of daily living, and an assurance of God's presence within the mystery of life.

There is a useful distinction here between *assurance* of God's presence and an immediate sense of *meaning* derived from that presence. Qoheleth is able to affirm God's presence without a strong sense of meaning arising from that assurance. Qoheleth leaves us with the advice that we should fear God who will bring every deed to judgment (Eccl 12:13 and 14). There is reverence here, and a conviction of the reality of God. But unlike Job, he seems to have no burning need or drive to relate to God in a personal and deeply engaged way. Whether we should call this sense of God "the silence of eternity" or God's "presence as absence" or simply a deep recognition of the transcendence of

---

[28] Harold Kushner, *When All You've Ever Wanted Isn't Enough* (London: Pan Books, 1987).

[29] Davidson, *The Courage to Doubt*, 189.

[30] Ibid., 200.

God, this view remains as one more form of faith, holding within it doubt, yet affirming itself as faith.

The figure of Qoheleth stands within the Hebrew tradition as a counterpoint to all other theologies, a challenge to every attempt to reduce the mystery of God to human proportions. Here is one further element in the divine conversation, faithful doubt "sifting" the silence. In the case of Job, the conversation is at first crowded by other voices who seek to explain God. Job himself focuses on the reality of God, and eventually through mutual questioning the conversation develops to the further level of theological insight. For Qoheleth, however, God remains silent. The resultant image of faith involves trusting the God who knows and approves, even while remaining elusive.

In this chapter we have drawn upon various sections of the Old Testament, finding examples of stories and situations in which doubt can be seen as a positive element in the people's relationship with God. The people of Israel witness to a God who is continually inviting them to engage in conversation. This divine-human conversation has called forth protest, pleading, and lament, as well as praise and proclamation. At significant times faithful servants of the Lord actively questioned and challenged the faith of their forbears. What was taught in the name of God is now questioned—also in the name of God. This faithful doubt is often a costly experience. For Jeremiah it seemed as if God was his enemy, while Job is repudiated by those who speak for God.

While our survey is in no sense exhaustive or representative—we have not, for instance, considered the apocalyptic stream in later Hebrew tradition—we will conclude our considerations here. We have seen that faith in YHWH can take the form of "the courage to doubt." The divine conversation poses questions and provokes questioning and doubt, as well as belief and obedience. All these are elements in Israel's story of faithful conversation with YHWH.

9

Faith in Jesus: Belief and Doubt

For Christian faith, the Israelite tradition of responsive relationship with YHWH takes a decisive turn with the coming of Jesus of Nazareth. In Chapter 7 we suggested that Jesus' life and ministry can be understood as the embodiment of the divine conversation. In Jesus, God offers us an evocative demonstration of the possibilities of human life—a life fully responsive to God. Jesus is what humanity is meant to be, a second Adam as Paul suggested. Humans are created to be responsive creatures engaged in dynamic conversation with God. Thus we suggested that Jesus explored the possibilities of being with God, offering his life to God throughout his ministry, as well as in his death. This exploration worked itself out in Jesus' openness to other people and their possibilities with God and, as a result, his life became an evangelical invitation to others to recognize the presence and reign of God among them. In so doing, Jesus also challenged and questioned some of the received teachings about God. He invited people to think in new ways about themselves and to recognize God's surprising presence and gracious purpose at the margins of their experience and expectations.

The New Testament is written from the perspective of faith *in* Jesus. The writers have become convinced that Jesus was not only a "demonstration" of faith as a conversation with God; rather, the divine conversation is now centered upon Jesus. He is proclaimed as a person in whom God was—and is—present. He is both human and divine, the "conversation" made perfect within the identity and life of a human being. Yet this faith in Jesus is not faith in a new God. The first Christians saw themselves as proclaiming the God of Israel, as for example the sermons of Peter in Acts make plain. The presence of God in and as Jesus of Nazareth is seen in continuity with the history of Israelite encounter with YHWH. Jesus is seen as the fulfillment and expression of Israel's hope for a decisive and saving act in which God will vindicate their faith before the nations. Though the earliest Christians eventually found themselves expelled from the synagogues, this was not their intention or choice. Indeed, the book of Acts suggests that the earliest doctrinal struggle for the Church concerned the question of whether Gentile people needed to become cultically Jewish in order to enter the Christian community. Much contemporary New Testament scholarship has been devoted to showing the continuity of Christian faith with the faith of Israel, perhaps to correct the overemphasis, especially in the reading of Paul, upon the distinction between justification by faith alone and the works of the Law.[1]

In this chapter, we will continue our exploration of the divine conversation as witnessed in the Bible, with specific emphasis upon the nature of faith in Jesus. We shall see that for the New Testament writers, faith in the God of Israel means following Jesus into a life of continuous responsiveness to God. To have faith in Jesus is to be responsive to the God of Jesus. We will consider the nature of this faith and its relationship to doubt, as indicated by a number of specific passages and themes within the New Testament.

Our study is complicated by a number of factors not evident within the Old Testament, resulting from the use and influence of Greek language and thought. In the New Testament we find a number of words which are commonly translated as "doubt." We will examine their usage and meaning in the few passages where they occur. The situation is also complicated, as we have noted earlier from Val Webb's work, by the existence in English of two nouns, "belief" and "faith," used to translate the one core idea of faith—from the Greek *pistis*. Though in English we have two nouns we have only one verb, "to believe," making it difficult for us to distinguish the relationship of believing and faith. As John Dunnill has observed, the term itself has a breadth of meaning: "The word *pistis* had a wide range of meaning in contemporary

---

[1] For a valuable summary of the issues here and the "new approach to Paul," see James D. G. Dunn, *The Theology of Paul the Apostle* (Grand Rapids, Mich.: Eerdmans, 1998) ch. 14.

writings, Jewish and Greek: from 'belief' to 'trust,' through 'trustworthiness' and 'certainty' to a 'mode of existence of those who live in relation
to the divine.'"[2]

A central issue for us to consider is, therefore, the role and nature of
belief in Christian faith. What does it mean to believe in Jesus? Does it
mean to believe certain statements *about* Jesus? Does it mean to *trust in*
what Jesus did, especially in his sacrificial death on the cross? Does it
mean to *enter into* the same kind of encounter with God as Jesus embodied—to be "in Christ," to use Paul's phrase? All of these seem to be
well-established candidates for the meaning of "faith in Jesus." All have
something to contribute to our exploration of the relation of doubt and
faith.

Through the course of the twentieth century, considerable scholarly
effort has been addressed to explaining the nature of belief, through
linguistic philosophical analysis. The classic work here, with an extensive survey of issues and approaches, is H. H. Price's *Belief*.[3] Price
makes a useful distinction between "belief-that" and "belief-in," suggesting that the former has as its object a proposition or statement,
while the latter is addressed to a person. Belief-in is more like trust
than a propositional attitude, though necessarily it implies some element of belief or conviction about the person or ideal in which we have
placed our trust. It is useful to distinguish these forms of belief, because
they show different relationships with doubt. Clearly one cannot both
believe and doubt a statement. To say, "I believe it will rain today, but I
doubt it," is nonsensical. On the other hand, it is quite common to say
that we trust someone or believe in them, but we also have some doubts
about them. The relationship of doubt to "belief-in" is different from
the relation of doubt to "belief-that."

All of the theologians considered in our preceding study have rejected the idea that Christian faith can be reduced to a propositional
attitude alone. Even Newman's concept of faith as assent was found to
depend upon a personal and "real" apprehension of God as the object of
the propositions of faith. Without this revelatory encounter, faith cannot be formed as real assent and is, in Newman's view, not genuine
faith at all. Nonetheless, Newman insists upon the propositional content of faith as an essential element, to which believers will offer their

[2] John Dunnill, "Saved by Whose Faith? The Function of *pistis Christou* in Pauline
Theology," *Colloquium* 30:1 (May 1998) 3–5.
[3] H. H. Price, *Belief: The Gifford Lectures for 1960* (London: Allen and Unwin, 1969).

assent if called upon to do so. Taking an opposite approach, Val Webb wants to distinguish faith from belief, in order to allow that doubt is a necessary element within faith. We found, however, that she had not adequately explained the role of belief within the life of faith. The question of the relationship of belief and doubt within Christian faith remains. In this chapter, we will attempt to explore this question from within the documents of the New Testament as witness to the continuing conversation with God, and specifically in the form of response to Jesus. What is the role of belief and doubt within faith in Jesus?

Believing in Jesus

It could be argued that the most immediate and basic response to Jesus sought by the New Testament writers is believing. Mark's Gospel presents Jesus as beginning with a call to believe the gospel (Mark 1:15). Paul writes that it is through believing that we are justified (Rom 10:10), and John presents Jesus as engaging in several disputes with his opponents because they will not believe what he says (John 5:47-48; 8:24-25; 10:26-27, etc.). There is much encouragement to believers, perhaps especially those suffering persecution and other trials of their faith, to hold fast to their beliefs. Thus while faith in the New Testament includes other elements, such as obedience, hope, and witness, all these imply some foundational element of belief.

One critical issue, however, is to explain the nature of this belief. Whereas the concept of belief can mean believing statements or propositions, this aspect is not the primary element in the New Testament use of this term. To believe is chiefly to believe in Christ, not so much to believe things about Christ. Faith, as we have seen, is essentially relational and attitudinal. Nonetheless, to "believe in" Christ is at least to imply certain beliefs about Christ: for example, that he is believable, trustworthy, and indeed merits the honor accorded to him. Christopher Marshall sees faith in Mark's Gospel as "a mixture of mental conviction and existential commitment." The personal and relational elements necessarily imply at least some content of belief about Jesus.[4]

What then is the character of faith sought by the Jesus of the Gospels? When Jesus says, "Believe the Good News," what is the belief he is

---

[4] Christopher Marshall, *Faith as a Theme in Mark's Narrative* (Cambridge: Cambridge University Press, 1989) esp. ch. 2.

seeking? Is Jesus calling for an attitude of belief such as that described by Newman, an assent which admits of no wavering? There seems good reason to argue that the faith Jesus is calling for is not an all-or-nothing stance which admits no doubts and no questions. Rather, in a number of episodes we see Jesus' positive response to people who admit to unbelief or who challenge his own statements.

The most significant example here is that of the Canaanite woman who seeks healing for her daughter (Matt 15:21-28). Arguably this story is the fulcrum in Matthew's narrative of Jesus' mission and his quest for faith in the house of Israel. The woman argues against Jesus, refusing to accept his claim that he is sent only to the people of Israel. Eventually Jesus declares that this is great faith. Here is an astonishing example of "divine conversation" in which, as some feminist scholars have suggested, Jesus learns from a Gentile woman.[5] The conversation develops because of her doubting response. Her great faith rejects the accepted theology which Jesus had articulated, calling him to a further development of his mission. In Matthew's narrative, that call leads Jesus to the point where his mission extends to all the nations and his presence to the end of the age. In this story, "great faith" is contrasted with a ready belief of what Jesus had previously said.

In Mark 9:14-29 we read a story of Jesus' response to an avowal of belief and unbelief, in the healing of a boy with an unclean spirit. Jesus says to the pleading father that all things can be done for the one who believes, and the man replies, "I believe; help my unbelief!" (v. 24). The narrative does not indicate Jesus' response to this statement, *except* to tell us that Jesus healed the boy. What we can conclude, however, is that the healing was not dependent upon the father's having the kind of faith that excludes doubt, hesitation, or unbelief. Indeed this incident would support the view that it is the faith of Jesus (rather than of other people) which heals and saves. What is required of others is that we should call upon him, trusting in spite of our own hesitation or doubts. This perspective will be developed further when we consider, later in the chapter, the "faith which can move mountains."

What seems clear from these few examples is that the Gospels call not so much for belief about Jesus as for an attitude of responsiveness

---

[5] For a detailed exposition and discussion of this passage, see Elaine Wainwright, *Towards a Feminist Critical Reading of the Gospel According to Matthew* (New York: Walter de Gruyter, 1991) ch. 5, esp. 222–44. See also Elisabeth Moltmann-Wendel, *A Land Flowing with Milk and Honey* (London: SCM Press, 1986) 121–4.

to him. This call seems to be in continuity with our findings in the Old Testament, where courageous faith included the possibility of doubt and protest as parts of a continuous responsiveness to God.

Nevertheless, as the gospel mission of the Church began to spread to other places, it was necessary to focus upon the actual content of the message of and about Jesus. When the evangelists called upon people to receive their testimony, what were they asking them to believe? It is interesting that in the New Testament generally there seems to have been no set standard of belief, such as a minimal statement of doctrine or anything like a creed. We find a number of short statements which seem to have a confessional status or history, such as "Jesus is Lord" (1 Cor 12:3) or the "Christological Hymn" in Phil 2:5-11, but overall there is no clear formulation of the "content of Christian belief" as such. That is not the purpose of these writings. On the contrary, the documents of the New Testament indicate considerable diversity on many matters of doctrine. The first epistle of John urges that we should not believe every spirit (1 John 4:1), and the letter to the Ephesians urges its readers not to be blown this way and that by every shifting wind of deceitful teaching (Eph 4:14).

Arguably more than any other New Testament writer, it is the apostle Paul who asserted the character of faith as involving a dynamic trust in God, which nevertheless allowed room for questioning and even doubt. What exactly did Paul mean by faith in Jesus? The history of interpretation of Paul's understanding of faith is perhaps one of the most extensive and divisive areas of Christian theology, and we cannot begin to chart this entire area. Rather, we will depend upon the work of several writers to provide us with some central insights into the field. James Dunn's study of Paul's theology helpfully demonstrates the continuity in Paul's Christian faith with what he, Paul, considered to be the meaning (though not the practice) of the law of God in Israelite faith. Central here is the idea of living continuously in dependence upon God. Paul's argument about faith uses Abraham as the paragon of faith. To be a follower of Jesus is to enter into a life of faithful dependence upon God, who has been shown—in the death and resurrection of Jesus—to be righteous, trustworthy, and therefore the proper object of our faith. We are brought into right relationship with God not by the law as such, but by the righteousness of God. To depend upon and trust God is therefore to be justified by faith. Dunn concludes:

> This, then, is what Paul meant by justification by faith, by faith alone. It was a profound conception of the relation between God and

humankind—a relation of utter dependence, of unconditional trust. Human dependence on divine grace had to be unqualified or else it was not Abraham's faith, the faith through which God could do his own work.[6]

With this idea of faith as an attitude of dependence upon God's trustworthiness, however, the question arises as *to whose faith it is that justifies* or saves. This is one area of current debate concerning Paul's idea of justification by faith, particularly as expressed in a number of texts where the formulation *pistis Christou* occurs. The question is whether saving faith is our belief in Christ or our participation in the faith of Christ. Morna Hooker has usefully summarized the issues and findings of recent research, suggesting that for Paul it is Christ's obedience and trust in God which is crucial, "though of course the response of the believer is necessary."[7] Hooker finds it no accident that in all the passages studied there is also a reference to the faith of believers. This response, however, is not simply a matter of believing, and is not best characterized as such. For Paul, to have faith is to be "in Christ" and that means responsive obedience, service, and joyous participation in the life of the Spirit.

James Dunn argues that human believing is a quite crucial and distinct element in Paul's idea of justifying faith, though of course such believing is not to be conceived as a kind of "work" by which people create or merit their salvation. Rather, this belief is an active trust in the righteousness of God, made known decisively in Christ.[8] For Dunn, however, the crucial element in such justifying faith is the freedom it permits and provides, in contrast to "the *restrictiveness* implicit in the counteremphasis on works of the law."[9]

I think Dunn is right to emphasize that to believe in Christ was for Paul to enter into Christ, to "participate" in Christ, through the liberating life of the Spirit. For Paul, Christ was not a person in the past, whose deeds and teachings gave rise to beliefs or doctrines which now people must believe in order to be saved. For Paul, Christ is a life-giving

---

[6] Dunn, *The Theology of Paul the Apostle*, 379.

[7] Morna Hooker, *From Adam to Christ: Essays on Paul* (Cambridge: Cambridge University Press, 1990) ch. 14: "Pistis Christou." A similar conclusion is reached by John Dunnill, who makes a careful study of the relevant texts and recent literature on this issue in Dunnill, "Saved by Whose Faith?"

[8] Dunn, *The Theology of Paul the Apostle*, 379–85.

[9] Ibid., 372–3.

spirit who meets us in the present. Our faithful response is to trust ourselves to Christ, to enter into his life and thus to participate in his faithfulness and salvation.[10] The life of faith was for Paul a life of continuous conversation with God and with his Hebrew tradition. Within this conversation he found great freedom, including what we have previously called the courage to doubt.

Faith, Doubt, and Freedom in Paul

Paul seems to have placed a strong emphasis upon freedom in faith. To remain in Christ enables both an unswerving *commitment to* Christ and a radical *freedom in* Christ, a freedom to express that faith in new ways, within or without the Jewish tradition. Within Paul's letters we can see several interesting ways in which his faith included doubt as part of his response to challenges and difficult situations.

One key issue for Paul seems to have been doubt about his apostleship. Though perhaps he shared these doubts at times, his response was to persist with his ministry. In 1 Corinthians, in particular, we find Paul's defense of his apostleship.

In 1 Cor 9:1-23 Paul does not refer to his calling as the basis of his apostleship, but to his continuing practice of ministry, and to the Corinthians themselves as the evidence that he has this ministry. In 1 Cor 15:9-11 he refers to his experience of meeting or seeing the risen Christ. In both these passages Paul rebuts the challenge to his apostleship with a reaffirmation of his faith. It is important to note, however, that this is not just an assertion. Paul invites his opponents to see what God has done and is doing. His own response to opposition is to keep on with his ministry and availability to God.

Another persistent issue for Paul was the question of freedom and strength. Paul seems to have been criticized for being weak, in his leadership as well as in some physical ways. The stereotype of a "strong leader" implied in this criticism involves uncompromising standards, clear-cut convictions, and always carrying through what one has proposed. For Paul, however, genuine strength is not like this at all. Strength in Christ involves the freedom to be subject to others and to tolerate

---

[10] Similarly, John Knox argues that for Paul the Christian life consists in "the shared life of love, faith and hope, which is the life of the Spirit." John Knox, *Chapters in a Life of Paul,* rev. ed. (London: SCM Press, 1989) 98.

moral ambiguity. Those who really are weak are those who may sound "strong" and may think they are strong, but who are unable to live with complexities and ambiguities. Thus to the Corinthians, as also to the Romans, Paul urges both freedom and subjection: because they are free in Christ, they can choose to be subject to those who really are weak (Rom 14:14, 23; 1 Cor 8:1-13; 9:19-20).

There are several significant passages where Paul recognizes and leaves room for moral and even spiritual ambiguity. Not every issue is clear-cut. In his teaching about marriage and divorce, Paul allows several important areas to remain open to judgment in varying situations. In 1 Cor 7, verse 10 is very definite: "I give this command—not I but the Lord. . . ." Here he is very definite, while in verse 12 he takes an opposite stance: "To the rest I say—I and not the Lord. . . ." He leaves open the possibility that the Corinthians may be led to a different judgment. In another very significant passage where Paul mentions his ecstatic experiences (2 Cor 12:1-6), we find a similar tolerance for ambiguity. Twice he says that he just doesn't know exactly what was happening, "whether in the body or out of the body I do not know; God knows." Here there is evidence of a kind of weakness that Paul's opponents would have criticized, whereas Paul himself is able to accept this uncertainty and leave it to God.

As a third example we turn briefly to Paul's references to the book of Job. While there is substantial literature on Paul's use of Old Testament texts and themes generally, very little attention seems to have been given to Paul's references to the book of Job.[11] In a recent study, David Hay has explored these passages, suggesting that "the book of Job influenced him [Paul] significantly."[12] We will consider here just one of these passages.

[11] Here a valuable early study was E. Earle Ellis, *Paul's Use of the Old Testament* (Grand Rapids, Mich.: Baker Book House, 1957, 1981), while a more recent critical study is Craig A. Evans and James A. Sanders, eds., *Paul and the Scriptures of Israel,* Journal for the Study of the New Testament Supplement Series 83 (Sheffield: Sheffield Academic Press, 1993). Of particular value in this discussion is the seminal work of E. P. Sanders, *Paul and Palestinian Judaism: A Comparison of Patterns of Religion* (Philadelphia: Fortress Press, 1977).

[12] David M. Hay, "Job and the Problem of Doubt in Paul," *Faith and History: Essays in Honor of Paul W. Meyer,* ed. John T. Carroll, Charles H. Cosgrove, and Elizabeth E. Johnson (Atlanta: Scholars Press, 1990) 209. Among these passages Hay identifies 1 Corinthians 1–4, Romans 11, and Philippians 1 as significant insofar as they provide an insight into Paul's understanding of religious doubt.

In the opening chapters of 1 Corinthians, Paul is engaged in a discussion of the wisdom of the world which is said to be folly to God. In this context we find a quotation from Job 5:13 (in 1 Cor 3:19). In discussing this text, Hay expounds what he believes to be the doubts Paul is addressing. They are doubts about whether the Christian faith can be combined with and consistent with the other forms of wisdom. But whereas Paul writes confidently of the wisdom given through Christ and of the conflict between God and human wisdom—so much so that from 1 Cor 2 we might gain the impression that he repudiates all forms of human understanding—he is not in this passage suggesting that faith involves a superior epistemology, which is free from doubt and not open to further questioning. On the contrary, *Paul is actually advocating an attitude of openness to doubt.* This is part of the character of divine wisdom. With this quotation from Job—"He catches the wise in their craftiness"—and the subsequent (altered) quotation from Ps 93:11, Paul is suggesting that Christians ought to doubt some things. On the basis of the genuine wisdom they have received, they ought to set aside judgmentalism and any pretense to "know it all." Hay says, "They must have sufficient doubt of their Christian understanding to make them avoid divisiveness and indifference to Paul's teachings."[13] The cumulative impact of Paul's quotations and reference to Job leads Hay to conclude that doubt is not always antithetical to faith. Rather, Christians must hold their own convictions with an appropriate humility, open to learn from others.

These examples indicate that while Paul consistently encourages faith in Christ, that faith has room for ambiguity and tolerance. Paul's vision of faith is governed by love and the freedom of the Spirit rather than a standard of belief.

From these preliminary considerations, we conclude that while Jesus comes preaching the gospel and calling for belief, the faith he seeks is not the kind of belief which excludes all doubt. Rather, it is a kind of belief which engages with him in a conversation that explores continually the meaning, freedom, and possibilities of God's saving presence. We now turn to consider a number of specific passages and themes in the New Testament witness which will further illumine our understanding of doubt and faith in the New Testament.

---

[13] Ibid., 211.

"Little Faith"

In all the Gospels, as throughout the New Testament, there are those who do not believe in Jesus. They are *apistoi*—unbelievers—who do not trust Jesus or receive his teaching about God. Perhaps the most interesting instance here is the community at Nazareth. Mark 6:5-6 tells us that Jesus could not perform works "of power" there and was "amazed at their unbelief."

Between faith and unbelief, we find in Matthew's Gospel the theme of "little faith."[14] In Matt 8:23-27 we find Matthew's version of the stilling of the storm. There are many interesting variations on Mark's text, including the transfer of the discussion about faith from after the miracle to before it. Most important, however, is the "softening" of Jesus' rebuke: "And he said to them, 'Why are you afraid, you of little faith?'" (v. 26). We note the polarity of faith and fear. Here the disciples are not absolutely without faith, but are of little faith, *oligopistoi.*

Another incident on the lake raises the same issue. In Matt 14:25-33, Jesus comes walking on the water, and Peter asks if he can do so too. When Peter begins to sink, Jesus addresses him—literally—as "Little-faith": "You of little faith, why did you doubt?" (v. 31). It is crucial to note that the word translated "doubt" here, *edistasas,* which occurs only here and in Matt 28:17, does not denote unbelief. It has more the meaning of a shift or movement in Peter's trust or focus, away from Jesus toward something else. It means to hesitate in the action one was taking, suggesting that Peter was indeed acting in faith, but now his focus is less absolute, it is mixed with hesitation or "second thoughts." This suggests that faith here means to trust completely in Jesus, and "little faith" or doubt means to trust partially in Jesus, while also attending to someone or something else. In these instances that something else is one's own fear.

On this basis we can agree with Held's suggestion that doubt and little faith are effectively the same thing for Matthew.[15] "Little faith" describes the life of believers insofar as it includes an element of unbelief or fear. It is important to note that the episodes we have discussed thus far do not so much concern belief as trust. The difficulty is not so

---

[14] An exceptionally valuable study here is Heinz Joachim Held, "Matthew as Interpreter of the Miracle Stories," *Tradition and Interpretation in Matthew,* ed. Günter Barth, Gerhard Bornkamm, and Heinz Joachim Held (London: SCM Press, 1963) 165–299.

[15] Ibid., 295.

much a lack of belief as the presence of fear. The disciples are overcome by fear and anxiety, so that they waver in their trust in Jesus, rather than deny their beliefs about Jesus. Indeed, even in his little faith, Peter calls out to Jesus and addresses him as Lord.

In Matt 16:8 we find an instance of "little faith" related to the disciples' anxiety about having no bread and their failure to *remember* the feeding miracles. Here perhaps what is lacking is more precisely *understanding* of what it means to journey with Jesus and to trust in God's provision. So "little faith" can mean a lack of believing and understanding, but this belief is not simply a matter of intellectual assent. It has to do with remembering, and then trusting themselves to the reality of God's provision already clearly demonstrated to them. This is further borne out by other passages where "little faith" is used in relation to anxieties about food (6:30) and about threats to the disciples' lives (8:26; 14:31).

Finally, we turn to the passages which suggest that even a small amount of faith can achieve great things. In Matt 17:20 Jesus says that faith as little as a mustard seed can move a mountain. This saying is repeated in Matt 21:21-22, in the context of Jesus' cursing of the fig tree. Here we find a specific statement opposing faith and doubt: "Truly I tell you, if you have faith and do not doubt, not only will you do what has been done to the fig tree, but even if you say to this mountain, 'Be lifted up and thrown into the sea,' it will be done."

The crucial contrast here is not between small amounts and large amounts of faith. It is vital to resolve this confusion that has led many people to be concerned about the quantity of their faith. Held says the contrast here is between faith in an absolute sense and "impaired" faith.[16] "Little faith" and doubt are "broken" faith, which has come to include some element of unbelief or hesitation within the life of discipleship. It is not outright or "complete" trust, but neither is it abandonment of that trust, in outright unbelief or distrust.

By contrast, the faith which can move mountains is strong, but its strength resides in its object—God. To have such faith—and perhaps Matthew and Mark both imply that only Jesus ever actually exercised such faith—is not a matter of the "proportions" or capacities of the believer or disciple. It is rather to be completely focused upon God, trusting in God and in that sense to forget entirely about how much faith one has or does not have. *For to be concerned about the measure of one's faith is actually to doubt,* to have "little faith."

---

[16] Ibid.

To have faith, in Matthew's sense, is to be open to the surprising possibilities of God and of ourselves. It is not about a strong adherence, by moral or intellectual effort, to what is already known. Rather, it is a trustful openness to divine possibilities as embodied in Jesus and his mission. Doubt as "little faith" may mean simply a hesitancy in trusting oneself to God, or it may actually reveal a preoccupation with one's own faith. There is a close association between little faith and fear. By contrast, faith involves a trusting response to Jesus, in spite of fears and the "measure" of one's faith.

"Doubting Thomas"

Of all the characters in the Bible, Thomas is the person most widely associated with the concept of doubt, so much so that the term "Doubting Thomas" has become a part of the language generally. Whether Thomas should be represented as a figure of doubt, and what significance we attribute to that doubt, is open to debate.

Apart from being named in the other Gospels as one of the twelve apostles, Thomas is mentioned only in three brief instances in John's Gospel. If we consider these stories together, in their Gospel context, we can understand better the nature of Thomas's response to Jesus.

We first meet Thomas in John 11, when Jesus proposes to go to Bethany because Lazarus is ill. While the other disciples object, on the grounds that the Jews had recently tried to stone him, Thomas says, "Let us also go, that we may die with him" (v. 16). Rudolf Bultmann sees here a statement of resignation to the fate that threatens the disciples as well as Jesus.[17] Raymond Brown makes no comment here, but later gathers this into his picture of Thomas's "obstinacy."[18]

Next we meet Thomas in chapter 14, where Jesus speaks of "the Way." Where he is going the disciples may go also, for they know the way. Thomas protests that they do not know where Jesus is going, so how can they know the way. Brown sees this incident within the overall theme of seeing and not seeing. For John, faith is a form of seeing, while its opposite is blindness. Thomas here expresses such blindness: he does not know the way.

---

[17] Rudolf Bultmann, *The Gospel of John: A Commentary,* trans. G. R. Beasley-Murray (Oxford: Basil Blackwell, 1971) 400.

[18] Raymond E. Brown, *The Gospel According to John,* The Anchor Bible, vol. 2 (New York: Doubleday, 1970) 1045.

If, however, we consider these two incidents together we see a person who speaks for his fellow disciples, expressing their natural human responses to Jesus. In the first situation, he may be "resigned" to dying with Jesus, or obstinate, or we might regard his attitude as one of courage. He is prepared to go with Jesus, even if it involves dying with him. Then when Jesus says they know the way Thomas protests that it is not clear to them.

It is important to note that in John 14 Jesus does not rebuke Thomas or repudiate his question. John's purpose is not to present Thomas in a bad light, as ignorant or recalcitrant, but as a typical example of all those who need to be drawn from a human way of seeing into the light of God. Thomas serves John's purpose of setting in contrast two ways of seeing. Much of the earlier material of the gospel identifies the spiritual blindness of "the Jews" and the teachers in the Temple. Now, however, John suggests that disciples too can fail to know the Way. Thomas at least acknowledges this.

Finally, we come to the incident for which Thomas is called a doubter. In John 20 we read of two incidents in an upper room. In the first the risen Jesus appears to the disciples, but Thomas is absent. Significantly, the others seek him out to tell him of their great discovery. Thomas declares that unless he can see the mark of the nails in his hands, and put his finger in the mark of the nails and his hand in Jesus' side, he will not believe (John 20:25). The detailed statement of "demand" has the effect of emphasizing Thomas' deep need to know. He will not believe just because others have said so: he must know for himself that Jesus is risen. Francis Moloney describes this as Thomas' conditioned faith. He does not rule out the possibility of resurrection, but he wants to believe on his own terms.[19] When next Jesus appears, he and Thomas "have it out." Jesus invites Thomas to see his hands and put his hand in Jesus' side, then says: "Do not doubt but believe." Thomas' response is a deeply personal declaration of faith, with a double "my": "My Lord and my God."

What significance do we attribute to Thomas' demand to know for himself that Jesus really is risen? Brown discusses this in terms of disbelief and demand. He says that John clearly disapproves of Thomas' attitude, expressing it in similar terms to that condemned by Jesus in 4:48:

[19] Francis J. Moloney, *The Gospel of John*, Sacra Pagina, vol. 4, ed. Daniel J. Harrington (Collegeville: The Liturgical Press, 1998) 537.

the Jews' demand to see signs and wonders or else they will not believe. In his comment here Brown uses strong words of disapproval, such as "reprehensible," and then says that Thomas, "despite his tendencies, is capable of being led to faith." Jesus is said to "accuse" Thomas of several failings.[20] The "tendencies" of which Thomas is guilty are taken to be inherently wrong. Brown seems to have overstated his case quite unnecessarily here. As he and other commentators have observed, the function of this story is indicated by the concluding statement of Jesus: "Have you believed because you have seen me? Blessed are those who have not seen and yet have come to believe" (John 20:29). This is John's main point: he is concerned for a community of disciples who cannot see Jesus or touch his side but are yet called to faith.[21]

Is it necessary to regard Thomas as a reprehensible character of bad tendencies because he wanted to know for himself that Jesus really is risen? I think not. We need rather to take the point John is offering: in faith, we are called to a "sight" which cannot always have the degree of proof we want. We may indeed be called to go with Jesus and die with him. We may be called to go a way we do not know, trusting in Jesus who is "the Way." We may also be called to a very deep personal encounter with Jesus. This is not a faith we can create or control; it is the gift of the Spirit, which blows where *it* wills.

What, then, is Thomas asked to stop doing, when Jesus says, "Do not doubt?" Should we say with Brown that Thomas is without faith? If we make such an absolute separation, in which Thomas' doubt indicates a total lack of faith, we are making belief the essential test and criterion of faith. But at no point has Jesus actually condemned or rebuked Thomas. Indeed, he grants Thomas his "demand"—though we are not told that Thomas actually carried it out by touching Jesus. It is important here to see that Thomas is part of the discipleship group, and Jesus is dealing with him as one of his own. On this basis, I think it more appropriate to represent the Thomas stories as part of the continuing process of faith. This is another episode in the conversation with God, embodied in Jesus, which helps us to see what faith is actually about.

Faith for Thomas involved going with Jesus. At times this faith was expressed as courage, or maybe even resignation. At times it was expressed in a deep questioning: what does it mean to follow Jesus? At

---

[20] Brown, *The Gospel According to John,* 1045–46.

[21] See, for example, Rudolf Schnackenburg, *The Gospel According to St. John,* vol. 3 (London: Burns & Oates, 1982) 330–1.

other times it involved a deep struggle, when Thomas was unable simply to go along with what the others said. The continuing conversation of faith, for all who read John's stories of Jesus and of Thomas, may involve each of these elements. Given these struggles, John wishes to encourage his community to trust even when they are unable to "see." When Thomas is asked to stop doubting and to believe, he is simply being asked to trust Jesus, to come the next step. Doubting is represented here as the penultimate, the form of faith from which Thomas now moves. It is not a move from "disbelief," if by that we mean an absence of faith, but from a form of faith which has not reached the peace and joy Jesus wishes to give him.

In offering us this story, John also indicates to us the potential of doubt. It is ambiguous. It might indeed involve the negative attitudes Brown and others have attributed to Thomas. Doubt has the potential to move in the opposite direction to Thomas—from doubt to unbelief. But John shows us that doubt does not have to separate us from the community of faith or from Jesus.

Here then is another set of possibilities and responses in the conversation of faith with Jesus. We may, like Thomas, encounter Jesus in such a way as to move from doubting faith to a deeper confession of Jesus as Lord and God. John's purpose and wish is that all disciples may be able to make this move. That is why he has written his gospel.

"The Double-Minded" in James

There are just a few verses in the epistle of James which speak about doubt in strongly negative terms, and which have contributed to the impression many people have that the Bible consistently disapproves of doubt. In particular, we find in James 1 the suggestion that a person who doubts can expect nothing from God. A careful study of these verses will help us to see yet another way in which faith can develop as conversation with God. In so doing we discover that the attitude James condemns, "double-mindedness," is not a state of intellectual doubt, but more a moral attitude or personal disposition. For the purposes of our discussion it will be helpful to quote these few verses in full:

> If any of you is lacking in wisdom, ask God, who gives to all generously and ungrudgingly, and it will be given you. But ask in faith, never doubting, for the one who doubts is like a wave of the sea, driven and tossed by the wind; for the doubter, being double-minded

and unstable in every way, must not expect to receive anything from the Lord (Jas 1:5-8).

Draw near to God, and he will draw near to you. Cleanse your hands, you sinners, and purify your hearts, you double-minded (Jas 4:8).

These verses must be seen in their context within the entire letter of James. The first chapter in particular deals with a series of problems which James' readers may be facing. It is like a check-list of issues, each being touched upon briefly, including the Christians' attitude to struggles, what to do when facing difficult decisions or a need for wisdom, dealing with poverty or wealth, with temptation and trials, and finally with the nature of true religion, "pure and undefiled before God." In relation to each, James hopes to show the character of true faith and to encourage his community to practice this "true religion."

Faith for James is an attitude of responsiveness to God, and his sayings draw the hearers and readers constantly to recognize God as the one who generously gives all they need, if they are open to receiving it from God. Faith, then, includes an appropriate receptivity and a spirit of thankfulness toward God. It includes a willingness to learn and a preparedness to act courageously and with trust in God, knowing that God will make good from every situation. Søren Kierkegaard summed this attitude up with the phrase "heart enough to be confident." He emphasized that the issues at stake in James' exhortation are "heart" issues, questions of attitude and personal engagement, not theoretical or intellectual issues.[22]

With this background we come to James's treatment of doubt. The question arises concerning those who lack wisdom, that is, the moral discernment which will enable us to live the Christian way. Wisdom enables us to know what to do, and clearly if faith involves active living we will need such wisdom. In this need, we can pray to God who will

---

[22] Søren Kierkegaard, *Edifying Discourses: A Selection,* ed. with an intro. by Paul L. Holmer (London: Collins, 1958) ch. 2: "Every Good and Every Perfect Gift Is from Above." See also Timothy Polk's excellent exposition and discussion of this discourse and its significance for our understanding of the epistle of James: Timothy Polk, "'Heart Enough to Be Confident': Kierkegaard on Reading James," *The Grammar of the Heart: New Essays in Moral Philosophy and Theology,* ed. Richard H. Bell (San Francisco: Harper and Row, 1988) 206–33. This essay has been reproduced in Timothy Polk, *The Biblical Kierkegaard: Reading by the Rule of Faith* (Macon, Ga.: Mercer University Press, 1997).

give us what we need. But we should pray without doubting. What is the character of doubt here?

James characterizes the doubting person with a term used here and in 4:8, and nowhere else in the Bible, and previously unknown in Greek literature: *diakrinomenos,* translated "double-minded." The metaphor of the wave tossed by the wind evocatively suggests the double-minded person's lack of direction and self-control. Ralph Martin explains: "The word speaks of a person marked by irresolution where moral choices are concerned, hence the indictment of that person's character as one controlled by the moods of doubting, hesitating to act decisively."[23] The verse is about praying for wisdom. Such prayer needs to have the quality of faith we have described earlier: it should be "engaged" faith, serious and willing to act, to "have a go." The doubt which James condemns here is a kind of praying which only partially expects that God will help. It is not outright unbelief, it is prayer without conviction, without "heart." James therefore wishes to direct his readers toward God and God's willingness to help everyone in need. All that is needed from the double-minded is to "purify" their hearts, and that means, according to 4:8, "to draw near to God."

This does not mean, however, that the one who prays must do so with absolute definiteness or clarity about what they are seeking. This is precisely James's point. He is addressing a situation where someone *lacks* this clarity, and he is saying they should not struggle for or wait for that clarity before they can approach God. God is generous, gracious, and willingly assists those who openly and unreservedly ask for help. The problem of double-mindedness is that some other concern is preventing an unreserved expectation from God and a total commitment to the way of God.

The letter of James is about the logic of the heart and the potential of faith that is pure in heart. All too easily the problem of doubt and "double-mindedness" are represented as intellectual problems, or as a situation where people trust their reason to direct them, rather than God. This sets up a destructive dichotomy between faith and thinking, between religion and reason. Kierkegaard's analysis of doubt has this potential, too, if we do not attend carefully to what he is advocating.

Timothy Polk has helpfully outlined the "anatomy" of doubt in Kierkegaard's thought, showing that it includes elements of carelessness or not addressing one's situation seriously. But it may also involve a form

---

[23] Ralph P. Martin, *James: Word Biblical Commentary,* vol. 48 (Waco, Tex.: Word Books, 1988) 20.

of sorrow. This I think is an especially helpful insight. In such sorrow, unresolved issues and pain from the various hurts of life cause us to expect less than we might from God or from the future: we are wary. The idea that everything comes from God is now changed: we now think that only the good things, or the things we think are good, come from God. For the rest we nurse our sorrow and perhaps even some quiet resentment.[24] What Kierkegaard calls for here, following James, is a singularity of heart, which accepts *everything* as a gift from God. Such an openness will be receptive, but will also move on from the regrets to new action and will discover afresh the generosity of God's care.

This analysis also suggests how doubt is to be dealt with. To "purify" one's heart does not require denying the issues, problems, or concerns which may have arisen. These questions are not to be ignored or repudiated as "unspiritual." They too are part of what God "gives." To allow them any other status is to have two "minds" or to live in two realities, one from God and another which is apart from God. I think it is crucial to see that much "religion" has precisely this character, separating matters of the "spirit" from other concerns of life. In effect, such religion is a form of double-mindedness. James is suggesting that faith receives and accepts all things from God, praying for the wisdom which enables us to live with God in all aspects of our experience.

Here we have seen another aspect of doubt, in its potential to distort faith or to hold us back from a continuing, open conversation with God. What is significant in this analysis of doubt is that any element in our experience, including our religious beliefs or special "spiritual" concerns, can do this. Doubt or double-mindedness is not the opposite of belief, but a particular stance or form of belief which separates the "things of God" from other aspects of life. If we divide our lives into that which relates to and comes from God and that which does not, we are already double-minded and in doubt.

How then is it possible to have that faith which is pure in heart? James confidently encourages his readers to trust God. Faith is not a state of perfection of belief, wisdom or love, but a continual responsiveness to God's presence and generosity. Such faith will most likely involve struggle and suffering. The challenge of faith is to engage with such difficulties as part of a living conversation with God. In the next section we see an illustration of such purity of heart in the suffering of Jesus.

---

[24] Polk, "Heart Enough to Be Confident," 222.

Suffering Doubt

A number of contemporary works in Christology have noted that Jesus was consistently resisting and opposing various ideas of God and God's reign. Marcus Borg, for example, plays on the expression "conventional wisdom" to argue that Jesus was a Wisdom teacher who sought to subvert the traditional and accepted view of God (and thus of wisdom) and to replace it with a more radical vision.[25] In his innovative work, *Jesus: An Experiment in Christology*, Edward Schillebeeckx has described the way Jesus resisted a "narrow and oppressive idea of God," which places a screen between humans and God. The people are burdened by legal obligations but are not able to see how these bring them into a saving relationship with God.[26] In contrast to this view of God was Jesus' own *Abba* experience, "the source and secret of his life and mission." God for Jesus is the welcoming, nourishing, and creative source of all things, the provider of all we need and the one who promises a new order or new creation. This is not a *new* understanding of God; it is the God known in the Hebrew Bible as both present and elusive. Yet this very intimacy with God also gives rise to a deep experience of alienation or abandonment by God, in Jesus' passion and death.

In Mark's account of the crucifixion, Jesus is heard to cry out, "My God, my God, why have you forsaken me?" (Mark 15:34). With this and an inarticulate "loud cry," Jesus dies. These are his last words to the God he has served and proclaimed all the way. This cry of dereliction sets Jesus right at the heart of the stream of doubting responses seen throughout the Bible.[27] Here from the mouth of the Christ, the Son of God, we hear the deepest possible cry of despair.

[25] Marcus J. Borg, "New Understandings of Jesus and Motives for Contemporary Evangelism," *Jesus in Contemporary Scholarship* (Valley Forge, Pa.: Trinity Press International, 1994). Borg sees Jesus as emphasizing God's holiness as compassion, in contrast to the received wisdom in which God's holiness is understood as purity. See also Marcus J. Borg, *Meeting Jesus Again for the First Time* (New York: HarperCollins, 1995).

[26] Edward Schillebeeckx, *Jesus: An Experiment in Christology* (New York: Seabury Press, 1979) 229–56. The quotation is from 256. A similar exposition of Jesus' ministry as a joyous celebration of being with God can be found in Leonardo Boff, *Jesus Christ Liberator: A Critical Christology for Our Time* (London: SPCK, 1980).

[27] An excellent survey of the history of theological interpretations of this cry can be found in Gerard Rosse, *The Cry of Jesus on the Cross: A Biblical and Theological Study* (New York: Paulist Press, 1987). Rosse's conclusion is that the cry of dereliction should be understood as revelatory. It shows us not only the saving love of God but also the character of the trinitarian life of God.

It is important to see this cry in continuity with the Gethsemane ex-perience. Here, too, Jesus is in great turmoil. He struggles with what has now become clear to him, that his devotion to God really does mean death, and very soon. Jürgen Moltmann has written in several places about this struggle, noting that here for the first time in Jesus' life he does not wish to be alone with his Father. Jesus asks the disciples to stay awake with him because it is terrifying to face this call of God. As Heb 2:9 sug-gests, he was "apart from God" for a time. Moltmann observes, "The Gethsemane story [Mark 14:32-42] reflects the frightening eclipse of God in which Jesus died."[28] This is the absolute nadir of Jesus' *Abba* ex-perience. Moltmann further comments that Jesus who had known him-self to be the child of God now experiences the silence of God.

The cry of despair from the cross makes a direct link with the psalms of lament, for indeed it is a direct quotation from Psalm 22. Like the psalmist, Jesus cries out to God, because the wicked are prospering, and he who has lived his life in the closest devotion and obedience to God is now suffering and dying. But this cry of dereliction also stands in conti-nuity with Job. Like Job, Jesus holds fast to God even as he shouts out in protest to God. His despair is addressed to the one who seems to have abandoned him. Eduard Schweizer has expressed this very nicely:

> The cry of Jesus summarizes in an extraordinarily meaningful way both aspects of what is happening here: it is a radical expression of the loneliness of Jesus' suffering. He has to bear not only the experi-ence of being abandoned by men [*sic*] but also of being forsaken by God. At the same time, however, it is a radical expression of a devo-tion to God which endures in every adverse experience—a devotion which continues to claim God as "my" God and will not let him go although he can be experienced only as the absent One who has for-saken the petitioner.[29]

In this cry of despair, as also in the anguish in the garden, we see Jesus struggling with what we may call the loss of all meanings. His life has been directed by an experience and vision of God, such as he has expounded in his preaching of the *basilea* of God, the coming of God's way or reign. But now all that seems to have come to nothing, and he

[28] Jürgen Moltmann, *The Way of Jesus Christ: Christology in Messianic Dimensions*, trans. Margaret Kohl (London: SCM Press, 1990) 166.

[29] Eduard Schweizer, *The Good News According to Mark*, trans. Donald H. Madvig (London: SPCK, 1971) 353.

who proclaimed life is confronted with death in its most agonizing and brutal form. It is not only Jesus' personal death that is expressed here, but the death of his life's mission and meaning. Yet the astonishing thing about Jesus' death is that this absolute desolation and despair is also a form of faith. This too is directed to God and offered to God as prayer of protest. Even here, the *Abba* experience expresses itself, albeit in the most paradoxical form. Like Job, Jesus will not give up on God.

In Jesus' cry from the cross we see another expression of faithful doubt. This doubting cry is part of his continuous responsiveness to God, divine conversation embodied. Here anguish and bewilderment are offered to God. This is courageous faith in the form of doubt. With such "courage to doubt" Jesus commits his life to God. The divine conversation has come to a confronting, haunting silence.

"But Some Doubted"

All the writers of the New Testament acknowledge that it is possible to doubt the resurrection. We have noted the experience of Thomas. Paul's argument in 1 Corinthians 15 directly addresses the suggestion that Christ is not raised. Clearly there is an element of apologetic in the empty tomb traditions.[30] All the writers recognize that here doubt is present and seek to bear witness to the presence of the risen Christ, to address that doubt.

In this context, it is interesting to consider the brief passage at the conclusion of Matthew's Gospel, where Jesus delivers a final missionary commission to the disciples. The eleven went to the mountain in Galilee as directed by Jesus, where he appeared to them. When they saw him, "they worshiped him; but some doubted" (Matt 28:17). Jesus then "came to them" and declared that all authority in heaven and earth has been given to him, and on this basis the disciples are sent to make disciples of every nation.

What significance do we attribute to the phrase, "but some doubted"? First, it is important to note that those who doubt are among the eleven, and not, as some exegetes over the centuries have wanted to suggest, an unnamed group of other people on the fringes of the group

---

[30] For a succinct summary of contemporary evaluations of the various resurrection traditions, see John Barclay, "The Resurrection in Contemporary New Testament Scholarship," *Resurrection Reconsidered,* ed. Gavin D'Costa (Oxford: Oneworld, 1996) 13–30.

of disciples. Charles H. Giblin has gathered significant textual arguments to rebut this suggestion.[31] We have seen already that Matthew's
picture of the disciples includes their "little faith." Doubt and little
faith do not disqualify them from being disciples.

Next we must note that Matthew is not here referring to unbelief,
nor even that mixture of faith and unbelief called "little faith." Here
again we meet the term *edistasas,* used only twice in the Bible, both
times by Matthew. Earlier, Jesus asked Peter why he had doubted while
walking on the water, and now a number of them doubt. *The Jerusalem
Bible* translates this verse, "but some hesitated," helpfully conveying the
nuance of the term Matthew uses. It is a word denoting hesitation in
action but does not carry the connotation of unbelief.[32]

Third, we can affirm with commentators such as Ellis that this is
part of Matthew's picture of discipleship. The life of the disciples of
Jesus does include times of doubt. As we have said, the reality of the
resurrection remains open to doubt. In this passage, Jesus' appearance
to the disciples does not involve such incontrovertible proof that doubt
is impossible. Nor does he annul their doubt by some demonstrative
proof, as is suggested in other appearance stories, such as Luke 24:24-
43 or John 20:27. Matthew has quite a different purpose. Indeed Ellis
suggests that this is not so much a resurrection appearance story as a
Matthean story about "the authoritative word of Jesus to the Church."[33]
Had it been Matthew's purpose to offer "proof" of the resurrection—
such as he has offered in the earlier part of the chapter—there might
have been some difficulty in mentioning the fact of doubt amongst the
disciples. But Matthew's purpose is otherwise. Indeed, as Leonora
Tidsdale has effectively argued, Matthew's argument in 28:1-10 does
not remove all basis for questioning the resurrection. Rather, Matthew's
account shows that it is not proofs of reason or historical details, but
only the presence of the living Christ that provides that assurance and
conviction which enables us to believe.[34]

[31] Charles H. Giblin, "A Note on Doubt and Reassurance in Mt. 28:16-20," *Catholic Biblical Quarterly* 37 (January 1975) 68–75.

[32] An excellent discussion of the terms available to Matthew and the significance of
his use of *distazo,* or the Latin *dubito,* can be found in I. P. Ellis, "But Some Doubted,"
New Testament Studies 14 (July 1968) 574–80.

[33] Ibid., 580.

[34] Leonora Tubbs Tidsdale, "Matthew 28:1-10: Expository Article," *Interpretation*
42 (January 1988) 63–8.

Why then does Matthew mention this doubt? Ellis argues that it serves to direct attention away from the subjective state of the disciples and toward "what Christ does with them." The crucial issue is not belief as such but discipleship. On the pathway of discipleship there will be difficulties; some will hesitate, but all are called and commissioned by Jesus.

In support of this conclusion we note that Jesus does not rebuke this doubt, nor even comment upon it. Rather, the immediate response is that Jesus "came to them." There is no selectivity here: the risen Christ comes to them all, including to those who doubted. Their mission is not based on their own faith, but entirely upon the call and commission of Jesus. They do not "merit" this call by the measure of their belief, nor forfeit it because of their doubt. Matthew's point is precisely that those who worshiped with single-hearted devotion *and* those who worshiped and doubted are all gathered into the community where Jesus is known as authoritative Lord.

Thus, Matthew's picture of the discipleship community makes no pretense about struggle and doubt. It will always be possible to doubt, and the only resolution of that situation is when Jesus comes to them, drawing forth worship and obedience. This is a crucial insight both into the nature of the resurrection as such and the dynamics of faith and doubt. For Matthew the risen Christ is known through the obedience of discipleship.

Those who doubt are not disqualified, for doubt itself is likely to be part of the journey. But the invitation is for all to continue in conversation with Jesus "to the end of the age." It is thus left as an open question whether those who have faith and doubt, and those who find themselves in "little faith," will go on in obedience of Christ's call, or if their hesitancy will resolve itself in unbelief.

With this question we conclude our peripatetic survey of scriptural witness to the divine conversation and the role of doubt within the response of faith. We have identified a range of doubting responses to Jesus as the embodiment of divine conversation. We have seen the potential of doubt as a creative element within faith, as well as some ways in which doubt may reflect a distortion or limitation of faith. While we make no claim to an exhaustive study, nor to having covered all aspects of biblical witness to faith, it can reasonably be concluded that the Bible envisages a continuing exploration of the divine conversation. In no sense has the questioning and inviting approach of God come to an end with the closure of the biblical canon. Rather, as Brueggemann suggests, YHWH continues to place before us the options and possibilities and "the choosing is not yet finished."[35] The Spirit of God is yet working to gather us and the whole creation, with our own consent, into the divine conversation.

The question which remains for us to consider, then, is how the conversation of faith, belief, and doubt is to be worked out today, in a vastly different world. This will be the subject of our next chapter.

---

[35] Walter Brueggemann, *Theology of the Old Testament: Testimony, Dispute, Advocacy* (Minneapolis: Fortress Press, 1997) 562, and further at 747–50.

10

Constructive Aspects of Doubt

In this chapter we will gather together a number of insights into the relation of doubt and faith, drawn from the various frameworks and perspectives we have studied. These insights provide us with constructive ways of understanding and responding to what has been a perpetual problem for theology and for many individuals in the modern period, the alleged tension or polarity between doubt and faith. We will identify a number of conclusions about the nature of doubt and its significance within the life of faith. We will offer a number of clarifications of concepts and experiences, which have practical and pastoral consequences for individuals and for communities of faith. Finally, we will offer some directions for further theological exploration of our theme.

Beyond Belief and Doubt

As we saw at the outset, in the modern period Christian faith has seen itself as under challenge from critical reasoning, which uses doubt as a method for discovering knowledge and furthering our understanding. If faith is understood as a form of belief which needs justification in the face of critical questioning, a polarity is set up between faith and doubt. It is now possible, however, to break this polarity by challenging the framework within which these ideas are formulated. In particular, it is necessary to challenge the identification of faith with a state of belief in which an individual person assents to a conclusion for which they do not or may not have sufficient evidence.

The modern polarity between faith and doubt is misleading in a number of ways. Though the modern "project" sought to make human experience the measure of all things, in fact the representation of faith as a state of belief without doubt fails to reflect the reality of human experience. In this study we have found that faith is more than belief and can include doubt as a meaningful and significant element. We will address each of these conclusions in turn.

Christian faith involves far more than belief and cannot be reduced to belief. Beliefs about items of doctrine, such as the existence and nature of God and God's relationship with the world, with human beings, and so on, are all elements in faith. But faith is far more than belief. It has been the identification of faith with belief that has created much of the personal and conceptual difficulty associated with the "problem" of doubt.

Belief *is* an important element in faith. We might call it an implicate of faith: it is something which is implied in faith. If for example someone has faith in God, that implies that they believe some things about God. To say that faith is more than belief is not to dismiss the element of belief as unimportant or nonessential. It is rather to insist that one essential element is not the only crucial aspect of this part of our experience. A school, for example, cannot function without teachers. They are essential to the life of the school, but they are not the only essential elements. Similarly with faith. There are a number of elements which are essential in the life of faith, properly understood. Although at times some of these elements may be absent or not as prominent, they are nonetheless essential to what faith is. Doubt is one such element, as also are belief, worship, and participation in a faith community. To reduce faith to any one of these elements is a mistake.

In Chapter 2 we discussed Newman's attempt to explain the character of faith as complex assent, based upon a real apprehension of an idea or proposition. Newman was right, I think, to stress the essentially personal character of faith-commitments. In faith we are involved as persons. We come to commitments which involve us not only in believing ideas or truths, but in living out those beliefs. A faith commitment is different from the conclusion of a process of reasoning. This is why Newman developed the idea of faith as assent. But Newman also sought to explain faith in terms of *certainty,* a form of assent which admits of no degrees. Here we found an inherent inadequacy in Newman's account of faith, for in the end his view of faith is dependent upon a personal encounter with the reality of God. It was this element in Newman's account which we found insufficiently explained and led us to explore other theological frameworks.

Newman's account of faith as unconditional assent also indicates other reasons we should not limit faith to belief. Newman makes faith an all-or-nothing matter, a perfection. If we have faith we have it maximally, and if we do not have such complete assent then we have no faith at all. Those who doubt have no faith at all, since doubt and assent are incompatible. We have found, however, that in a number of ways doubt may be an expression of faith. Both in Old and New Testaments we found indications of "faithful doubt." This suggests that the all-or-nothing view of faith is inappropriate. Indeed I would suggest it is positively harmful, leading people into much deception, suspicion, and fear. People pretend that they have a strong conviction when really they do not, while others who have doubts think that they have no faith at all. Furthermore, this all-or-nothing idea of faith is contrary to the facts of our experience, to which Newman also appealed as an adequate basis for his ideas of faith. People consistently speak of their faith as being strengthened by experiences they have undergone. If we can speak of faith being weaker or stronger in these ways, faith can exist in degrees; to this extent it is different from assent.

We also found in the theology of Harry Williams the description of what we might call "fearful belief." Williams contrasts faith, which can live with doubt and uncertainty, and a fearful state in which belief is maintained as a wall of protection against genuine engagement with other people and with the truth about ourselves. What appears as certainty and strength is really fear and self-deception. Though Williams sometimes seems to suggest that all enthusiastic professions of faith have this nature, we do not have to make this generalization. But we can agree that at least sometimes what appears to be fervent belief in God is in fact more focused upon the maintenance of an essentially protective and self-serving attitude. As a result, it is too simplistic to reduce faith to the idea of individual avowals of belief.

Another reason to reject a simple identification of faith with belief is that it implies a static view of faith and of personal life. It does not take account of the dynamics of personal life, in which we change through time: we mature, we are unsettled and later become more "mellow" or "philosophic," and so on. It is for this reason that Val Webb emphasizes the aspect of process or journey in faith. Though she expresses some reservations about the possible implication that a journey has a definite destination, her concept of faith as "adventure" emphasizes the dynamic aspect of personal life. For Webb, doubt is an essential part of what keeps faith "moving," alive and free to change. Our faith is *us,* engaged in the on-going exploration of life and its meaning, in response to God.

It is in this context that we can identify one of our most important findings about doubt and its relation to faith. Many who struggle with questions of faith are not struggling with propositions and their credibility, at a reflective level. They are struggling with God, with the "content" of their faith as a reality. They are struggling to grasp what this is really about. As such, to doubt is not to deny the importance or the reality of God. Rather, as Tillich suggests, it may be precisely the expression of a person's seriousness about faith, their deep passion for God and concern about what it means to have faith in God. Faith may take the form of a quest for truth and integrity, rather than assent to what is said to be the truth but does not appear as coherent or credible.

Faith, then, is a more complex dimension of our lives, individually and collectively, than is suggested by a simple identification of faith with assent or belief. *Faith can include doubt as well as belief.* Indeed Tillich and Williams suggest that all faith includes an element of doubt. We may not necessarily experience this doubt as such, but in every act of faith there is a courageous commitment, taking on a risk. In the life-story theologies of Williams and Webb we found valuable accounts of how doubt can be part of the on-going dynamics of personal life. In our own development of a theology of divine conversation we proposed a framework for understanding faith as a continuous responsiveness to God, in belief, doubt, protest, searching, and many other elements.

What is common to all these arguments is the idea that faith includes an essential element of mystery and thus requires that we maintain an appropriate sense of "reserve" or qualification in all our theological assertions, doctrines, and belief statements. Even Barth, whose theology centers on the idea of a self-revealing God, insisted that what is revealed to us is the hiddenness (or mystery) of God. One outcome of these arguments is the suggestion *that doubt can help us to preserve faith as faith.* To accept and welcome doubt may help faith to remain faithful, rather than lead to an abandonment of faith. Where all doubt is eschewed, in pursuit or defense of a state of certitude, faith loses the element of mystery, the sense of the holiness or "otherness" of God. Without doubt, faith ceases to be faith and in so doing it centers upon a reality other than God, something less than God. The "knowledge" available to us through such "faith" may provide us with a satisfying sense of certitude, for a time, but it will not mediate to us the life-enhancing presence of God. By contrast, a faith which genuinely embraces doubt is open to the surprising presence of a creative God, who both uses and transcends the recognized "mediums" of the divine presence.

These arguments lead us to stress the ambiguity of doubt. From the outset, I have suggested that doubt is an ambiguous phenomenon. It can be destructive, undermining the confidence of individuals and causing them great anxiety, perhaps even debilitating them so that they no longer know what to do or how to respond to the religious dimension of their lives. Equally, doubt may be as liberating and life-enhancing as Val Webb has found it to be. Doubt can have these different consequences or impacts on an individual's life and in the life of a group or community. But doubt is not only a force from "without," which can impact upon us. Doubt is something we do and here too there is much potential for ambiguity. A person may doubt because they are unwilling to face the consequences of commitment in faith, or precisely because they are genuinely concerned to understand and commit themselves fully to that faith. Furthermore, these elements can be mixed together in our lives, occurring at different times and perhaps also at the same time. Given these ambiguities, it is crucial to recognize these features in our understanding of the relationship between doubt and faith.

These considerations bring us back to the crucial question of how faith can include or embrace both belief and doubt. Earlier I asserted that belief is an important element of faith. Yet there is also a definite incompatibility between doubt and belief. How then is it possible to maintain both belief and doubt as elements in faith?

Doubt can be seen as an integral part of faith only when faith is not too closely identified with doctrinal or propositional belief. In the preceding chapters we have identified several different ways of understanding how faith can incorporate doubt. Harry Williams uses metaphors such as faith "living with doubt," doubt being a "traveling companion," and doubt being distributed through the life of faith in many "little heaps" rather than as a constant presence. Val Webb celebrates doubt as the "nudges" of God, luring us along the journey of faith. Taken together, these metaphors suggest that the relationship between faith and doubt needs to be seen within the time-frame and process of our lives.

Within the changing processes of a person's lifetime, faith can include many phases, stages, styles, different forms of response and practice. Underlying all these elements, however, and expressed within them, is an engagement or "concern" with God and the meaning of faith in God. This indicates a significant difference between the concept of faith as assent or belief and the concept of faith as a journey or process. In the former, the emphasis is upon the *truth* of faith, which is to be believed and maintained, despite the changing circumstances of life. The continuity rests in the truth, which is external to the life process of the believing person. In the journey or life process model, the emphasis is much more upon the *meaning* of faith, which necessarily changes in relation to changing situations. In this process, faith quests for meaning and thus for truth. But the truth which is sought here is not considered to be external to the process; the truth is known and lived. As such, in questing for truth-as-meaning, or truth-as-integrity, previous expressions and ways of understanding are called into question. That is to say, they are called into doubt because they are no longer meaningful; they no longer relate to the changed situation. To try to preserve such "truth" of the past would be inauthentic, and as such a denial rather than an act of faith. In this way, the dynamic processes of life and faith bring our beliefs into doubt, as a way of calling forth new forms of faith. Far from being a loss of faith, then, doubt here indicates faith at work, faith that is living and growing.

Exactly how such doubt expresses itself, what form it takes and how it is used, "resolved," or incorporated into new forms of faith will vary from situation to situation, person to person, and phase to phase in a person's life. Thus, for example, in adolescence doubt can lead to exploration and discovery of new insights and possibilities, as inherited forms of faith are strenuously called into question. In later years, doubt may take a more reflective or "philosophic" form, yet may also lead to more focused commitment and action. We may question our youthful conviction about how we would change the world, but may become more determined to act in the areas we can influence, and simply have to leave the rest to the mystery of providence.

It is also important to add that doubt can have a less productive, even a quite negative, meaning in some situations. This possibility causes me to temper the enthusiastic celebration of doubt found, for example, in Webb's book and also to question Tillich's one-sided analysis of doubt as a necessary element in all faith. Sometimes people experience doubt as a turmoil which disturbs their religious convictions and sense of assurance in God. Not everyone is equipped or enabled to deal with this disturbance. In these situations, they may simply feel they have to endure, to hold fast to what meaning or convictions they do have; or, sadly, they may abandon this aspect of their lives altogether, regarding it as something they thought they understood, but now it is too confusing or perhaps too painful to go on with. These experiences of doubt are real and, I would suggest, quite common, and should be recognized as part of the character and potential of doubt.

The range of possible forms and outcomes of doubt was also seen in the New Testament. James urges the wavering or indecisive person to engage more genuinely in faith. Jesus in some aspects of his ministry is clearly presented as challenging existing "certainties," yet also called people to a faith which trusts God in the face of danger and uncertainties. Paul clearly "pushes back" the frontiers of ideas and the received wisdom, distinguishing between some areas which he saw as central articles of faith and others where he recognized a wide scope for individual differences.

All these factors suggest that there is no single state which is the ideal of faith, in which doubt or questioning is absent. We do not grow in faith toward some such final position and then we have "arrived." There is no time when faith is doubt-free, although there may be many times—and for some persons almost all the time—when faith is not troubled by doubt. For some people, doubt may be experienced as a lively challenge, the spice of life which keeps faith alive, while for others of a different disposition the times when doubt emerges are periods of struggle and growth.

We have been considering the dynamic and personal nature of faith and the complex and sometimes ambiguous character of doubt within the life of faith. These elements lead us to conclude that faith should not be reduced to a static ideal of belief or assent. Another reason for rejecting the strict identification of faith with belief is that it fails to take sufficient account of the *communal aspects* of personal life and of faith. Faith certainly involves us as individuals. We must make our own response, in whatever form. But as persons we are not only individuals. The personal is not limited to the individual, even less the private. Our personal lives include all our personal relationships: I am not only an individual, I am a son, brother, husband, father, colleague, and friend. Our faith interpenetrates all these aspects of our personal lives: it is communal as well as individual.

In the analysis offered in this book, faith is understood as an essentially *responsive* activity. Our faith, along with our entire existence, occurs within the context of God's creation, presented to as an invitation to relationship and conversation. God's revelatory approach to us, illustrated through the form of divine questions, calls us into an exploration of life together. As God's own trinitarian life is communal, so too the life God creates and nurtures through the continuing creativity of the Spirit is communal. The Spirit invites, questions, gathers, and challenges us into a responsive life and a life together. We are drawn into a conversation with each other, with the past, and with the future. We are drawn also to hope, to imagine, and to explore what might be. God is continually posing the questions of meaning and value so fundamentally posed within the Bible, and we are continually offering our responses in a community of faith and doubt.

A Community of Faith and Doubt

In this section we will seek to outline some insights into the nature of the Church which flow from the preceding discussion of doubt and its relation to faith. These may be seen as contributing to the continuing theological inquiry into the nature and mission of the Church, rather than as an alternative ecclesiology as such.

In the light of the foregoing discussion of God the conversationalist, we might describe the Church as the community in which the divine conversation occurs "out-loud." Here the conversation comes to conscious expression. The Church is a community of people who recognize their participation in the cosmic conversation with God. All the elements we saw earlier in the divine-human conversation may be expected and should be included in the life of the Church. Here too God can be seen as inviting response and as embodying the conversation, seeking to gather a genuine consensus. In continuity with Jesus, the life of the Church is to be a life of continuous responsiveness to God, through participation in the divine conversation. In continuity with Israel, we should also expect expressions of trust, adoration, and praise, but also perplexity, protest, and doubt.

The Church as a community of response is essentially a community in process, not having arrived but participating in a journey of faith. This community is not only defined by where it has been but also by where it has not yet been. It is made up of those who know they are members of the community, but includes in its conversation and its reflections even those who do not presently want to be part of the Church. For the Church here is understood as a symbol of the entire human family, an expression of all life. This is not to say that everyone is a member of the Church, or an "anonymous Christian," to use Rahner's famous phrase. Rather, I mean to suggest that the life of the Church gives expression to elements of all human life and all the ways in which humans respond to God. What distinguishes the Church from the rest of human life in the world is the self-consciousness with which the Church participates in the conversation. Understood in this way, the Church is that part of the human community which acknowledges the God who asks questions and seeks to engage actively with them.

The Church as a community of response will understand itself and recognize its life in these terms. It will acknowledge God as inviting source, and celebrate the whole creation as an invitation to life with God. It will acknowledge Jesus Christ as the presence of God, a participant in the conversation, indicating to us the possibilities of human life fully responsive to the divine invitation. It will recognize itself as an element of the Spirit's mission seeking to gather the entire community of creation into a dynamic consensus. As such, the Church will seek to live within the faith it has received. Its life will be guided by the Scriptures, including their witness to the God who asks questions. These characteristics of the Church's life will not be regarded as optional, characteristics of the present phase, but will rather be considered life-defining. The questions God asks *constitute* the Church, defining its identity and direction within the context of God's life as conversationalist.

As the community in which the divine-human conversation comes to self-consciousness, the Church knows itself to be an *open community*. The Church has no exclusive rights to participate in the conversation. Neither does such a Church have "all the answers." It knows itself to be questioned by God, and is more characterized by these questions than any of its attempted responses. The Church thus recognizes itself as but the tip of the iceberg of human response to God. The mission of the Church is to invite all people to recognize and participate in the conversation, not to define and determine how everyone may participate.

What, then, does the Church have to contribute to the conversation? In the light of the God who ask questions, what does the Church have to say for itself? There are two parts to our answer to this question. First, as a community shaped by the biblical witness the Church will set forth and proclaim not itself but Jesus Christ. It will identify him and commend him to all human beings as the one who exemplifies human life at its highest, a life lived wholly conscious of God's presence and responsive to God's purposes. But because it proclaims Christ as such, the Church itself will also seek to live as Christ lived and to order its life toward those four things we recognized earlier about Jesus' life.

Following its Lord, the Church also will seek to explore the conversation with God, following the truth wherever it may lead. The Church will allow itself to be led into the desert, and there tested and tried. The Church will not always seek its comfort, somewhere to "lay its head," but will know itself to be on pilgrimage with Christ. The life of the Church will be open to new explorations, new questions, and new challenges, not claiming to define in advance what can be known about God or limit its adventures of faith to well-worn pathways.

Like Jesus also, the Church will invite others to join the conversation of response to God. Its evangelical witness will remain an essential part of its life. The character of the Church's witness, however, will be influenced by the remaining features of the Church's life in following Christ. As Jesus' life was open and available to others for their questioning, for their interruption and testing, so too the Church will be available to society and to people who wish to challenge its claims and test its witness. The Church which has become used to the surprising presence of God questioning it will welcome these challenges, for among those who question its present ways it may be that God is also provoking the Church to fresh insights.

At the same time, the Church itself will also initiate its own questions, as Jesus did. Ched Myers has argued that the Church needs to question the "imperial" authorities of our own time, as Jesus challenged the established authorities of his day.[1] In addition, the church must question itself and its systems of power, to ensure that it remains responsive to God's call to justice and genuine community. The Church will also, by its very existence as well as its overt statements, challenge the secular interpretation of life and all those values and ways of living that diminish human worth and close off the inviting possibilities inherent in God's creativity. The Church's witness must champion freedom and hope, by repudiating sin and shallowness and by witnessing to the creativity inherent in God's world. It is in these ways that the Church will see its life defined by the way of its Lord and his responsiveness to God.

To further explain the Church's life as self-conscious conversation with God, it is important to add that this conversation will include or relate to all elements of human society. The questions God asks are not

---

[1] Ched Myers, "'I Will Ask You a Question': Interrogatory Theology," ch. 5 in *Theology without Foundations: Religious Practice and the Future of Theological Truth*, ed. Stanley Hauerwas, Nancey Murphy, and Mark Nation (Nashville: Abingdon Press, 1994).

religious questions, if by "religion" we mean a separate domain of human experience relating to "sacred" subjects or rituals. The questions God asks are *life questions,* practical life-style questions dealing with everything from how brothers relate to each other, what we can do about hunger and poverty in the world, right through to our attitudes to ourselves, our illnesses ("Do you want to be healed?"), and our approach to worship. In response, the life of the Church should relate to and draw upon all elements of society and culture. This will involve, I suggest, a two-way protest against secularization. The Church will protest against the designation of particular aspects of life as "sacred," as if these define the arena of God's presence and activity, while also protesting against the idea that other areas of life are "secular." The Church's life will insist on relating to politics and economics, the way laws are made and enforced, just as it will also express itself in prayer for the dying and seeking food for the hungry. The God who challenges all religious idols calls us to engage in life with God in every aspect of our culture and society, and no aspect is outside the agenda for conversation.

Arising out of its life of exploration with God, the Church will offer its convictions both to God and to the wider world. In so doing the Church will articulate its faith. This is possible, however, only as the Church itself engages in the continuing conversation of faith, and this means the struggle of belief and doubt. Quite specifically, the Church will seek to articulate its faith through *formulating the questions* which it believes God is asking, in its present context. Tillich's notion of the method of correlation is of particular help here. He believed this to be the essential method of the Church's theological task in every context and time. Before the Church can formulate "answers" it must articulate the questions. I have suggested, however, that the questions to be considered are not simply to be seen as questions arising from the contemporary context. They are divine questions. In exploring the possibilities and forms of the conversation of life with God, the Church will seek to articulate its faith. This means it will formulate statements of belief and also of doubt. It will identify questions, offer some tentative directions or "answers," recognizing and valuing the contributions of former generations but also allowing doubts and questions to remain if those previous "answers" are not entirely appropriate in the present. In this way, the Church itself will be a living theological community, a conversation about and exploration of the truth of God.

This aspect of the Church's life has immediate implications for local congregational life. I will mention three aspects here. The first concerns the faith of the Church community. The community of faith includes both believers and doubters, or rather, people who at times believe and at other times may doubt. Collectively, the faith of the community includes a dynamic mixture of assurance and perplexity, conviction and questioning. Sometimes these elements are corporate experiences, sometimes they are concentrated in specific individuals or subgroups. But they are all parts of the life of the community of faith.

It is important to remember that in the Bible doubt was given direct expression in the communal life and worship of the Hebrew people—especially through the lament psalms, which as we noted earlier are the largest group of psalms. Similarly, in the New Testament stories of Thomas it is significant that he was sought out by his fellow disciples and brought into the "circle" where he met with Jesus. It is within the community life that faith grows and that doubt can be constructive. Only when it is given expression, in contexts where questioning is welcomed, can doubt be experienced as an invitation to growth. Otherwise individuals feel alienated from the community by their questions, thinking that only they have these questions or only they are troubled by them. Doubts can be constructively dealt with and used as a helpful contribution to the life of the group. In this process, the acceptance of the person who expresses doubt affirms them as a person of faith. The community or group thus upholds them, we might say believing for them while they may not be able to believe for themselves. This can be a very significant source of growth for the entire group.

Second, a local community which sees itself as exploring the divine-human conversation will need *leadership* which evokes and facilitates this process, rather than seeks to control it. In this respect at least, those who lead are to function as facilitators and enablers, drawing forth the contributions of many and enabling them to receive and value each other's different perspectives. As Val Webb has argued, such a community will be a context in which people do not expect their leaders to have all the answers. They will freely acknowledge their own perplexities and limitations, as parts of a common life in which love of one another, rather than maintaining a standard of belief, is the defining purpose.

Finally, in a Church which sees itself as consciously participating in conversation with God, *worship* becomes a central medium of that conversation, including a means by which God confronts the Church with questions. Worship might be defined as the experience or foretaste of the conversation God seeks with all creation. In that worship, the questions God asks will be articulated in an inviting way, thus giving expression to the character of our context. The forms of worship will mirror the creation, seen as God's invitation to response. The whole world is thus offered up to God in worship, as it is recognized as the context of conversation. Similarly, the elements and forms of worship are drawn from the world of our experience, as we express to God what our lives are about, in their fullness and busyness, in their shallowness and shabbiness. But in worship also, what we offer to God is transformed by encounter with the divine life. Our priorities and concerns are set in a different perspective. Our values are challenged, our beliefs *and* questions are called into question, our idols shattered under the impact of the divine presence. All this takes place as we offer, each to the other, a conversation in which faith engages without fear. Following the example of the psalms, laments and protests are offered, and past certainties are questioned, in the search for authentic response. Out of this worship, itself a form of quest, faith emerges and is encouraged and motivated to journey further, to engage in further cycles of witness and challenge, doubt and fresh articulation. In short, the conversation goes on.

These aspects of the life of the faith community raise serious questions, however, about how we are to relate to those who do not believe or who follow a different understanding of God and God's purpose in the world. How does a community of faith which includes and welcomes doubt preach its own message and maintain its identity in the face of the different, people of other faiths and of none?

Welcoming the Other

One of the critical issues for the theology we have advanced in this book concerns the way Christian faith understands and relates to those who are different—the "other." Historically Christians have labeled those who are other as "heretics," meaning that their teaching and worship was "heterodox," something other than the teaching and worship of the one true Church. In this century, however, we have become much more aware of and affirming of difference, welcoming the plurality of forms of worship and polity within the Christian community. The "ecumenical movement" sees the whole Church as the people or household of God, not just one segment or stream of it. The same movement of thought and spirituality is now raising the question of how we respond to other faiths. Our Muslim or Hindu neighbors also worship God and engage in a spiritual journey similar in many ways to our own. What questions and implications does this raise for our understanding of the divine conversation and for the relation of doubt and faith?

Encountering these questions raises numerous practical and theological questions which we cannot address here. But there are two specific aspects which need to be considered, albeit briefly. The first of these concerns the distinctive doctrines of the Christian community. Can a community of faith exist and grow if its defining teachings are subject to question and doubt? If, as we have urged, a local church welcomes questions and indeed fosters exploration and the expression of challenges to existing teachings, will it also be able to proclaim its message unequivocally, in evangelism and prophetic witness? The danger envisaged by this question is that a church which welcomes doubt will be a church without evangelical conviction, a church which is so hesitant in its faith that it is unlikely to attract anyone to believe it and join it. This concern is popularly expressed by evangelical Christians who see doubt as a threat to the missionary activity of the Church. Clearly an unhelpful solution is the suggestion that the Church *en famille* can permit the expression of questioning and doubt, while publicly it articulates an unequivocal message.

On a broader level, these concerns address the role of doctrine within the life of the Church. Newman's position here was very clear. He insisted that those who assent to faith do so on the basis of the Church's teaching and if they assent to any of the Church's doctrine they must assent to it all. Faith is therefore incommensurate with doubt of Church doctrine. Karl Barth's position was characteristically dialectical. In one sense, he would also say that faith excludes doubt of the word of God formulated in the teaching of the Church, since faith is created and determined by that word. But Barth refused to identify the word of God with the Church's doctrine. Rather, he insisted that the Church—and all people of faith—must be continually open to question by the word of God and willing to be responsive to that living word. On this basis Barth himself insisted on the freedom to change his theology. ("If there are Barthians, I am not one of them.") As a result it would seem that Barth would agree that the Church must include both a categorical commitment to its present understanding of God's word, including, for example, active evangelical witness, and a perpetual openness to question, correction, and reproof of our understanding and teaching of that word. To exist in this tension is part of what he called the "existentials" of faith.

The difficulty we saw with this position, as expressed by Stephen Sykes, was that Barth denies the Church, its leaders, and its theologians any ground or standpoint from which to evaluate and judge whether its present doctrine and practice is in conformity with God's word. Barth seems to eschew any subsidiary or temporal criteria by which the Church can, in any specific time and context, test its theology or the questions and proposals which might be put forward for changes in the Church's teaching.[2]

What is needed is a constructive theological framework for the critical evaluation of what we have called faithful doubts, as well as an ongoing evaluation of the Church's faithful belief. How can a community of faith positively include and learn from the challenges to its doctrine from within and without?

One helpful proposal arises from the work of Christopher Morse. In his book *Not Every Spirit: A Dogmatics of Christian Disbelief,* Morse argues that when we are called to faith in God we are called not only to believe some things but also to reject and resist some other things. In faith there is both belief and disbelief. Following the urging of 1 John 4:1, not to believe every spirit, Morse argues that we must refuse some ideas and approaches in order to follow authentically the way of the Spirit of Christ. If we fail to recognize what we should disbelieve, focusing only on what we believe, we are committed to truth that contains a lie. "My thesis is that the truth in Christian doctrine harbours a lie whenever the faithful disbeliefs these doctrines entail go unrecognized."[3] The result is that people are often led into misguided ways of living and acting. In the main body of his work, Morse examines the major doctrines of the Christian faith by indicating what is denied, as well as what is affirmed, by these doctrines. Like Aquinas, he identifies a series of objections or possible misunderstandings of each doctrine, in order to make explicit what is to be faithfully disavowed. Morse seems convinced that in order to be authentic in their faith, people need not

---

[2] See Chapter 3 above. A similar difficulty seems to me to obtain with George Lindbeck's proposal that Christian doctrine should be understood as the cultural-linguistic "grammar" of the Church community. George Lindbeck, *The Nature of Doctrine: Religion and Theology in a Postliberal Age* (Philadelphia: Westminster Press, 1984). Doctrine here makes no truth-claims; rather, it expresses the governing rules of the internal conversation of the Christian community. There seems to be no basis, other than community consensus, by which such a church can establish that its own teaching is valid or that any alternative doctrine is inappropriate. While this view has many strengths, not least its candor, it seems profoundly earth-bound, denying the Church any prospect of grounding its life in the reality of a transcendent God.

[3] Christopher Morse, *Not Every Spirit: A Dogmatics of Christian Disbelief* (Valley Forge, Pa.: Trinity Press International, 1994) 13.

only to know what they believe but also to understand clearly what they may faithfully disbelieve.

Whatever we make of this approach to dogmatic theology, one very valuable part of Morse's work is his discussion of a series of criteria or tests of doctrinal faithfulness.[4] He offers ten such criteria, which together function as "rubrics of accountability within which dogmatic assessments under the constraints of God's Spirit and the mysteries of God's coming are made."[5] The ten factors are: continuity with apostolic tradition, congruence with Scripture, consistency with worship, catholicity, consonance with experience, conformity with conscience, consequence, cruciality, coherence, and comprehensiveness.

With the first two criteria, Morse appeals beyond the Reformation division over Scripture and tradition, to argue that the "traditioning" of the apostles hands on a gospel of freedom, a common ecumenical teaching to which the Scriptures bear witness. With the third test, Morse appeals to the Church's worship as a criterion for evaluation of doctrine. The historic formula *Lex orandi, lex credendi,* the rule of prayer is the rule of belief, suggests that the God we know in worship is a guide for our teaching of who God is and how we should live. But given that there are many diverging forms of Christian worship, we need other criteria. Thus Morse turns to the idea of catholicity. This criterion is not an appeal to an empirical finding, but to what is found to be essential to Christian identity. Doctrines satisfy the criterion of catholicity if they are found by all Christians to be central to their identity. The fifth test appeals to what "rings true" to our experience. Here Morse follows Wesley's suggestion that people can discern what is useful or fruitful teaching, as it enables them to live holy lives and do the most good. The appeal to conscience draws on both Catholic and Protestant traditions to argue for faithful disbelief: no one should be required to act against their conscience, and therefore conscience is a further test of doctrinal validity. To have consequence, Christian doctrine must make a difference. There must be forms of living and acting which flow from valid doctrine, which make a difference to the world and for the good of the world. As a further refining of this test, cruciality requires that a doctrine should address what is central and matters most in the present situation. This is not the same thing as addressing what is most urgent

---

[4] Ibid., ch. 4.
[5] Ibid., 46.

in the popular media. Rather, Christian doctrine must provide us with a basis for recognition of "what time it is" in the divine perspective, enabling us to see what really is crucial and what is not. The test of coherence requires an internal consistency in our doctrinal formulations, while the requirement of comprehensiveness gathers together all the other tests, to ask whether the doctrinal formulation being evaluated takes into account the broadest possible range of factors or aspects.

Taken collectively, these criteria help us to flesh out a vital implication of our theology of divine conversation. If, as we have suggested, the Church is to be the community in which the divine conversation occurs "out loud," then the Church is called to be continually responsive to God, actively engaged in answering God's questions, witnessing to God's wisdom, and proclaiming God's grace. All this suggests a quite fundamental criterion for critical appraisal of the Church's life, its doctrine, activities, and worship. The question is whether the Church is *being responsive to God,* faithfully engaging with God's call, questioning, "nudging"—to use Val Webb's phrase—or whether the Church is allowing itself to rest with penultimate concerns, even if these concerns are its own teaching and the maintenance of its life as a religious institution. This broad, critical criterion applies to the expression of belief as it does to the challenge of doubt. In responding to this doctrine or that doubt, are we engaging in the divine conversation? What does it mean for us to be faithful here? It may be that faithful conversation with God requires a respectful rejection of the different, in the light of our understanding of Scripture, the apostolic tradition, and our own experience of God's nature and purposes. On the other hand, we may sense the possibility that God is inviting us toward new insights and fresh forms of discipleship or service, or the discovery of a new level of consensus.

It is in this way, too, that a Church which acknowledges doubt as a part of its life of faith can encounter *other religions* and can work with God's Spirit toward what we called the consensus of the entire creation. Again there are many complex issues here and we can only make a few tentative observations. Reflecting on many years of engagement in ecumenical dialogue, Reinhold Bernhardt argues that a major difficulty in the encounter of one faith community with another is the conviction that one's own position and commitment is "absolute."[6] Bernhardt

---

[6] Reinhold Bernhardt, *Christianity without Absolutes,* trans. John Bowden (London: SCM Press, 1994).

examines the psychological and sociological factors which can give rise to exclusive attitudes between religious groups. He suggests that a claim to absoluteness can be a form of self-assertion, designed to overcome an inner uncertainty or sense of guilt. On the other hand, Bernhardt recognizes situations where it is necessary for a community to take an absolutist stance. A group may be forced to declare an absolute protest against a totalitarian regime, for example. This situational absolutism is to be distinguished from dispositional absolutism, an exclusive attitude which is grounded in anxious uncertainty.

Bernhardt traces a long tradition of Christian theological reflection which has sought to be inclusive, beginning with Justin and Clement who argued that in the *logos* all human quests for truth and life find their fulfillment. Here there is an "inclusive absoluteness," rather than an excluding and repudiating attitude to other movements or religions. Bernhardt's objective is to propose a Christianity without absolutism. He argues for a dialogical approach which, he contends, arises from the Christian faith itself, properly understood. The absolute to which we are committed is God. Bearing witness to God's revelation in Christ means participating in God's reaching out to all peoples. On this basis, Christians may stand in God's truth, on the way to God's truth. We do not possess all of God's truth and therefore can engage in dialogue with "peoples of God on the way."

Bernhardt is right to assert that a Christianity without absolutes in this sense is not a soft option. It requires a rigorous openness to God and to the demands of truthfulness in every situation. It does not involve a negation of our own Christian conviction and witness. On the contrary, as followers of Christ we are called to tell our story of God's redemptive engagement with us, but we are also called to listen to the stories of others and to consider critically whether their story might be for us part of God's call to the responsive conversation of faith.

In genuine dialogue, the primary objective is not the discovery of a "core" of belief which we hold in common about the nature of God or the meaning of salvation, though this may be a desirable goal. Our purpose is to meet with God and to engage more fully in the divine conversation, responding to the Spirit's purpose of gathering the whole creation into a consensus, a life together in God. If we maintain this perspective, I suggest, we will be saved from the excesses of absolutism or exclusivism, as well as from a bland religious relativism. We will engage with the other as other. But we will also be open to the genuine possibility that in the other we may also meet with something of the truth of God. We will be constantly reminded that our purpose is not to achieve some kind of religious treaty of understanding, but always to acknowledge the mystery and glory of the God who has created us, who has encountered us in Christ and invites us to respond by participation in faithful conversation. In this way, dialogue with "the other" can involve faithful doubt as well as the positive witness to our belief and doctrine. All may be parts of the divine conversation.

Doubt in Search of Understanding

In this book we have been investigating the significance of doubt as an element in the life of faith. We have argued that doubt can be seen as a positive and constructive aspect of faith. But this finding is paradoxical, for doubt exists only in response to some assertion of belief which is considered inadequate, incoherent, or in some way inappropriate. Doubt is raised as an expression of faith—faith in search of understanding, in search of a more appropriate form of belief. Doubt, then, is a form of faith searching for understanding.

There is another sense also in which doubt itself is in need of understanding. The nature of doubt and its relationship to faith has not been understood. As a result many confusions and difficulties have emerged in our study of doubt. We have found that doubt is an ambiguous phenomenon. As a form of questioning, a search for understanding, doubt can lead to further deepening of faith, further insights into the character of our life with God. But doubt also has a negative potential and may lead to the abandonment of faith, through a skeptical denial of any form of meaning. Our argument has been, however, that this negative outcome is not necessary and seems to result where doubts are repressed or suppressed by authoritarian leadership or a community which seeks to stifle inquiry or maintain a static form of faith.

We have also seen that belief, the opposite of doubt, is subject to a similar ambiguity to doubt. Faith should not be strictly identified with doctrinal belief, for there may be forms of belief which express fear and a resistance to God, attitudes which are the opposites of faith.

Positively we have argued for the importance of doubt as a constructive ingredient in the life of faith, preserving faith from the tendency to idolatry and stimulating faith toward further inquiry and hope. This perspective on faith and doubt requires, however, that we set aside a number of common ideas about faith, which seem to be the causes of much confusion about doubt. Faith cannot be simply identified with belief, nor should we consider faith to be an all-or-nothing concept. There may be degrees of faith, involving both belief and doubt. This is possible, however, only if we think of faith as a dynamic aspect of our lives and as having social dimensions, rather than as a static situation in our individual lives. We have found it most helpful to pursue the image of faith as a journey undertaken with others. Within the corporate journey of faith, doubt and belief interact constructively and creatively.

Finally, these dynamics of doubt and its quest for understanding have given rise to the theological metaphor of God as conversation-alist, a God who asks questions, invites responses, and is continually seeking a living consensus. The life of faith thus essentially involves questioning and being questioned. Doubt, protest, and a quest for new ways of responding to God are appropriate expressions of a living faith. At the core of the Christian faith is the invitation to respond to Jesus Christ, in whom the divine-human conversation is embodied. The invitation to the Christian journey of faith is expressed in the question: *But who do you say I am?* In faith, belief, and doubt, we offer our living response to this the most central of the questions God asks.

The "resolution" of doubt is not through finding a form of belief without questions or struggle. Rather, as we journey with the questions we discover that doubt and belief, perplexity and praise, struggle and rest are all gifts of the same Spirit who bears witness with our spirit, gathering us into the eternal, divine conversation.

Did not our hearts burn within us while we were talking along the road?

Index